HUMANIST PIETAS

THE PANEGYRIC OF IANUS PANNONIUS ON GUARINUS VERONENSIS

Indiana University Uralic and Altaic Series

Editor: Denis Sinor
Volume 151

Medievalia Hungarica Series

Editor: Emanuel J. Mickel
Volume I

UMANIST
PIETAS:

THE PANEGYRIC OF IANUS PANNONIUS ON
GUARINUS VERONENSIS

By
IAN THOMSON

Research Institute for Inner Asian Studies
1988

This translation and commentary of Janus
Pannonius' *Panegyricus* was supported by
a grant from the Translations Division
of the National Endowment for the Hu-
manities, an independent federal agency,
as well as by the Office of Research and
Graduate Development at Indiana Uni-
versity. We must also thank Professor
Denis Sinor and the Hungarian Chair at
Indiana University for their generous and
unfailing support of this volume and the
series it initiates. We are also in debt to
Karin Ford, who organized a working con-
ference of scholars from Hungary and the
United States in 1985 to discuss the work
being done in the three projects of this se-
ries. Gratitude is also due to Lisa Mosele,
Suzanne Thurman, and Camellia Hoene,
who played an important role in bring-
ing this volume from manuscript to book
form.

ISBN 0-933070-21-7
Library of Congress Card Number 88-082270
———
Indiana University Uralic and Altaic Series
Research Institute for Inner Asian Studies
Goodbody Hall
Bloomington, IN 47405

CONTENTS

PREFACE

N HIS 1951 EDITION OF the elegies and epi-
grams of Ianus Pannonius, Mihovil Kom-
bol states that of all the humanists of the
fifteenth century, Ianus most deserves to
have his Latin poems translated.[1] Kom-
bol was justifiably proud of one whom he
considered a fellow-Croat, just as the Hun-
garians, in whose country Ianus spent most of the last thir-
teen years of his short life (1434-1472), claim him as their
greatest Latin poet. Born in eastern Slavonia in the king-
dom of Hungary-Croatia, Ianus rose to be Bishop of Pécs
and an important literary and political figure in the reign
of Matthias Corvinus (1458-1490).

Ianus had the misfortune to participate in an unsuccess-
ful rebellion against Matthias in 1471, and died near Zagreb
on March 27, 1472, while fleeing from the king's wrath. If he
had lived longer, and had not offended the king, his collected

---

[1] Ivan Česmički/Janus Pannonius, *Pjesme i Epigrami* (Poems and
Epigrams), ed. M. Kombol, with Croatian translations by Nikola Sop
(Zagreb, 1951), Introduction, p. xxii.

poems would perhaps have been published in his lifetime. There is some evidence that about 1470 he had begun to collect them for a definitive edition.[2] It was not, however, until fifteen years after Matthias' death (1490) that Stefan Brodarich, later chancellor of Hungary but in 1505 only a rising civil servant, tried to have a collection of Ianus' poems published at Venice by Aldo Manuzio. Such an edition did not materialize, but there was a great demand for Ianus' work. In 1512 an edition by the Polish-born scholar, Paulus Crosnensis, of Ianus' panegyric on his teacher, Guarino, came out at Vienna.[3] This was followed by another edition of the same poem, by Sebastian Magyi, at Bologna in 1513. As many as nine separate editions of works by Ianus are reported for the period 1512-1523, but the most important in that group was Beatus Rhenanus' edition of the panegyric on Guarino and a number of the epigrams, printed by Froben at Basel in 1518. It was dedicated to Jakob Sturm

---

[2] Codex 82-4-8 in the Biblioteca Colombina y Capitular in Seville, discovered by Csaba Csaopodi, contains poems by Ianus, and 101 hitherto-unknown Latin letters written by him on behalf of the king. There are corrections in Ianus' own hand in fol. 14r: see Klára T. Pajorin's note and the appended bibliography to item 35 (Janus Pannonius: Poemata et epistulae, mit Korrekturen des Autors, Fol. 14r) in *Matthias Corvinus und die Renaissance in Ungarn* (Katalog des Niederösterreichischen Landesm useums, Neue Folge Nr. 118, Wien 1982), 157. This codex may have been in Ianus' possession when he died at Medvedgrad in 1472. It appears to have been a companion volume to Codex 7-1-15, also in the Biblioteca Colombina y Capitular, which was purchased at Basel in 1531 for Fernando Colon (the natural son of Christopher Columbus) and willed by him to the library. Presumably, both codices had somehow come into the possession of a seller at Basel. Codex 7-1-15 contains poems by Ianus and, at the end, one by Péter Garázda, which was discussed by Marianna D. Birnbaum, "An Unknown Latin Poem, Probably by Petrus Garazda, Hungarian Humanist," *Viator* 4 (1973), 303-309. Birnbaum (p. 307-308) also gives a general analysis of the codex, which is described by Mária Horváth in *Janus Pannonius Tanulmanyok* (Budapest, 1975), 445-58.

[3] The title appears as *Panegyricus in laudem Baptistae Guarini Veronensis* showing that Paulus Crosnensis had confused Guarino with his youngest son, Battista.

of Strassburg, and had a wide distribution among Cerman and Dutch humanists, including Erasmus, whose praises of Ianus did much to popularize his work throughout Europe. Notable editions after 1523 have been: that by Hilarius Cantiuncula of the panegyric on Guarino and many of the epigrams and elegies (Venice, 1553); an enlarged second edition at Basel (1555); an *omnium* edition by Iohannes Sambucus (Vienna, 1569), a facsimile of which, with a long critical article by Tibor Kardos, was printed at Budapest in 1972, to mark the five-hundredth anniversary of Ianus' death; a selection of his poems, with others by György Túri, Janos Sommer, and János Filiczki, in *Delitiae poetarum Hungaricorum regis Matthiae Corvini,* edited by Iohannes Philippus Pareus (Frankfurt, 1619 and 1727); Conrad Norbert's edition of the epigrams and elegies (Buda, 1754), the text of which was the basis for Kombol's edition of 1951; and *Iani Pannonii poemata,* edited by Samuel Teleki (Utrecht, 1784). The last, which has generally been considered the standard edition, is in two volumes, the first of which includes the panegyric on Guarino, the second a *vita auctoris* life of the author), various *testimonia doctorum de Pannonio* (testimonies of scholars on the Pannonian), and a critical apparatus on the text of the poems claimed to be based on a total of thirteen manuscript sources and printed editions. Eight pages in double columns and small print refer to the panegyric on Guarino.[4]

These older editions kept Ianus accessible to scholars of all nationalities, whose medium of learned discourse was Latin until at least the end of the eighteenth century. A recent study by László Mezey has traced his influence in

---

[4] I must thank the Widener Library and the Houghton Library of Rare Books at Harvard University for access to all of the editions listed in this paragraph.

the sixteenth century.[5] It appears, for example, that Rabelais knew his works, and may have borrowed from him in coining the expressions *tor-coulx* and *torty-colly*.[6] Erasmus praised him for his humanist skills and political idealism, as did the seventeenth-century Czech educator, Comenius (Jan Komenski); and Jan Kochanowski, the greatest Polish poet of the sixteenth century, who wrote in both Latin and his native language, used him more than once as a model, notably in his poem–cycle, *Treny*, on the death of his baby daughter, Orszula, which shows the influence of Ianus' magnificent elegy on the death of his mother, Barbara.[7]

On a more popular level, Ianus became a symbol of lost glory. As Leslie Domonkos has shown, in the thirty-six years between the death of Matthias Corvinus and the defeat of Louis II (1516-1526) by the Turks at Mohács (1526) education continued at a high level in Hungary, but in every other respect there was decline.[8] Matthias' successor, the Pole Wladislaw II, and Wladislaw's son, Louis, lost control of their nobles; the royal treasury was depleted; taxes became an intolerable burden, and there was much resistance to their collection; the nobles oppressed the peasants, who revolted in 1514, only to be defeated and pressed into serfdom; population decreased in the cities, and with it their prosperity. Even before Mohács there had been nostalgia for the strong rule of Matthias. Those who remembered him, seeing the decline around them, contrasted it with his

---

[5] László Mezey, "Janus Pannonius XVI. századi utóéletéröl (The Sixteenth Century *Nachleben* of Ianus Pannonius), *Janus Pannonius Tanulmányok* (1975), 523-533.
[6] León Dorez, "Rabelesiana," *Revue des Bibliothèques* 13-14 (1903), 140-144.
[7] *Elegiae* 1. 6 (Kombol, 10-19), *De morte Barbarae.*
[8] L. S. Domonkos, "The State of Education in Hungary on the Eve of the Battle of Mohács (1526)," *Canadian-American Review of Hungarian Studies* 2, No. 1 (1975), 3-20.

more stable government; those to whom he was only a name invested him in their minds as lord of a vanished golden age, when literature and the arts had flourished. This was no less the case after 1526, when most of Hungary passed into the possession of the Habsburgs. Ianus, as the greatest poet of that lost time, also took on romanticized associations, even outside what was left of Matthias' former dominions. Opponents of absolute monarchy saw him as a young hero, who had died young fighting royal tyranny, and Hungarian protestants seized upon a number of poems in which Ianus had ridiculed the Pope and criticized the greed of the Roman curia as further confirmation of their own choice in rejecting Catholicism. Even in our own time Ianus has reemerged as a potent symbol, representing a particular point of view. Ivan Supek, the Croatian author of *Heretic on the Left* and other political works, has depicted Ianus as a somewhat victimized, but passionate freedom-fighter in his play, *Pjesnik i Vladar* (The Poet and the Ruler), published in the Zagreb periodical, *Forum* (Nos. 1-2, 1980). With scrupulous attention to the historical background, Supek deals with Ianus' gradual disenchantment with Matthias, the rebellion in 1471 led by Archbishop János Vitéz and his nephew, Ianus, its failure, and Ianus' fevered death in the fortress of Medvedgrad a year later. By using Ianus as a symbol of reasonable opposition to tyranny, Supek also covertly attacks what he perceives to be repressive policies on the part of the present regime in Jugoslavia. [9] In this present study, however, our concern is not with Ianus as a politician, but as a Latin poet. There is a considerable amount of

---

[9] Supek's play is discussed by Ante Kadić, "The Poet and the Ruler, a Play by Ivan Supek," *Journal of Croatian Studies* 21 (1980), 67-76, reprinted in A. Kadić, *The Tradition of Freedom in Croatian Literature* (The Croatian Alliance: Bloomington, Indiana, 1983), 346-355.

modern scholarship on his life and works. The groundwork was laid in Jenö Ábel's *Analecta ad historiam renascentium in Hungaria litterarum spectantia* (Budapest, 1880) and in later revisions of this work, which provide many documents relating to the spread of humanism in Hungary.[10] Of the earlier scholars, Vilmos Fraknói made contributions to the biography of Ianus, but the first full-length biography was József Huszti's *Janus Pannonius* (Pécs, 1931). László Juhász published an excellent text-edition of the *Panegyricus in Guarinum Veronensem* (Budapest, 1934), on which I have based my own English translation. Hungarian translations of many of the poems, by Lajos Áprily and others, are to be found in the *Opera latine et hungarice* (Works in Latin and Hungarian), edited by Sandor V. Kovács (Budapest, 1972), and Hungarian versions, with no Latin text, are in *Janos Pannonius versei*, edited by Tibor Kardos (Budapest, 1972). This latter work includes some translations from earlier publications, among then *Janus Pannonius válogatott versei*, edited by Tibor Kardos, with an introduction by Rabán Gerézdi (Budapest, 1953). The 1953 edition contained a partial version by Gyözö Csorba of the panegyric on Guarino (p. 141-52), and brief notes to it (p. 85-88). Kardos has also edited *Carmina selectiora/Poèmes choisis* (Budapest, 1973), which contains a selection of Latin poems, with French translations by a number of French poets. Worth mentioning, too, is *Galle und Honig*, edited by Harry C. Schnur and Rainer Kössling (Leipzig, 1982), which includes fourteen of Ianus' best epigrams, with renderings into German verse by Schnur.

    Within the past seventeen years, Hungarian scholars

---

[10] The revisions are *Analecta nova ...spectantia*, ed. Eugenius Ábel and Stephanus Hegedüs (Budapest, 1903), and *Analecta recentiora ... spectantia*, ed. Stephanus Hegedüs (Budapest, 1906).

have greatly advanced our knowledge of Ianus. Of the lit-
erary and historical studies, I would mention especially:
Rabán Gerézdi, "Janus Pannonius," in *Italia ed Ungheria
Dieci secoli di rapporti letterari*, ed. Mátyás Horányi and
Tibor Klaniczay (Budapest, 1967), 91-112; Csaba Csapodi,
"Die Bibliothek des Janus Pannonius," *Acta Litteraria* 14
(Budapest, 1972), 389-400; Rabán Gerézdi, "Der Weltruf
des Janus Pannonius und die deutsche Vermittlung," in
*Studien zur Geschichte der deutsch-ungarischen literari-
schen Beziehungen* (Berlin, 1969), 32-43; Klára Csapodi-
Gárdonyi, "Ein unbekannte Erstausgabe von Epigrammen
des Janus Pannonius," *Gutenberg-Jahrbuch* (1979), 53-57;
Ágnes Ritoók-Szalay,

"Janus Pannonius kiadója, Hilarius Cantiuncula" (Hi-
larius Cantiuncula, editor of Janus Pannonius), *Iro-
dalomtörténeti Közlemények* 84 (1980), 125-36; the articles
in the periodical *Jelenkor* (Contemporary) for April, 1972,
a spe cial issue devoted to Ianus; and the important articles
in the issue of *Janus Pannonius Tanulmányok* (Budapest,
1975) edited by Tibor Kardos and Sándor V. Kovács. Use-
ful, too, for its concise, authoritative articles and up-to-date
bibliographies is *Matthias Corvinus und die Renaissance in
Ungarn*, the superb catalogue of the exhibit of Corviniana,
held as a joint venture of the Austrian and Hungarian gov-
ernments at Schallaburg in Austria from May 8 to November
1, 1982.

In Croatian, the best critical work has been that of
Kombol in his introduction (p. vii-xxii) to Ivan Česmički,
Pjesme i Epigrami (see footnote 1). Kombol's Latin text
is excellent, and the facing Croatian translations by Nikola
Šop are also good, though occasionally too far from the lit-
eral meaning of the Latin. Unfortunately Kombol omits all
sexually-explicit epigrams; his numbering of the poems does

not correspond with that of Teleki's 1784 edition; and he does not number the lines in the poems. His edition, however, is available in most good university libraries in America, and for that reason I have given page-references to it, as well as the poem-references in Teleki, in citing particular works of Ianus. Also widely available is *Hrvatski latinisti: Croatici auctores qui latine scripserunt*, edited by Veljko Gortan and Vladimir Vratović, 1 (Zagreb, 1969), which includes a good selection, though sometimes only in excerpt, of Ianus' poetry. It also contains facing Croatian translations. Worthy of mention, too, are Gortan's entry on Ianus in *Enciklopedija Jugoslavije* 4 (Zagreb, 1960), 461-63; Erwin Šinko's article, "Janus Pannonius," in *Rad*, 333 (1963), 518-26; and Miroslav Krleža, "O pojavi Jana Pannonija," *Eseji*, 3 (1963) in *Sabrana Djela* 20.

The comparative lack of books and articles on Ianus in English is attributable to the inability of most British and American scholars to read Hungarian or Croatian, and to the neglect of humanist literature by professional Latinists. Another reason is that specialists in the Renaissance have concentrated on its manifestations in England, France, Spain, The Netherlands, Germany, and Italy. In Britain and America, however, there is a growing awareness of the vitality of humanism in fifteenth and sixteenth century Europe east of Germany and Italy, and of the need to integrate the achievements of Poles, Croats, and Hungarians into our picture of the larger Renaissance.[11] There are many brief

---

[11] This opinion was commonly expressed among the almost two hundred participants in the conference, "The Polish Renaissance in its European Context," held at Indiana University, May 25-28, 1982, and by many of those who attended the two sections devoted (for the first time) to the Renaissance in Eastern and Central Europe at the Central Renaissance Conference of The Renaissance Society of America, also at Indiana University, April 7-9, 1983.

references to Ianus in books written in English, but only re-
cently have more extended treatments of him become avail-
able. Tibor Kardos has an article, "Janus Pannonius, Poet
of the Hungarian Renaissance," *New Hungarian Quarterly*
14 (1973), 79-93, as does Marianna D. Birnbaum, "Janus
Pannonius, Bartholomeo (*sic*) Melzi, and the Sforzas," *Re-
naissance Quarterly* 30, No. 1 (1977), 1-7. Leslie Domonkos,
while addressing larger issues , brings out Ianus' funda-
mental importance in two articles, "Ecclesiastical Patrons
as a Factor in the Hungarian Renaissance," *New Review
of East European History* 14, Nos. 1-4 (1974), 100-16, and
"Archbishop Johannes Vitéz, the Father of Hungarian Hu-
manism," *New Hungarian Quarterly* 15 (1975). Michael B.
Petrovich gives two pages to Ianus in "The Croatian Hu-
manists: Cosmopolites or Patriots?" in *Journal of Croat-
ian Studies* 20 (1979). In Ante Kadić's article, "The Poet
and the Ruler, a Play by Ivan Supek," in *Journal of Croa-
tian Studies* 21 (1980), 67-76, the first six pages contain a
brief sketch of Ianus' life, with sensitive interpretations of
key passages in his poems. The most important work, how-
ever, has been Marianna D. Birnbaum's biography, *Janus
Pannonius, Poet and Politician* (Zagreb, 1981). Part One
(p. 1-110) is mainly concerned with Ianus' education and
literary works; Part Two (p. 111-208) deals with him af-
ter 1459 in Hungary-Croatia, with emphasis on his political
activities. I gratefully acknowledge the help this book has
provided in the preparation of my own.

My own study concentrates on Ianus' most often printed
poem, and on his relationship with Guarino. I hope that a
close, particular study of this kind will prove useful in the
wake of Birnbaum's more general work. I have included
much information on Guarino, in the belief that the more
the reader knows about Guarino, the better he will under-

stand Ianus. This is particularly necessary in the notes to
the *Panegyricus* and its *Praefatio*, since Ianus is concerned
only to bring out Guarino's successes and positive qualities,
and his statements do not always accord with the facts. I
have also extensively annotated the mythological and ge-
ographical allusions in which the poem abounds, because
otherwise it would be largely incomprehensible. The main
classical and post-classical sources on which Ianus drew are
also indicated. The *Panegyricus* is much more than a mine
of information on Guarino's curriculum and teaching meth-
ods. It deserves to be read as a whole, and appreciated as a
carefully crafted tribute from a gifted pupil to the teacher
who shaped his artistry. It could be called Ianus' master-
piece as an apprentice humanist, the culmination of all that
seven years of intense study under the best teacher of his
time could add to his natural poetic gifts. Its defects are
therefore as interesting as its virtues, whatever the reader
perceives either to be. In Ianus' poetry, form rarely takes
precedence over content, but his style in the *Panegyricus*
is sometimes so artificial and inflated that the translator
is tempted to misrepresent the manner of the original in
the interests of readability. I cannot, however, accept the
view that a paraphrase which explains rather than trans-
lates the original Latin (what humanists called an *immu-
tatio*) is preferable to the old-fashioned attempt to render
the meaning, manner, and spirit as accurately as possible.[12]
But there are passages, a strict rendering of which would
be intolerably grotesque in English. In these, a looser ren-
dering is called for, not merely to avoid repelling the reader

---

[12] For a refutation of the view that accurate, faithful translations
are an error in taste or an anachronistic delusion, see L.R. Lind, "On
'Modern' Translation," *Classical and Modern Literature* 3, No. 2 (1983),
69-74.

but also because the genius of Latin is more tolerant of verbal pomposity than English, and expressions that sound absurdly mannered in a literal English translation may not convey this effect in Latin. A certain amount of artificiality, I think, must be retained (for instance, in rendering *nova Minerva* as "the new Minerva" rather than "the new learning," or *Alcides* as either "Alcides" or "the descendant of Alceus," rather than "Hercules"), because otherwise the effect the author intended, indeed labored for, would be distorted. Though prose is the medium of translation, I have tried to convey the impression that the original was a poem.

It remains to thank Professor Denis Sinor and Professor Emanuel Mickel, without whose initiative this study would not have appeared; Professor Richard Counts, Professor Felix Oinas, and Professor György Ranki for assistance with Hungarian passages; my ex-student, Dr. Michael Lowery, for xeroxing the Latin texts I needed, and providing me with his own first-draft version of most of the poem, done independently of my own, which I have found useful as a check; and most of all, Professor Ante Kadić, who not only translated many passages in Croatian for me, but has throughout been an unfailing source of encouragement. *Gratum est fateri per quos profecerim.*

INTRODUCTION

Y THE MIDDLE OF the fifteenth century there was no city in Europe more important for the training of humanists than Ferrara in the north of Italy, and no humanist teacher more famous than Guarino Veronese (1374-1460).[1] Little is known about Guarino's early life. The son of Bartolomeo Guarini, a metal-worker of Verona, and Libera di Giannino, he had probably received his early education under Marzagaia da Verona, whose curriculum seems to have been thoroughly medieval in nature. About 1392, Guarino moved to Padua or Venice. It is often said that he studied at Padua under Giovanni di Conversino da Ravenna, but

---

[1] The best sources for Guarino's biography are: Remigio Sabbadini, "Vita di Guarino Veronese," *Giornale ligustico* 18 (1891) and *La scuola e gli studi di Guarino Guarini Veronese* (Catania, 1896), both of which are reprinted in *Guariniana* ed. Mario Sancipriano (Torino, 1964); and Guarino Veronese, *Epistolario* ed. R. Sabbadini, 1-3 (Venice, 1915-1919; reprinted Torino, 1959). Now mostly out of date is Carlo Rosmini, *La vita e disciplina di Guarino Veronese e di'suoi discepoli* 1-3 (Brescia, 1805-1806).

the evidence for this is tenuous.[2]

It is likely, however, that he knew Giovanni and a few other scholars at Padua, such as Pier Paolo Vergerio and Paolo Veneto, who had caught the spirit of Francesco Petrarca (1304-1374), and were striving towards a cleaner and more classical style of Latin. Popular at first mainly among lawyers and notaries who merely wished to improve their style, this movement gradually expanded and became identified with what Cicero had called *studia humanitatis*, meaning that immersion in the works of the great poets, orators, historians, and philosophers of antiquity, both Greek and Roman, which made up the education of a Roman gentleman. By the end of the fourteenth century, however, very few scholars in the West knew Greek; the universities clung to the traditional disciplines of law, medicine, and theology, and lucrative positions could hardly be attained without a doctorate in one of these; and there were no teachers who offered the kind of education described by Cicero or Quintilian.

Guarino's name appears in a document of 1403 as a teacher at Venice. About April of that year, he took employment with the Venetian merchant and politician, Paolo Zane, and went with him to Constantinople as a *notarius* (notary or secretary). Zane paid his fees to learn

---

[2] It consists solely of a remark by Leonardo Bruni quoted by Flavio Biondo in his *Italia ilustrata* (Venice, 1503) f. G. III: "Joannes Ravennas ...suopte ingenio et quodam dei munere, sicut fuit solitus dicere Leonardus, eum Petrumpaulumque Vergerium, Omnebonum Scholam patavinum, Robertum Rossum et Jacobum Angeli filium florentinos Poggiumque, Guarinum Veronensem, Victorinum Feltensem ...Si non satis quod plene nesciebat docere potuit, in bonarum, ut dicebat, litterarum amorem Ciceronisque inflammabat." Sabbadini, who quoted this passage in Guarino, *Epistolario* 3. 54, accepted it as proof that Giovanni had been Guarino's teacher. Guarino, however, mentions Marzagaia (G., *Epistolario* 1. Ep. 133) and Manuel Chrysoloras (*Epistolario*, passim) as his teachers, but not Giovanni.

Greek at the school of Manuel and John Chrysoloras. Guarino was later to claim that Zane's motives were altruistic, but the truth may be that Zane merely wished to have a Greek-speaking scholar to help him with his business and political affairs. By 1406 Guarino was working full time for Zane, but his schooling under the Chrysolorae had ensured his conversion to the literature and thought of the ancient world.

He returned to Italy in 1408 or 1409, but found no ready market for his skills. After a miserable period (1410-1413) as a protégé of the Florentine bibliophile, Niccolò Niccoli, and a lack-lustre year as a lecturer in Greek at the University of Florence, he went to Venice in the summer of 1414, where he taught Greek to Francesco Barbaro, Leonardo Giustinian, and several other patricians interested in the humanist movement. In 1415 or 1416 he opened a *contubernium*, that is, a community of fee-paying student-boarders, in his own home. Plague interrupted his work, the venture was far from lucrative, and his spirits ebbed. In 1418, however, his fortunes improved, when he married Tadea Zendrata, a Veronese woman of good family. In 1419 he moved to Verona, and in 1420 became public professor, with freedom to teach the ancient authors. At the same time, he founded another and much more successful *contubernium*.

By 1429 he had produced many letters, orations, pedagogical works, and translations of Greek works,[3] but his fame as a humanist scholar and teacher was still confined mainly to northern Italy. In 1429, however, he was invited to Ferrara by the marquis Niccolò III d'Este. As tutor to Niccolò's heir, Leonello, from 1430 to 1434, he be-

---

[3] See n. on *Panegyricus* 695.

came famous throughout Europe, his scholarly reputation being enhanced by a wider diffusion of his writings, which were passed around in Italy and abroad as models of style. Leonello helped to have him appointed in 1436 as professor of Rhetoric in the University of Ferrara. Guarino lost no opportunity of associating himself with the House of Este, especially in the controversy over the relative merits of republican and monarchical government, in which he emerged as Leonello's champion.[4] From 1436 onwards, too, Guarino maintained a *contubernium* in his own large house near the Estense palace.[5] In 1442, Leonello, now marquis, reconstituted the university, chose Guarino to deliver the inaugural lecture, and installed him as its recognized leader.[6] He had already become "il più grande maestro del suo secolo," and "l'immagine esemplare del professore laico."[7] In 1459, Enea Silvio Piccolomini (Pope Pius II) recorded in his Commentaries that Guarino had been "the teacher of almost everyone in his time who achieved distinction in the humanities."[8] When Guarino died on December 4, 1460, his ex-student, Lodovico Carbone, composed a magnificent funeral oration,[9] in which he compared his master's school

---

[4] See n. on *Panegyricus* 794.

[5] See n. on *Panegyricus* 591.

[6] For the re-organization, see Werner L. Gundersheimer, *Ferrara: The Style of a Renaissance Despotism* (Princeton, 1973) 101. Extracts of Guarino's 1442 lecture are published in *Il pensiero pedagogico dell' Umanesimo* ed. Eugenio Garin (Firenze, 1958) 488-90. This work is hereafter referred to as Garin, *L'Umanesimo*.

[7] "The greatest master of his century" and "the model figure of the lay professor": see, respectively, Sabbadini, *La scuola e gli studi di Guarino* 37, and E. Garin, *L'Educazione umanistica in Europa 1400-1600* (Bari, 1957) 148.

[8] *Memoirs of a Renaissance Pope: The Commentaries of Pius II.* Translated by F. A. Gragg, with Notes and Historical Introduction by L.C. Gabel (London, 1960) 115.

[9] Latin text with facing Italian translation in *La letteratura italiana: Storia e testi* 18: *Prosatori latini del quattrocento* ed. E. Garin (Milano, 1952) 382-417.

to the Trojan horse, "from which poured forth princes without number." Carbone paints a dismal picture of the state of Ferrarese education before the arrival of Guarino.[10] "It was disgraceful," he says, "how little our countrymen knew about literature. Far from there being anyone who knew the art of speaking or taught rhetoric, or could deliver a weighty and polished oration, or would dare speak at a public meeting, there was nobody who knew the correct rules of grammar, or understood the proper meanings and usages of words, or could explain the poets. Priscian lay neglected, Servius was unknown, the works of Cicero were unfamiliar; and it was counted a miracle, if anyone spoke the name of Sallust, Caesar, or Livy, or had any desire to understand the ancient authors. Something like their fortieth year found our fellow-citizens still in the elementary school, forever tied up and laboring over the same basic lessons." This is probably an exaggeration, but it was true that Guarino's presence made an enormous difference within a very few years, and that his "swan-like voice" (as Carbone describes it) and great reputation as a teacher and scholar attracted so many students to Ferrara that "their names alone would fill a huge volume." The numerical claim is borne out by the enrollment figures at the University of Ferrara:. using the statistics compiled by Pinghini in 1927, Werner L. Gundersheimer has calculated that during the marquisate of Leonello d'Este (1442-1450) an average of 388 students attended, of whom 78 were enrolled in the law school, the

---

[10] For a fairer view of Ferrarese culture before the arrival of Guarino, see G. Carducci, "Della coltura Estense nei secoli XIII e XIV fino alla signoria di Niccolò III," in *Edizione Nazionale delle Opera di G. Carducci* 13 (Bologna, 1954) 1–54 (essay first published in 1895); F. Novati, "Donato degli Albanzani alla corte Estense," *Archivio storico italiano* ser. 5, 6 (1890) 365-85; Giulio Bertoni, *Guarino da Verona fra cortigiani a Ferrara 1429-1460* (Genova, 1921), which has a survey of protohumanism before 1429; and Gundersheimer, *Ferrara* 39-65.

remaining 310 in the faculty of arts.[11] The number and quality of Guarino's works speak for themselves, [12] and the excellence of his teaching is attested to by the large numbers of his students who achieved eminence in later life.[13]

Among Guarino's students were a number from abroad: William Grey, Robert Flemmyng, John Gunthorpe, John Free, and John Tiptoft, from England;[14] Henri Jouffroy from France;[15] Peter Luder, Georgius Boemius, Gaspar Schmidhauser, and the sons of Samuel Karoch from Germany; [16] Henri de Bruges, from Flanders;[17] a certain Vale-

----

[11] Gundersheimer, *Ferrara* 102. The enrollment figures are in C. Pinghini, "La popolazione studentesca dell'Università di Ferrara dalle origini ai nostri tempi," *Metron: Rivista internazionale di statistica* 7: 1 (1927) 120-44.

[12] For the number, see n. on *Panegyricus* 695. For the quality of his translations, see Sabbadini, *La scuola e gli studi di Guarino* 128-29, where samples of Guarino's translation of Strabo are favorably compared with Gregorio Tifernate's. Sabbadini discusses Guarino's contributions to grammar, orthography, lexicography, rhetoric, prosody, metre, epistolography, and textual and literary criticism in *La scuola e gli studi di Guarino* 38-97.

[13] About 150 known students are listed in *Biographical and bibliographical Dictionary of the Italian Humanists* ed. Mario Emilio Cosenza (Boston, 1962) vol. 5, under "Guarinus Veronensis." (Several are included who were actually students of Guarino's son, Battista.) The most famous were Jacopo Ammanati, Francesco Barbaro, Ermolao Barbaro, Basinio da Parma, Bernardino da Siena, Lodovico Carbone, Pandolfo Collenucio, Angelo Camillo Decembrio, Bartolomeo Fazio, Battista Guarini, Leonardo Guistinian, Giovanni Lamola, Ianus Pannonius, Pietro del Monte, Tito Vespasiano Strozzi, Georgius Trapezuntius, Galeotto Marzio, Vittorino da Feltre, and Raffaele Zovenzoni.

[14] The English students are extensively discussed in Roberto Weiss, *Humanism in England during the Fifteenth Century* (Oxford, 1941). See also R.J. Mitchell, "English Students at Ferrara in the XV Century," *Italian Studies* 1 (1937-1938) 75-82, and, by the same author, *John Tiptoft* (London, 1938) and *John Free: From Bristol to Rome in the Fifteenth Century* (London, 1955).

[15] Nephew of Jean Jouffroy, Bishop of Arras: see Guarino, *Epistolario* 2. Ep. 913. 13-18. Jean Jouffroy (ca. 1412-1473) met Guarino while attending the Council of Ferrara in 1438. In 1473 part of his large collection of codices passed to his nephew, Henri: see Charles Fierville, *Le cardinal Jean Jouffroy* (Paris, 1874) 13.

[16] See notices in Guarino, *Epistolario* 3. 502, 512.

sius, from Portugal, and several, whose names are un-
known, from Spain;[18] the Cypriotes, Lodovico, Filippo, and
Carlo Podocatero; [19] the two nephews of the Polish Bishop,
Mikołej Lasowski; [20] and a number from the kingdom of
Hungary-Croatia, including the poet known in Croatian as
Ivan Česmički, in Hungarian as János Cesinge or Czesmicze,
but most commonly by his Latinized name, Ianus Pannon-
ius. All of these foreigners were aristocrats, protégés of aris-
tocrats, or the sons or wards of wealthy men. Their numbers
were not great, nor did any of them, save Ianus Pannonius,
achieve spectacular success as humanists, or markedly pro-
mote the new learning in their own country, but their pres-
ence in Guarino's school was symptomatic of the increasing
flow of humanist ideas and methods from Italy to the other
countries of Europe.[21] It is noteworthy that of all the for-

---

[17] See Guarino, *Epistolario* 3. 512.
[18] For Valesius and his brother Alfonsinus, see Guarino, *Epistolario* 3.
26-27, 39, 77-78. Neither may actually have been students of Guarino,
since their contacts with him date from 1414 and 1415 (G., *Epistolario* 1.
Ep. 20, and 1. Ep. 31. 20). There were, however, Spanish students at
Ferrara, because in a letter of 1449 (*Epistolario* 2. Ep. 813. 227-231)
Guarino quotes samples of Spanish he had heard from two separate
Spanish students at the university of Ferrara: "Vade in malas horas
cum carnes assadas anseres et anserinos" ("Go to hell with the beef,
the roast, the geese and the goslings") and "esta civitat habe formosas
mulieres" ("This town has some nice-looking women").
[19] See Guarino, *Epistolario* 3. 512. Filippo Podocatero, a protégé of
János Vitéz, was sent to Ferrara before Ianus (Huszti, *Janus Pannonius*
12). Birnbaum (p. 54) suggests that Lodovico helped Ianus in the early
stages of Greek, and reports (p. 64, n. 15) that *Epigr.* 2. 6, one
of Ianus' first translations from Greek, appears in "the Seville codex"
(see n. 2 to my Preface) as "Hymnus in Musas, Iovem et Apollinem a
Homero adhuc puero editus, de greco in latinum traductus per Joan. ad
Lodovicum Cyprium" ("Hymn to the Muses, Jupiter, and Apollo, done
by Homer when he was still a boy, translated from Greek into Latin by
Iohannes and dedicated to Lodovico Podocatero of Cyprus").
[20] Jan and Michal Lasowski, both students at the same time as Ianus.
See the notices in Guarino, *Epistolario* 3. 411, 413-14, 416-17 on Jan
(Giovanni Lassocki), and 3. 411-13 on Michal (Michele).
[21] On contacts between Italy and Hungary from the Middle Ages to
the end of the Renaissance, see the essays by J. Lajos Csoka (on Benedic-

eign students, Carbone mentions only the five Englishmen and Ianus Pannonius.[22]

With the possible exception of Carbone's funeral oration, no laudation of Guarino is more eloquent than Ianus' *Panegyricus in Guarinum Veronensem*, or, as it is sometimes entitled, *Silva panegyrica ad Guarinum Veronensem, praeceptorem suum*. Barely thirteen when he first arrived in Ferrara in the late spring of 1447, Ianus spent seven years as a student at the University and as a boarder (*socius*, companion, or *contubernalis*, literally, tent-mate) in Guarino's home. The *Panegyricus* was presented as a parting gift to Guarino, almost certainly in May or June, 1454. It consists of a *praefatio* (preface or prologue) of 18 elegiac couplets, and 1,073 hexameter verses in the *Panegyricus* proper. Ianus romanticizes Guarino's career, glossing over his set-backs and disappointments,[23] and presents him as a paradigm of virtue, the ideal scholar and teacher. The poem is extremely laudatory, but in an age when Guarino himself once suggested that the virtues of Manuel Chrysoloras would make a better subject than Achilles for an epic, and criticized Homer for choosing a ruffian like Achilles for a

tine contacts with Hungary), Andor Csizmadia (on Galvano da Bologna, a law professor in the university of Pécs), Ilona T. Berkovits (on the Budapest Codex of Dante), Laszlo Mezey (on Lorenzo Giustinian and medieval culture in Hungary), Tibor Kardos (on Petrarch and the beginnings of humanism in Hungary), Raban Gerézdi (on Ianus Pannonius), Csaba Csapodi (on the library of Beatrice, wife of Matthias Corvinus), and O. Szabolcs Barlay (on the history of Hungarian Petrarchism) in *Italia ed Ungheria: Dieci secoli di rapporti letterari* ed. Mátyás Horanyi and Tibor Kardos, (Akadémiai Kiadó: Budapest 1967) 9-145.
[22] At Padua Ianus became a friend of Tiptoft and Free (Weiss, *Humanism in England*, III). In 1460 Tiptoft was considering Carbone for employment, and Carbone would not have risked Tiptoft's displeasure by omitting Ianus' name. For the relations between Ianus and Carbone, see my Introduction, p. 34-35.
[23] See notes on *Panegyricus* 32, 53-56, 83-87, 123, 158, 298, 325-29, 331, 390-92, 401-05, 404.

hero, [24] adulation of the magnitude that Ianus heaps on his teacher was not merely acceptable, but expected in a panegyric. The poem, however, is so well planned and well written, and its virtuosities are such, that it is difficult not to admire it. Its saving grace is that Ianus seems genuinely to have admired Guarino. After seven years with Guarino, he seems truly to have felt that he was living in a new springtime of the world, and to have seen Ferrara as the centre of a new Golden Age of culture, symbolized by the god-like master who had "opened the way to Pieria" (*Praefatio* 36) and "taught the lyre to speak" (*Panegyricus* 7).

Ianus was sent to Ferrara by his uncle on his mother's side, János Vitéz de Zredna, bishop of Várad since 1445. As a proponent of humanism, Vitéz had probably discussed the matter of a tutor for his nephew with Pier Paolo Vergerio (1370-1444), who had lived in Hungary since 1418. Vergerio had learned Greek from Manuel Chrysoloras at Florence (1397-1400), and in 1404 had published a treatise *De ingenuis moribus et liberalibus studiis adulescentiae* ("On good morals and the liberal education of the young"), the first since ancient times plainly to set forth the ideals of humanist education.[25] Though not himself a humanist teacher, he provided the basis on which the great practical educators like Guarino and Vittorino da Feltre (1378-1446) built their curricula.

As a close friend of Guarino, Vergerio had probably sug-

---

[24] "You see what a vast number of excellent verses Homer, the greatest of poets, puts out before he can get rid of that demi-god of myth, whom he had taken it upon himself to praise, a bad-tempered, lustful, bloody savage, a brigand born to lay waste to cities. What do we think a really philosophic poet would do with a non-fictional subject and with solid virtue to write about?" (G. *Epistolario* 1. Ep. 27. 40-46). Guarino was trying to persuade Pier Paolo Vergerio to write an epic on Chrysoloras.
[25] See note on *Panegyricus* 797 for a summary of Vergerio's suggested curriculum and his recommendations to teachers.

gested his name to Vitéz, but he might also have mentioned Vittorino. As head of the court school at Mantua, Vittorino was Guarino's equal, perhaps superior, as a teacher. His school, moreover, embodied Vergerio's recommendations in at least two ways that Guarino's did not.[26] Vittorino taught the "seven liberal arts" (grammar, rhetoric, logic, arithmetic, geometry, astronomy, and music) of Hellenistic, Roman, and medieval education,[27] each as virtually a separate subject; he also took seriously, as Guarino never did, Vergerio's insistence on the old Greek idea that education should be a harmonious blend of *mousikē* (intellectual training) and *gymnastikē* (physical exercise). Vittorino, however, died in 1446, a year before Ianus came to Italy, and his successor, Sassolo da Prato, had nothing like his master's prestige. Guarino stood alone as the obvious choice.

Unlike Vittorino, who wrote almost nothing [28] Guarino was an established author. Vitéz must have recognized the superiority of Guarino's Latin to anything that Hungary could produce at that time. Guarino, moreover, was a renowned Hellenist, who had translated widely from

---

[26] Biographies of Vittorino by four of his pupils and several other sources are published, with facing Italian translations, in Garin, *L'Umanesimo* 504-718. The standard work on V. in English is still William Harrison Woodward, *Vittorino da Feltre and Other Humanist Educators* (Cambridge, 1897; repr. with a preface by Eugene T. Rice by Teachers College, Columbia University, New York, 1963).

[27] The Greek *enkylios paideia* (all-round education) embraced the seven subjects that a free-born person should master. The *trivium* (grammar, rhetoric, logic) and *quadrivium* (arithmetic, geometry, astronomy, music) were medieval concepts.

[28] Platina states in his Memoir on Vittorino (Garin, *L'Umanesimo* 696) that "he left no monument of his genius, saying that it is better to act well than to write well," but adds, "There are a few letters of his to friends, faultless in their serious tone, sincerity, and scholarship." For texts of eight surviving letters, including one in Italian, see *L'Umanesimo* 713-17. An *Orthographia* by Vittorino was published by A. Casacci, "Un tratatello di V. da F. sull'ortographia latina," *Atti del Reale Instituto Veneto* 86, No. 2 (1926-27), 911-45.

Isocrates, Lucian, and Plutarch. His personal character was unstained, and he had a reputation for turning out first-rate Latin writers, which is exactly what Vitéz wanted his nephew to become. Much as professors had done in ancient and medieval times, Guarino commented on his texts line by line, even word by word, as Ianus tells us (*Panegyricus* 521-22). The texts, of course, were not those popular in the late Middle Ages, which Guarino himself studied as a child and had come to abhor, [29] but the Latin and Greek classics, and the better stylists among the Church Fathers.[30] Believing that the moral correctives supplied by such Church Fathers as Augustine and Jerome, could provide a full education, Guarino saw no need to introduce specialized reading, such as Euclid's geometry or Aristotle's works on logic. He did not deny such books to advanced students, but they were never part of his regular curriculum. The only books he forbade were those on love–making, magical spells, and the art of delicate cooking.[31] In general, he was opposed to censor-

---

[29] In a letter of 1452 to his son, Niccolò, Guarino deplores the loss of Latin eloquence during the long period "when the great Cicero was unknown," and mentions, as examples of the kind of barbaric textbooks popular in his boyhood, the *Epigrammata* of Prosper of Aquitaine (versified *sententiae* from the works of St. Augustine), the *Dittochaeon* of Prudentius (a guide to the Old and New Testaments), and the *Chartula* (a moralistic poem of uncertain authorship); he also quotes a sample of the "barbaric" Latin then in vogue: "Vobis regratior quia de concernentibus capitaniatui vestri vestra me advisavit sapientitudo" (Guarino, *Epistolario* 2. Ep. 862. 20-31). Other texts, for which humanists had a particular aversion, were: the *Disticha Catonis*, the *Eclogue* of Theodulus, the *Facetus*, the *Tobias* of Matthew of Vendome, the *Parabolae* of Alain de Lille, the *Liber Aesopi*, the *Floretus*, the *Physiologus* of Theobaldus, the *Liber derivationum* of Uguccione of Pisa, the *Catholicon* of Giovanni da Genova, and the *Graecismus* of Evrard de Béthune. These are all described in Garin, *L'Umanesimo* 91-103. Garin also lists the *Elementarium doctrine erudimentum* of Papias, Donatus' *Ars minor* (and its abridgement, the *Ianua*) and the *Doctrinale* of Alexander de Villa-Dei; but these four were all approved of by Guarino.
[30] See remarks of Battista Guarini in Woodward, *Vittorino* 170, 173.
[31] Guarino, *Epistolario* 2. Ep. 823. 370-74.

ship, since without access to an author's full text a student could not discriminate between what was wholesome and what was not; he was prepared to trust the reader's own sense of decency to make the choice.[32]

His lecturing method was to impart information on diverse matters of grammar, syntax, style, history, myth, geography, and the various sciences as opportunities to do so presented themselves in his line-by-line commentary. Thus a note on some point of astronomy might directly follow one on an etymology, and it might be superficial or detailed, as he saw fit. Even his "scientific" notes, however, showed his literary bias, since they were never detailed, but usually called attention to some literary source where some broad scientific principle was mentioned. He was never interested in scholastic philosophy, or even in a close examination of the tenets of ancient philosophy; his conception of "philosophy" was as a series of moral precepts, with it exempla (illustrative anecdotes) which could be used to grace a poem, letter, treatise, or oration. Following Cicero and Quintilian, he believed that the union of *eloquentia* (good style) and *sapientia* (wisdom) made up the complete orator, or thoroughly educated man. In that sense, his curriculum was "balanced," but the overwhelming emphasis was on the literary skills in which he himself excelled. His teaching was entirely representative of what Italians have generally meant by *umanesimo*.[33]

---

[32] See n. 31 above for the reference. Battista Guarini makes the same point: see Woodward, *Vittorino* 170 and 175.

[33] Cf. the remarks of Monique Sprout in her introduction to Garnis Markham's English version (1608) of Ariosto's Sixth Satire, in *Umanesimo* 7, No. 3 (1967) 69-70: "The work (Ariosto's satire) is in fact the most genuine expression of humanistic writing. It is more so since the poet does not aim at writing a treatise with the pretense of being complete and encompassing all aspects of education ...Ariosto had only to speak of what he wanted a preceptor to give his son. He expressed

Guarino's students were expected to respond to his lectures with systematic study. One of his virtues, as Ianus recognized (*Panegyricus* 377; see also n. on 170-77), was his tripartite scheme of education, designed to take a student through an elementary, an intermediate, and an advanced stage. Thus a student could enter at any age or level of preparation. He educated his own sons from infancy, and at times accepted very young students as *contubernales*. [34] The students worked in pairs, helping and emulating each other. They made thorough notes, arranging the material in ways that would make retrieval of it easy. No doubt Ianus had many notebooks filled with a miscellany of historical and geographical facts, *exempla*, mythological data, grammatical rules, and graceful turns of phrase culled from his reading. In the absence of good dictionaries, handbooks, annotated texts, and encyclopedias, Ianus would have to create his own, or add to the few already in existence. Not only was this material set down, it was also learned by heart, until it became second nature. Guarino provided recommendations, inherited from Chrysoloras, as to how this could best be accomplished. Regular practice in speaking and writing Latin and Greek was also given. Ianus paints a charming picture of the evening discussions between Guarino and his pupils, with Guarino acting as judge (*Panegyricus* 601-03). Even more touching is the reminiscence of himself and his room-mate, Galeotto Marzio, rising before dawn from their warm beds to study, while the stars in heaven wondered at

---

what was really important to him: no science; no Aristotelian thinking or study of metaphysics; no practical training; no absorption into the divine; just goodness and "studio umano," that is, moral values fused with Christian religion, classical training not for the purpose of erudition and learning, but because classicism is the basis of religion and humanity."

[34] Giovanni Lamola was only nine when he first came to Guarino. See note on *Panegyricus* 645.

their lights below (*Panegyricus* 607-09).

In one of Ianus' earliest poems, addressed to Leonello d'Este, Ianus tried to give the impression that coming to Ferrara was his own idea:

> About my recent arrival in your city, Prince Leonello, from the chill axis of the Arctic sky: pardon me, but the attraction was not the lustrous fame of your deeds, nor your house, decked out with august forebears, nor your Ferrara with its glittering culture, nor the seven delightful tributaries of the twin Po. I came here not to feast my eyes, but my avid ears, food for which flows from the lips of Guarino.[35]

This poem, like many others of his addressed to dignitaries, has a confident ring. Ianus did not suffer from feelings of inferiority. It is clear that he was already making a hero of Guarino. Obviously he was receptive to the new learning. Like Guarino, he was not insensitive to the beauties of nature, civilized surroundings, and man's artistry, but literature was for him the supreme art.[36] The poem is also valuable, because it suggests that he had come to Italy directly from Hungary, the "chill axis of the Arctic sky." [37] Though born in Croatia, Ianus had been taken by his uncle to live in Hungary.

In Ianus' most famous elegy, *De morte Barbarae* (on the Death of Barbara), written after his mother's death in 1463,

---

[35] *Epigr.* 1. 185; Kombol, 190. Although the poem is addressed "Ad Leonellum Ferrariae Ducem" in Kombol's text, Leonello was not a duke (*dux*), but a marquis (*marchio*).

[36] For Guarino's view of the non-literary arts, see note on *Panegyricus* 443. For Ianus' similar views, see Birnbaum, 75.

[37] Ferrara is situated 44 degrees, 50 minutes N. and 11 degrees and 38 minutes E.; Budapest is 47 degrees, 30 minutes N. and 19 degrees, 20 minutes E. There is little difference in climate between Italy and Hungary, but if Ianus could say the Poles live in the Arctic regions (*Panegyricus* 483), he could say much the same about the Hungarians.

he acknowledged that Vitéz paid for his education in Italy for eleven years:

> I had scarcely drunk in the first elements
> of the tender Minerva, and was already
> showing no slight promise of what was to
> come, when your brother sent me to the
> shores of Ausonia, and bade me seek the
> muses in a distant world. At his expense
> I toured the cities of Venetia, while the
> sun went eleven times through the Zo-
> diac.

Vitéz might have sent him to Prague or Kraków, both of which had universities, but these institutions were usually attended by the children of the minor nobility. As bishop of Várad, the richest diocese in Hungary, Vitéz doubtless wished to follow the tradition of the higher aristocracy, who often had their sons educated in Italy.[38] Besides, only an Italian school like Guarino's could offer the humanist skills that Vitéz wanted his nephew to learn. Ianus was to be part of Vitéz' policy for the cultural revitalization of Hungary. To understand this, we must briefly review Vitéz' career.[39]

Born in 1408 at Sredna in Slavonia, Vitéz (whose name in Croatian means "knight") seems to have been of minor nobility. He was related to the Garázda and Szilágyi families, and hence distantly to the great nobleman, János Hunyadi, whose wife was a Szilyági. The details of his early career are not clear,[40] but he appears to have impressed

---

[38] See Birnbaum, 21-22 and 33, n. 2.
[39] The standard biography is still that of V. Fraknói: see n. 73.
[40] The date of his birth is variously given. Birnbaum (p. 124) and Peter Kulcsar in his article "Der Humanismus in Ungarn," *Matthias Corvinus und die Renaissance in Ungarn* (Schallaburg, 1982) 55, give 1408, while 1400 is the date given in Iohannes de Zredna, *Opera quae supersunt* ed. Ivan Boronkai (Budapest, 1980) Introduction, sec. 1, p. 11. Birnbaum (p. 18-19, n. 41) cites the suggestion of Csaba and Klara

Mátyás of Gothalocz, provost of Zagreb, and through him to have advanced rapidly as a servant of the Hungarian crown. He seems to have studied at Vienna in 1434, and thereafter worked in the chancery at Buda until 1444, where he made the acquaintance of Vergerio and the Polish humanist, Gregor Sanok. In 1443 he was made provost of Várad, and after the death of King Wladislaw I in 1444, he became secretary to János Hunyadi, who as voivode (governor) of Transylvania since 1442 and *capitaneus* (constable) of the southern marches, was the richest and most powerful noble in Hungary. Through Hunyadi, Vitéz became bishop of Várad in 1445. When Hunyadi was appointed regent in 1446, Vitéz ruled the kingdom with him, taking care of its administration and diplomacy, while Hunyadi attended to its military defence.

Since 1439 at least, Vitéz had been attempting to bring humanists into the Hungarian chancery. Hungary was emerging as a great power, and to help build and maintain her prestige, more was required than victory on the battlefield. Vitéz saw the need to train young men, selected from within the kingdom, whose Latin style would be as good as that of their foreign counterparts. Loyal to himself, they would provide the propaganda he foresaw would be needed, and add lustre to Hungary's emerging greatness. His own Latin was graceful and vigorous, but far from Ciceronian, as his letters and orations show.[41] Clearly, he expected his nephew to acquire the classical style which he

---

Csapodi that Vitéz was Ianus' paternal, rather than maternal, uncle, but indicates that the matter requires further investigation.

[41] For Boronkai's modern edition, see n. 40. Between 1448 and 1451 Vitéz' secretary, Paulus de Iwanich, collected and annotated 78 of Vitéz' letters. This collection (Cod. 431 of the Österreichische Nationalbibliothek in Vienna) was published in *Johannis de Zredna ... Epistulae per Paulum Iwanich ... congestae* (n.p., 1746).

himself lacked, and then return to assist him.

Early in 1451, Ianus paid a brief visit to his uncle in Buda. From two letters written by Vitéz, both dated March 17, 1451, we gather that Ianus had been in debt to Guarino, who had not permitted him to leave Hungary until the money was paid, or surety for it had been provided. Ianus had appealed for help to Giovanni Antonio della Torre, bishop of Modena, who had promised to make good the debt, if Ianus did not return. Both of Vitéz' letters show his tact, wry humor, and somewhat stiff, formal manner. The first, to Guarino, bears the salutation, "To the excellent gentleman, Guarino of Verona, Esquire, etc., our sincerely beloved friend," and is subscribed in the medieval manner, with the bishop's name and title. It reads:

> We have seen our John (*Iohannem*),[42] whom we recalled to us, once a boy, but now with the signs of a master's care and learning about him. We loved him in the person of a brother,[43] but much more as the picture of his teacher.[44] So having learned how much we owe for the diligence, affection, teaching, and goodwill that have been expended upon him, we must pay immediately. As we shall love a learned brother, so we shall not scorn to reimburse a teacher who does his job. We now send the same John back to his former place and position of trust, and commend him once more to your care.

---

[42] For Ianus' change of name, see n. 80.

[43] Paulus de Iwanich's note (in Boronkai's ed., p. 159) states that "John" was the brother of Vitéz, obviously using *frater* in its ecclesiastical sense, as Vitéz uses *fraternam* here.

[44] Vitéz knew what Guarino looked like, because in Guarino, *Epistolario* 3. 440-41 there is a letter of Ianus to Vitéz, dated 1449 by Sabbadini, in which he mentions sending a "bronze likeness" of Guarino to Vitéz. But here Vitéz is referring to spiritual rather than physical qualities.

Despite the complimentary tone, there is perhaps a note of resentment that Ianus had been regarded as untrustworthy. As we shall see later, Ianus, too, had been annoyed by Guarino's distrust, but did not handle his resentment so maturely. The second letter was addressed to the bishop of Modena, whom Vitéz had never met:

> Reverend Father, "Reverend Fatherhood"[45] shows its strength in that egregious "faith" of yours (which is the foundation and foremost of the other virtues), when it shows "faith,"[46] without a formal promise-to-pay, in strangers from abroad, whose acquaintance it has not yet made. Hence the saying that virtue cannot think of anyone except in virtuous terms.
>
> We have, then, seen your Reverend Fatherhood's letter, and we have also seen our beloved John, who was brought to account before us[47] by what you wrote and the strength of it. We gladly welcomed both, the letter just as much as our brother, and we were equally delighted by its kindness and the sight of him. We thank your Reverend Fatherhood very much, and also that virtuous and kind heart of yours. We are in your debt. Would that we could offer our own person as an acceptable settlement of this favor! That, at any rate, is what we intend to do, if the opportunity arises, and we are able to take it. We now remit and offer John in person to your Reverend Fatherhood, and we ourselves will come after him via a suitable

---

[45] *Paternitas vestra* was a common form of address to a bishop.
[46] There is a pun here. *Fides* can mean "religious faith" and "financial credit."
[47] The Latin "ad nos usque demissum," conveys a picture of a naughty child who has been sent to higher authority for chastisement.

courier.[48] In the meantime, please look
after him again, just as you trusted him
before, when your Reverend Fatherhood
chose to protect him of your own free
will, rather than to indict him, when you
were asked to provide his bond.[49] Dou-
bly, we commend him to your care.

Vitéz had not taken the matter lightly, and he was grate-
ful to a fellow-bishop for helping Ianus out of an embarrass-
ment. The offer of friendship, which might show itself in
future favors, would not have been lost on the bishop of
Modena, who continued to keep a watchful eye over Ianus.
In return, Ianus thanked him with two epigrams.[50]

In 1451 Ianus was made a canon in the cathedral of
Várad.[51] From then on, he was clearly designated for ad-
vancement in church and state, and his relationship with
Guarino seems to have improved.

After leaving Guarino's school in 1454, Ianus took an-
other vacation in Hungary before entering the University of
Padua in October of that year, to study canon law. Vitéz
had been made royal chancellor the year before, and was
now more powerful than ever. Clearly, he wished Ianus to
be qualified in every way for high office. Ianus' enrollment at
Padua was no reflection on Guarino's ability to impart ad-

---

[48] He means only that a further letter would be sent.
[49] The Latin is, "cui eciam (=etiam) hucusque reverenda paternitas
vestra prius ultro ferre, quam rogata deferre patrocinium maluit." The
Latin rogare can mean "to propose a stipulation," i.e. to ask someone if
he will promise something in accordance with some agreement; the verb
deferre (=deferre nomen ad praetorem) can mean "to inform against,"
or "bring to law." Vitéz means that the bishop of Modena could have
refused to help and left Ianus to the mercies of the authorities, had
Guarino chosen to prosecute Ianus.
[50] Epigr. 1. 81 and 82.
[51] Birnbaum, 111. The oft-repeated story that Ianus was also Provost
of Titel is challenged by István Tóth, "Janus Pannonius genealógiája,"
Janus Pannonius Tanulmanyok 68-69.

vanced knowledge, nor on the University of Ferrara, which awarded doctorates in both arts and law: it was simply that the prestige of a law degree from Padua was greater. According to a letter of Battista Guarini, Guarino's youngest son, Ianus took his doctorate in the unusually brief period of four years.[52] As Huszti has pointed out, there is no record in the archives of the University of Padua that Ianus took his doctorate, but this may be because the records of the university are defective for the year 1458.[53] Whether Ianus actually took his doctorate or not, the vast amount of correspondence he handled in the period 1460-1464, when he worked in the chancery of Buda, is proof that he used his legal training. He does not seem, however, to have enjoyed being a lawyer. In the *Panegyricus* he belittles the legal profession and lists it among those callings which Guarino had spurned for himself.[54]

After leaving Padua, Ianus visited Narni (the birthplace of his friend, Galeotto Marzio), Florence, and Rome, before returning to Hungary. He could not have chosen a more propitious moment for his own advancement. King Wladislaw V had died, and in January, 1458, Vitéz had secured the throne for Mátyás Hunyadi (1443-1490), the younger son of János Hunyadi (d. 1456). Mátyás (Matthias Corvinus) was grateful and disposed to reward Vitéz. When Nicolaus de Barnis, bishop of Pécs died early in 1459, Vitéz enlisted the king's help in obtaining the see for his nephew.

---

[52] A letter of Battista Guarini of 11467 to Giovanni Bertuccio, published by J. Abel, *Analecta* 203-11, provides a major source for Ianus' biography. Battista states that "he earned the insignia of a lawyer in four years, because after hearing him dispute, the whole college of lawyers at Padua thought that it was a stupendous and absolutely incredible performance, and they were hardly able to believe what they had seen and heard for themselves" (*Analecta* 207).

[53] Huszti, *Janus Pannonius* 356.

[54] *Panegyricus* 56.

By March, 1459, Ianus was being referred to as *episcopus electus* (bishop-elect), but Pope Pius II seems to have hesitated over confirming the appointment, perhaps because Ianus was only twenty-five.[55] Next to that of Várad, the bishopric of Pécs was the richest in Hungary. In a key position on the trade route between north and south, it drew its wealth from farming and the mining of gold, silver, and other ores. Matthias and Vitéz prevailed over the Pope's scruples, and by 1461 at the latest Ianus was installed as the twenty-sixth suffragan bishop.[56]

Over the next eleven years he played an active part in the politics of Hungary. His first love, however, was poetry, which he continued to write, though not at the elevated level he had earlier set for himself in *Panegyricus* 645-81. His projected epic on János Hunyadi was never written.[57] He did, however, glorify the martial exploits of Matthias in his sixth Elegy, which describes the capture of the city of Jajce from the Turks on Christmas Day, 1463. An eyewitness to the battle, he paints a vivid picture of the battle itself and the landscape of Bosnia:.

> Eagerly I rush through the enemy's fields. Behind me the lament is heard and in front the sound of fear. The Turkish power is destroyed, and everywhere there is killing, fire, destruction and ashes ...It used to be part of Illyria, but is now called Bosnia, a wild land, but opulent with silver ore. There did not stretch spacious fields with deep furrows, nor meadows that would bring

---

[55] This is Huszti's view (*Janus Pannonius* 188), and Birnbaum's (p. 111). Ante Kadić has suggested to me that the real reason may have been the Pope's dislike of nepotism.

[56] Birnbaum, 111-12 and 121, notes 5 and 6.

[57] See *Panegyricus* 675-81 and note on 677.

an abundant harvest, but naked, men-
acing mountains, inaccessible rocks and
elevated towers built on their rugged
edges...[58]

Ianus also accuses the other European powers of being too
selfish to help:

France sleeps, nor does Spain care about
Christ: England is ruined by rebel-
lious noblemen, and neighboring Ger-
many wastes its time in endless meet-
ings. Italy continues to be interested in
her commerce. . . We shall remain loyal
to our homeland and faith, no matter if
we get much help from you or a trifle.

ln 1463 and 1464 Matthias seemed to Ianus the hero of
Christendom.

The fortunes of Ianus and his uncle were never higher
than in 1465. Vitéz was made Archbishop of Esztergom and
Primate of Hungary, enabling him to increase his cultural
benefactions. He continued to believe in a strong central ad-
ministration and financial reform, but advised the king not
to over-tax his nobles or attempt absolute rule. Matthias
still trusted him, but was becoming less inclined to listen
to advice. On February 20, 1465, Ianus was sent as head of
an embassy to Italy, mainly to seek aid from Pope Paul II
and the other great powers for a crusade against the Turks.
Because of bad weather, he did not reach Venice until April
9, and from there he travelled to Padua, Ferrara, Florence,
and Rome.   The Pope promised 57,500 ducats, Florence
10,000, and Venice sundry contributions in kind, but Ianus

---

[58] Translation by Ante Kadić in his *Tradition of Freedom in Croatian
Literature* 349.

had hoped for much more. He was more successful in obtaining certain minor objectives: possession of some lands and livestock in the diocese of Zagreb, to which he laid claim; the right to rule on controversies over the collection of tithes within his own diocese; various titles and benefices for Péter Garázda and Clement of Nagyvát, Hungarian protégés of Vitéz, who were then studying at Ferrara; and a papal bull for the founding of a new university in Hungary, the statutes of which were to be drawn up by himself and Vitéz.

The trip to Italy revitalized his spirit. In Hungary, which he considered a barbaric land, he had to attend the king on his campaigns, a task unsuited to Ianus' hatred of bloodshed and increasingly frail health.[59] In Ferrara, he renewed his friendship with Battista Guarini, now professor of rhetoric and head of the *contubernium* since his father's death in 1460. He also met for the first time his own relative, Péter Garázda,[60] and Gaspare Tribraco, a poet from Modena.[61] In Florence, one of his missions was to buy books for himself and Vitéz. He therefore called at the *bottega* of Vespasiano da Bisticci, who later wrote a laudatory biog-

---

[59] For his sickness, see, e.g., *Epigr.* 1. 9 (*De se aegrotante in castris*) and 1. 3 (*Blasio militanti Janus febricitans*); for his detestation of war and bloodshed, *Epigr.* 1. 2; 1. 5; 1. 7; 1. 8; 1. 12.

[60] Garázda (1448/50?-1507) was regarded by his contemporaries as almost Ianus' equal as a Latin poet. His output was large, but only his own epitaph and a fragment of another poem remain. See S. V. Kovács, "Garázda Péter," *Irodalomtörténeti közlemények* 61 (1957) 48-62; M. D. Birnbaum, "An Unknown Latin Poem, Probably by Petrus Garazda, Hungarian Humanist," *Viator* 4 (1973) 303-09.

[61] Tribraco (1439-ca. 1493) was born at Reggio (Emilia), but spent his youth at Modena, where he became a teacher of grammar before moving to take up a similar post in 1464 at the university of Ferrara. On him in general, see A. Della Guardia, *Gaspare Tribraco de 'Trimbocchi* (Modena, 1910). His best-known work is a narrative poem in honor of Borso d'Este. In *Ad Trimbrachum poetam* ("To the poet, Tribraco"; *Epigr.* 1. 49) Ianus says that only Italian poets can write well, and compares himself to a goose amid swans. Other poems later exchanged between the two men are published in Abel, *Analecta* 120.

raphy of him.[62] We may doubt Vespasiano's claim that he introduced Ianus to Florentine society, but there is no reason to disbelieve his description of the magnificently-attired young Pannonian as very handsome ("di bellissima presenza"). Unfortunately, there are no reliably-authenticated portraits of Ianus in existence.[63] Vespasiano calls him the most talented man, foreign or Italian, he had ever known, uninterested in material things, and by repute a virgin. He insists that Ianus' life as a student was free from vice and full of virtue ("aliena da ogni vizio, e ripieno d'ogni virtu"). It was the kind of compliment he frequently included in his biographies of churchmen, but in Ianus' case he may have wished to counteract rumors, arising from the erotic epigrams Ianus had written in his student days, that the young Pannonian was unchaste. Ianus also met other notable Florentines, the most stimulating being Marsilio Ficino, the Platonist philosopher. After returning to Hungary, he maintained contact with Ficino.

When he returned from his embassy to Italy, Ianus fell into temporary disfavor with the King, for reasons that are not clear.[64] Some scholars have pointed to a pair of epigrams in which Ianus ridiculed the Pope, [65] but Birnbaum seems to me right in claiming that Matthias would have minimized

---

[62] Vespasiano da bisticci, *Vite di uomini illustri del secolo XV* ed. P. D'Ancona and E. Aeschlimann (Milano, 1951), 173-78.

[63] Birnbaum (p. 13-15) has an excellent discussion of several possible likenesses of Ianus. Of all of them, she considers a stone head (Plate II in her book), found by Ede Petrovich in the lapidary collection of Pécs Cathedral, most likely to be a portrait of Ianus.

[64] Huszti, *Janus Pannonius* 242-43, denies that there was any serious estrangement.

[65] *Epigr.* 1. 53 (a sneer at the Pope for having an illegitimate daughter) and 1. 58, *Quare nunc, ut quondam, summorum pontificum testiculi non explorantur* ("Why the Pope's testicles are not searched for now, as they once were"). Other epigrams mocking Paul II are 1. 52; 1; 54.

their importance.[66] It is more likely that Ianus had tried to sabotage Matthias' wishes, first, by suggesting to the Pope that Vitéz, rather than the King, should be allowed to choose the site of the new university, and second, by urging that Vitéz be made cardinal instead of Stefan of Warda, the king's nominee.[67] Presumably, Vitéz would have chosen to found the university at Esztergom, thus concentrating more power around himself . Matthias, however, chose Pozsony in Slovakia, and Stefan of Warda became cardinal in 1467. Matthias was beginning to sense stirrings of rebellion among his nobles, and it was his policy not to vest too much power in one man, however trustworthy he seemed to be. He might, however, have done better to promote Vitéz, who remained loyal to him until 1471, whereas Stefan de Warda aligned himself with the dissident nobility as early as 1467.

Kadić has pointed out another possible reason for the king's alienation from Ianus: the jealousy of certain Hungarians that a Slav had achieved such favor with Matthias.[68] This was the opinion of Ludovik Crijević (1459-1527) and Vespasiano da Bisticci, the latter of whom says that there were plots to poison Ianus[69]. Neither author states who these jealous men were, but Vespasiano refers to "a German bishop" whose machinations, he says, encompassed the ruin of Vitéz[70]. This bishop was probably Johann Beckensloer, bishop of Eger 1468-1472, and Vitéz' successor as Archbishop of Esztergom (1473), but at the time of Ianus' mis-

---

[66] Birnbaum, 161. She believes, however, that the Pope would have been so offended by the epigrams, if he had seen them, that it would have affected the outcome of his talks with Ianus.
[67] These points are well argued in Birnbaum, 159-161.
[68] Kadić, *Tradition of Freedom in Croatian Literature* 351, where he cites as evidence a passage from Ludovik Crijević (Tubero).
[69] *Vite di uomini illustri* 175.
[70] *Vite di uomini illustri* 171.

sion to Rome still provost of Pécs, a post to which he had been appointed in 1459. Birnbaum (p. 160, 177-78) suggests that Beckensloer and Girolamo Lando, Archbishop of Candia, who for some reason disliked Ianus, reported unfavorably on his mission to the Pope, and this is what aroused the king's wrath in late 1465. Neither of these men, however, was Hungarian, and Ianus could have had other enemies. Ianus regained Matthias' favor in 1466, but he was tired of the king's constant wars, and wanted only to pursue his scholarly interests and write poetry. Nevertheless, he could not escape political involvement. In an uprising of the nobles against Matthias in 1467, occasioned by increased taxation, Vitéz and Ianus remained loyal to the king, despite their growing anxiety over his arbitrary rule. Ianus was rewarded by being made Ban of Slovania in 1469. By 1470, however, it had become obvious that Matthias was bent on absolute power. The army, the courts, and the tax and monetary systems had all been reformed to further this end; the king was at war with Bohemia, and plotting to have himself made Holy Roman Emperor; he had attenuated the power of the magnates, and was relying more and more on an obedient bureaucracy of his own making; and, worst of all from the viewpoint of Ianus and Vitéz, he had left his southern borders vulnerable to the Turks. Ianus was removed from power as Ban of Slovania, and Vitéz was publicly slapped on the face for daring to question the king's policies. In 1471 both of them joined a conspiracy to replace Matthias with Casimir, the younger son of King Casimir IV of Poland. The plot failed, Vitéz was imprisoned, and Ianus fled, first to Pécs, which he fortified and then abruptly abandoned, then to Zagreb, where he took refuge in the fortress of Medvedgrad with Oswald Thuz, his relative and fellow-conspirator. According to Birnbaum (p. 201-202), his ultimate destination was Venice, the government of which may have been secretly backing Vitéz and his faction. Ianus, however, fell ill, probably from tuberculosis, and died at Medvedgrad on March 27, 1472. Vitéz died, probably of a stroke, on August 9 of the same year.

Despite its tragic end, most humanists would have considered Ianus' career enviable. He was born on August 29, 1434, near the confluence of the rivers Danube and Drava.[71] Most authorities agree that his family was of minor nobility.[72] Modern scholars are divided about his nationality, some claiming him for Hungary,[73], others for Croatia.[74] Vespasiano da Bisticci specifically called him a Slav,[75] but Battista Guarini seems to have thought of him as Hungarian.[76] The elder Guarino always called him "Pannonian." Ianus himself is explicit about his birthplace near the con-

---

[71] For the place, see *Panegyricus* 486-88; for the year, see authorities cited in Birnbaum, 16, note 1; for the day and month, see *Epigr*. 1. 107 and 208 (Kombol, 316).

[72] The best works on Ianus' family origins is by István Tóth, "Janus Pannonius származása," *Irodalomtörténeti Közlemények* 69 (1965), 603-13, and "Janus Pannonius genealógiája," in *Janus Pannonius Tanulmányok* (1975).

[73] For example, V. Fraknoi, *Vitéz János esztergomi érsek elete* 9-10; Huszti, *Janus Pannonius* 2; T. Kardos, "Janus Pannonius, Poet of the Hungarian Renaissance," *New Hungarian Quarterly* 14, No. 49 (1973) 84.

[74] For example, T. Klaniczay in *History of Hungarian Literature* ed. Miklós Szabolcsi (Budapest, 1964), 28; M. Kombol, *Ivan Česmički* p. xxii; V. Gortan in *Enciklopedija Jugoslavije* 4 (1960) 461; Andras Dávid, "Janus Pannonius a délszlávoknál," *Janus Pannonius Tanulmányok* 1975, 511.

[75] Birnbaum (p. 11) cites Enea Silvio Piccolomini, Tubero (Ludovik Crijević), Raffaello Ransan, and Vespasiano as calling him a Slav. The most important evidence is Vespasiano's, who calls both Ianus and his uncle, Vitéz, "dinazione schiavo" (*Vite* ed. D'Ancona and Aeschlimann, 169 and 173).

[76] Birnbaum (p. 11) rightly discounts this as an attempt by Battista to increase his friend's importance "by connecting him to the Várad bishopric and his uncle." Birnbaum also cites Rafaello Volaterrano and the elder Guarino as calling Ianus Hungarian.

fluence of the Danube and Drava, but not about his nationality. In one passage he uses the phrase *nos Hunni*
("we Huns"), but this was not necessarily a claim to be
Hungarian.[77] He was proud to be "Pannonius," but he
used this epithet for its associations with the ancient Roman province of Pannonia, which embraced the southwestern part of what is now Hungary, and all of Croatia that
lies outside Dalmatia. Almost certainly, he cared less about
his strict nationality than do his modern admirers.[78]

Even if, as seems likely, he was Croatian, he was born
a subject of Sigismund of Luxemburg, king of Hungary, because the Hungarian crown had ruled Croatia Proper and
Slawonia since 1102, and was not to relinquish either until 1527, when they passed to the Austrian Habsburgs. He
owed his advancement, moreover, to the Hungarian crown,
and remained loyal to it most of his life. Following the
theory of Vilmos Fraknói that Ianus' family originated in
Česmice, a village near Časma, a little to the east of Zagreb, Kombol and most Croatian scholars refer to Ianus in
Croatian as Ivan Česmički, "Česmički" being a masculine

---

[77] *Eleg.* 13. 87 (Kombol, 52) "Sin soli, luimus communia crimina,
Chuni" (But if we Huns alone are expiating the sins of all). Birnbaum
(p. 11) points out that "during the reign of Matthias the mistaken identification of the Hungarians with the Huns (based on Kezai's chronicle)
became an important part of the lesser nobility. For them it meant the
natio Hungarica, which was not the people, but the new, hybrid ruling
class of which Janus also considered himself a member." She also states
that Ianus "speaks for a heterogeneous political group who used the
Hun parallel as a slogan."
[78] See n. 71, also *Epigr.* 1. 338 (*De se ipso*; Kombol, 220), where he
says he was "Dravum generatus ad altum" (born near the deep Drava).
His most "nationalistic" poem is *Epigr.* 1. 61 (*Laus Pannoniae*): "Once
the land of Italy gave forth poems which everyone read; now Italy reads
poems sent from Pannonia. This brings great glory to me, but greater
glory to you, my country, ennobled by my genius." The epigram *in
Sclavoniam* (Kombol, 194) is not necessarily a slur, but simply a statement of fact: That part of Pannonia which is called Slavonia has many
villages, but no towns.

adjective in the nominative case, meaning "of Česmice." The Hungarian form of "Česmice" is "Czesmicze," hence the form of Ianus' name in Hungarian, János Czesmicze. In the fifteenth century it was not uncommon for the place of a person's birth or family origin to be used as a surname. Fraknói's theory, which Huszti adopted, has two weaknesses: first, Česmice is about two hundred kilometres from the confluence of the Danube and Drava; and second, the theory was based on what seems to be a reference in a papal document to Ianus as coming from Česmice. István Tóth, however, believes that this reference is actually to another nephew of János Vitéz.[79] More plausible is the theory that "Cesinge," used in another papal document definitely referring to Ianus, is an Italianization of the Hungarian "Kesince," a place in Slavonia on the southern bank of the Drava, near its confluence with the Drava. The Croatian form of "Kesince" is "Kesinec." Since its location fits Ianus' description of his birthplace, and several of his contemporaries refer to him as "Kesinac" (Birnbaum, 9 and 16, n. 10), the case in favor of Kesince is strong. When he first went to Italy, he used the given name, "Iohannes," but changed it, as he tells us in *Epigr.* 1. 130 (Kombol, 184):

> Lest you say, gentle reader, that you were not warned, I who am now called Ianus used to be called Iohannes. I did not reject that name out of dislike: none rings with greater fame throughout the world. Golden Thalia made me change it, against my will, when she washed me in the waters of Aonia.

He means by this that "Ianus" fits more easily into most Latin metres than "Iohannes." Birnbaum (p. 47) says that

---

[79] Tóth, "Janus Pannonius genealogiája," 67-69.

this change was made in 1454, but it is clear from Guarino's references to him as "Ianus" in letters of 1452 and 1453 that the change occurred earlier.[80]

Ianus' father, about whom nothing certain is known, died in 1440, leaving his wife, Barbara, sister of János Vitéz, to raise Ianus and his sister and two older brothers. In *De morte Barbarae* 85-84, Ianus says that his birth almost killed her, and she cherished him like an only child (90-94). "Perhaps," he says (95-100), "mothers have presentiments. Or does their love dwell more on the child who is born late? As soon as I took my first steady steps, and my tongue was no longer stammering and lisping, you started me, nothing loath, on the liberal arts, and did not let me be idle at home." He records (101-102) that she paid for his first lessons with money earned by spinning and weaving. One is reminded of a similar devotion on the part of the father of the poet Horace (*Satires* 1. 6. 71-92), and there is a curious parallelism in *Panegyricus* 40-44 between Ianus' upbringing by his mother and Guarino's by his. One might suspect a poetical *topos*, were it not for the deep sincerity which seems to inform the poem as a whole. Ianus never loved anyone more deeply than his mother. Could his affection for Guarino have stemmed in part from the fact that he, too, was given his early education through the selfless devotion of a widowed mother?[81]

---

[80] Guarino, *Epistolario* 2. Ep. 858.20 and Ep. 870.32.

[81] Cf. Guarino, *Epistolario* 2. Ep. 904.15-32: "Once long ago I got this advice [to be proud of his name] from my mother, a really wonderful woman, who loved and respected God and was an outstanding example of chastity and clean living among wives, and then later among widows. I used to be very happy and, as soon as I began to grow up and understand these things, I was not a little proud that I bore the name and distinction of my family and ancestors. This was the way my mother really inspired me to follow honorably in their footsteps, and she repeated the lesson often. For I had been left an orphan from my tenderest years, my father being already dead. I have only a dim,

Ianus does not say who his first teachers were. Vitéz had perhaps moved her and her children to Várad, when he became provost there in 1443. Ianus seems to have been in his direct care before he went to Italy. When Ianus became bishop of Pécs, he brought his mother to live there. When she fell ill in 1463, Ianus provided her with every care, but she died, aged sixty, on December 10. In *De morte Barbarae* he mourned her passing just when his career was so promising, and he had the means to provide every comfort. "The little sisters (*pupillae sorores*)," he laments (*De morte Barbarae* 135-138), "are not yet married, a throng that was to have been instructed by you. Who will now imbue their tender years with the arts? Who will now guard their tender virginity?" Birnbaum (p. 115) says that Barbara "ran a sort of private boarding school for young girls:" The word *pupillae*, however, does not mean "pupils," but simply "little girls." Barbara's arts are more likely to have been those of the household,[82] and the "throng" of unmarried girls were probably cousins and nieces of Ianus, the same *cognatae* (female relatives) he refers to in line 119 as being recently in his mother's care (*nuper tua cura*). He speaks of her as preparing tasty dishes, and spinning and weaving (lines 113-114), but not as an educated woman. Ianus missed his family sorely when he first arrived in Ferrara, but he was soon befriended by Galeotto Marzio, a twenty-one-year-old poet

---

dream-like memory of him. He fought in that battle which took place between the two rulers of Padua and Verona, and was taken prisoner. Later, as I learned afterwards, he died in enemy hands. The Veronese army lost because of the bungling and incompetence of a general, who had no experience of battles, save what he had seen in paintings or read about in books. So for those reasons, which I learned not from my father, but, as I said, from my mother..."

[82] Cf. *Epigr*.1. 135; Kombol, 184), the epitaph on Guarino's wife, Tadea, in which she is said to have surpassed Palas (Athena) in the arts, clearly meaning the domestic arts.

and former soldier from Narni, who studied with Guarino from 1447 to 1449. Ianus refers to him almost passionately in the *Panegyricus* 637-39, and in his 122-line *Elegia ad Galeottum Narniensem* (Eleg. 2. 4; Kombol, 112-18), the latter written in 1454, soon after their re-union at the University of Padua:

> We shared the same room, and one ta-
> ble always provided the food we shared.
> Often enough, the two of us were up un-
> til midnight, although our weary eyes
> longed for the gift of sleep. Often, when
> we had been lying warm and comfortable
> in bed, we rose before dawn at three in
> the morning. I had no one to trust, no
> one willing to look after me, but you.
> You took the place of uncle and brother,
> and were like a father and mother to me.
> (Eleg. 2. 4. 57-66)

Perhaps Guarino had asked Galeotto to act as Ianus' protector. Ianus adored him, but we cannot tell how deeply Galeotto reciprocated this hero-worship. Galeotto had a splendid physique, but Ianus professed to admire his mind even more (30-32); he helped Ianus with the intricacies of Latin metre, and dazzled him with his poetic gifts and moral character (69-108). The two remained friends for life, but there are indications that Galeotto's feelings were not entirely selfless, once Ianus had attained wealth and power.[83] Ianus had few real friends at Ferrara, or indeed at any time in his life. In the *Panegyricus* he omits mention of Elia Czepes and Zavissius Operowski, students from his own part of the world.[84] Perhaps, as Birnbaum suggests, he may have

---

[83] See note on *Panegyricus* 637.
[84] Operowski, nephew of the Polish archbishop, Wladislaw Operowski, came to Ferrara about August, 1449 (Guarino, *Epistolario* 1. Ep.

wished to avoid being identified with the many foreigners in Italy, against whom there was considerable prejudice,[85] but perhaps he omitted the names of compatriots from the *Panegyricus* only because none of them was important enough. He regarded this poem as his first major work, the "first fruits" of his "tender lyre."[86] Those he would "immortalize" in it could not be selected haphazardly. He must have had some bonds with fellow-Croatians or Hungarians at Ferrara and Padua, but he seems not to have maintained them, and to have been lonely most of his life. Even his uncle, whom he loved, was often too busy to have much time for him.[87]

The omission of certain eminent names from the *Panegyricus* suggests that he was jealous of them. For example, he may have been piqued because Raffaele Zovenzoni had been invited to contribute to Guarino's *Chrysolorina*, but

---

817.14). A letter of 1453, from Simon of Hungary to János Vitéz, attests to the presence in Ferrara of Simon himself and Giorgius Polycarpus (Kosztolanyi), both protégés of Vitéz Guarino, *Epistoario* 3.442-43). A letter from Giorgius Augustinus Zagrabiensis to Nicolaus Ostphus (Guarino, *Epistolario* 3.441), dated 1454 by Sabbadini, tells of a visit that Giorgius had made with Elia Czepes (or Czepez) to Bologna, where Ostphus (Sabbadini suggests) was in the service of Cardinal Bessarion. Giorgius in the same letter says that Ianus had been absent from Ferrara, but had returned, to the joy of his compatriots, on June 29th.

[85] On the hostility of Italians to refugees from the Turkish aggressions, see Deno J. Geanokoplos, *Byzantine East and Latin West* (Oxford, 1966; repr. by Archon Books, 1976), 1-6, 17-18, 49, 52, 87, 88, 94 n. 41, 105, 173, 193. On specifically anti-Slav feelings, Birnbaum (p.64, n. 16) points out that as late as the second half of the fourteenth century, Christians from Bosnia were being sold as slaves in Florence, and instances the high proportion of Slavic names in criminal records in Italy (for brawling and thievery) as proof of prejudice against them. According to Tubero (see n. 68), Ianus suffered from similar prejudices in Hungary.

[86] *Panegyricus* 1-7, and *Praefatio* 8.

[87] In the epigram, *Ad Joannem Archiepiscopum Strigoniensem* (Kombol, 184), Ianus chides his uncle for giving so much time to official business, and ends with the warning (lines 11-12): "If you are wise, be your own man some of the time, and don't live so much for others that you die to yourself."

he himself had not.[88] By 1454 Zovenzoni had made his mark as a poet, and it is noteworthy that Ianus ignores him.

Similarly, he ignores Lodovico Carbone (1435-1482). Huszti, on the basis of harsh comments about Ianus made by Carbone in his *Dialogus,* written long after 1472, maintained that the two men had always been enemies.[89] The epigrams in which Ianus pokes fun at Carbone neither support nor cancel out this view. He calls him a "hermaphrodite" in one (*Epigr.* 1. 90), because he is both an orator and a poet (in myth, Hermaphroditus was the child of Hermes, god of eloquence, and Aphrodite, goddess of beauty); in another (Kombol, 274) he puns on his second name:

> You who are now charcoal (*carbo*) were
> once a living coal; lose heart, Lodovico,
> you will soon become ashes.

Birnbaum (p. 53) sees no particular harshness in such jokes about Carbone, and considers the fact that Ianus took Carbone's poems with him to Hungary proof of his appreciation of them.[90] She also discounts the negative remarks about Ianus in Carbone's *Dialogus,* on the grounds that they were made to please Matthias Corvinus, and cannot be

---

[88] For the *Chrysolorina* and Zovenzoni's contribution to it, see note on *Panegyricus* 155. Zovenzoni (1431-ca. 1484) was born in Trieste, and received his early education there. He studied under Guarino 1450-1454, and thereafter taught in Capodistria, Trieste (1466-1470), then again at Capodistria, where he married into the family of Pier Paolo Vergerio. In 1471 he moved to Venice and remained there until his death. His best-known work is a poem, *Istrias,* in three books. He was crowned poet laureate in 1470 by the Emperor Frederick III. See B. Ziliotto, *La cultura letteraria di Trieste e dell'Istria* (Trieste, 1912) 1. 133-40, and Guarino, *Epistolario* 3. 465-66; also B. Ziliotto, *Raffaele Zovenzoni, la vita, i carmi* (Trieste, 1950).

[89] Huszti, *Janus Pannonius* 140.

[90] For the transportation of Carbone's poems to Hungary, see Csaba Csapodi, "Janus Pannonius könyvei és pécsi könyvtára," *Janus Pannonius Tanulmányok* 201.

taken as evidence of Carbone's feelings in his youth. Per-
haps by 1459 each had a more mature attitude towards the
other: Ianus recognized Carbone's literary merits, and Car-
bone those of Ianus, whom he mentions in the 1460 funeral
speech on Guarino as "fit to be numbered among famous po-
ets." We know nothing about Carbone's attitude towards
Ianus in his student days, but the omission in 1454 of Car-
bone from Ianus' list of famous pupils of Guarino in the
Panegyricus seems pointed.

Most conspicuous, however, is the omission of Basinio
da Parma (1424-1457).[91] Basinio had studied Latin under
Vittorino, and Greek under Theodore Gaza, at Mantua.
When Vittorino died in 1446, Gaza moved to Ferrara, and
Basinio went with him, becoming Guarino's student until
1451. At Ferrara he wrote a long mythological poem, *Melea-
gris*, which established his reputation. The first two books
were dedicated to Girolamo Castello, whom Ianus mentions
in *Panegyricus* 636. Since Castello and Basinio were close
friends, and Basinio was far from a non-entity, Ianus' re-
fusal to pair them looks like a calculated insult, all the more
pointed by the inclusion in line 640 of Tobia dal Borgo, a
much less famous poet, who, like Basinio himself, became
one of the resident humanists of Sigismondo Malatesta at
Rimini.[92] In what seems to be an early epigram, *In Bas-
inum* (Kombol, 314), Ianus had played on Basinio's name,
which according to Ferrante Borsetti[93] was actually Basino

---

[91] The only major work on Basinio is F. Ferri, *La giovinezza di un
poeta. Basinii Parmensis carmina* (Rimini, 1914), in which Basinio's
lyrical poems are published; see also the notices in Guarino, *Epistolario*
3. 210, 218, 382-83, 392, 395, 441, 475, 488-90, 507.
[92] For Basinio's friendship with Castello, see Guarino, *Epistolario* 3.
382. For Tobia dal Borgo, see note on *Panegyricus* 640.
[93] Author of *Historia almi Ferrariae gymnasii* 1-2 (Ferrariae, 1735).
I have not located Borsetti's statement about Basinio's real name, re-
ported in Birnbaum, 49, n. 13.

(Latin, *Basinus*): "Since you are Basinus, why do you want
to be Basinius? It would be more fitting, if the first let-
ter were to drop out." Without its first letter, "Basinus"
becomes "asinus," meaning "ass." There may be another
play on "Basinus," which could be taken as a diminutive of
the vulgar Latin *Basus*, meaning "penis." Ianus' dislike for
Basinio was unremitting, especially in the period 1451-1457,
when the latter was at Rimini. Basinio wrote much excel-
lent poetry in those six years, but this only added fuel to
the fire.[94] Particularly offensive to Ianus was a covert attack
on Guarino in Basinio's *Hesperis*, Canto 10. 170-230.[95]

The pupils of Guarino specifically named in the *Pan-*

---

[94] His works included the *Liber Isottaeus*, a collection of elegies cele-
brating Sigismondo's love for Isotta, the author of which was proved to
be Basinio by F. Ferri, *L'autore del Liber Isottaeus* (Rimini, 1912), and
"Il testo definitivo del Liber Isottaeus," *Giornale storico della letteratura
italiana* 3 (1913) 50ff.; the *Astronomicon*, modeled on the *Phaenomena*
of the third-century B.C. poet, Aratus of Soli; an epic, *Argonautica*,
based on the work of the same name by Apollonius of Rhodes; and
the *Hesperis*, an epic with Sigismondo Malatesta as its hero, in which
episodes from Vergil and Homer are ingeniously adapted to create a
vigorous and fast-moving narrative.

[95] In 1455 Basinio wrote Guarino an affectionate letter (Guarino,
Epistolario 2. Ep. 891), at the end of which he promised to send him a
copy of a satire he had written against "the swine," meaning Porcelio
Pandone, who in a debate at Rimini in 1455 over the usefulness of Greek
had joined Tommaso Seneca against Basinio (for whose satire, see F.
Ferri's article in *Athenaeum* 5 [1917] 33-43, with Sabbadini's note, p.
40-41). Like Guarino, who held strong views on the necessity of Greek
(see n. on *quicquid spectabile* in *Panegyricus* 109), Basinio defended
the language. Why, then, did he suddenly turn and attack Guarino in
the *Hesperis*? Sabbadini proposes (Guarino, *Epistolario* 3. 490) that
Guarino had been negotiating, through Basinio, the possibility of dedi-
cating his translation of Strabo in 1455 to Sigismondo Malatesta; when
he dedicated it instead to Jacopo Antonio Veneto (for the involved cir-
cumstances, see n. on *Panegyricus* 732-33), Sigismondo was offended,
and Basinio, loyal to his employer rather than his teacher, inserted a
passage in the *Hesperis* in which he mocked an aged teacher named
Carinus, living near the Po. This was clearly an attack on Guarino. My
suspicion is that since Ianus hated both Basinio and Sigismondo, but
was a close friend of Jacopo Antonio Veneto, he persuaded Guarino to
change his plan for the dedication of the Strabo translation, in order to
spite Basinio and Sigismondo.

egyricus are: Leonello d'Este (421, 714-15) and his son, Niccolò (592), Francesco Barbaro and Leonardo Giustinian (630-31), George of Trebizond (632-35), Girolamo Castello (636), Galeotto Marzio (637-39), Tobia da Borgo (641), Tito Vespasiano Strozzi (642-43), Bartolomeo Fazio (644), Pietro del Monte and Giovanni Lamola (645), Vittorino da Feltre (795), Battista Guarini (839-53), and Ianus himself (486-88, 675-82).[96] He could not have met Vittorino da Feltre or Giustinian, since both died before he came to Italy, and it is unlikely that he knew Tobia dal Borgo (d. 1448?), Lamola (d. 1449), Fazio, Pietro del Monte, or George of Trebizond other than by reputation.[97] Francesco Barbaro he met only in 1453.[98] The only "notables" he could have known at Ferrara were Leonello d'Este, Niccolò d'Este, Tito Vespasiano Strozzi, Galeotto Marzio, and Battista Guarini. Leonello, as marquis, was probably a comparatively remote figure, although Ianus had met him through the Bishop of Modena, wrote poems to him, and must have seen him often; Niccolò d'Este was "notable" only for his rank, and his name was included only to show that Guarino was trusted as a tutor by the Este familiy; Strozzi was an older poet, whom Ianus admired and exchanged verses with, but does not seem to have been particularly close to.[99] In the *Panegyricus* there is no reference to Borso d'Este, marquis of Ferrara since 1450 and duke of Modena and Reggio since 1453. By contrast, Ianus heaps praise upon his predecessor,

---

[96] For information on these individuals, see notes to *Panegyricus* at the passages cited.
[97] All of them had left Guarino's school by the time Ianus had arrived there.
[98] Guarino, *Epistolario* 2. Ep. 870.82-84.
[99] See Huszti, *Janus Pannonius* 122-31, where he analyzes the poems exchanged by Ianus and Strozzi on the subject of love. Birnbaum (p. 148) states that Ianus was probably only trying to get "some attention from the famous poet."

Leonello. The explanation may be that Borso had offended Guarino in 1450 by cutting Guarino's salary by more than half.[100] Guarino retaliated in two ways: by threatening, over the period 1450–1453, to leave Ferrara, and by ignoring Borso in his writings. Ianus, too, had threatened to leave Ferrara with Guarino,[101] and by ignoring Borso in the *Panegyricus* he may again have been following the master's lead. Birnbaum states (p. 52, note 52): "Had Janus kept a diary in Ferrara, we would proably not know more about his life and experiences than what has transpired through the epigrams to, and about, friends, and in the panegyric about Guarino."

Some of those to whom his epigrams are addressed, such as Leonello d'Este,[102] Giovanni Aurispa,[103] Theodore Gaza,[104] Giovanni Antonio della Torre,[105] and Francesco Durante da Fano,[106] were real people, but others may not have

---

[100] See note to *Panegyricus*, 390–392.

[101] In his elegy to the Veronese lawyer, Bartolomeo Cevola (Cipolla), he wrote: Ecce parat patrias remeare Guarinus ad arces/ Non potero tanto non comes esse viro. ("See, Guarino is preparing to return to his native city; I cannot but accompany such a great man.") (Notice in Guarino, *Epistolario* 3.456).

[102] *Epigr.* 1. 178, 179, 185, 233 (the last an epitaph).

[103] *Epigr.* 1.111 (*De docto simulato*) and 112 (*De Aurispa*; Kombol, 242). Aurispa (1376–1459) made two trips to the Greek East (1413 and 1421–1423), from which he brought back over 250 Greek manuscripts. After teaching at Savona, Bologna, and Florence, he went to Ferrara in 1427 or 1428 as tutor to Meliaduse d'Este. Thereafter, he divided his time between Rome and Ferrara. Ianus seems to have had little respect for his scholarship.

[104] *Epigr.* 1. 109 (Kombol, 242). Gaza (1398-1475), a native of Salonika, came as a refugee from the Turks to Italy in 1444. He taught Greek in Vittorino's school at Mantua, then at Ferrara (1447-1449), before moving to Rome as a protege of Nicholas V. After 1455, he moved to Naples, where his new patron, Cardinal Bessarion, made him Abbot of San Giovanni di Piro at Salerno.

[105] *Epigr.* 1. 81, 82, 259.

[106] The exchange of epigrams between him and Ianus is published in Abel, *Analecta* 145. Birnbaum (p. 53) states that Durante was the first of Ianus' schoolmates to praise him in poetry.

been. Moreover, it is hard to date the poems exactly, and impossible to know the full circumstances behind them. We do not know, for example, why Ianus said Aurispa was a "sham scholar," or whether the mutual admiration in the poems exchanged between Ianus and Francesco Durante was sincerely meant.

Many of the epigrams are addressed to characters with names like Lupus, Gryllus, Ovillus, Ornitus, Anellus, Crispus, Linus, Ladvancus, Gallus, Petrus, Ugo, Iulius, Philiticus, Agapetus, Lucia, Ursula, and Thecla. In some cases he was probably writing about a real person: for example, "Agapetus" in *Epigr.* 1. 71 may be Agapito Romano Cenci, who was a friend of Enea Silvio Piccolomini and appears as one of the characters in Lorenzo Valla's *De Voluptate*[107], and "Philiticus" in *Epigr.* 1. 25 may be Marino da Filettino, a student at Guarino's school until 1454.[108] In most cases, however, the addressees were probably fictitious.

We can never be sure that Ianus' epigrams were based on real experiences. Many are so sexually explicit that some scholars have assumed that he was drawing from actual sexual encounters. Domonkos, for example, states: "Vespasiano was obviously wrong when he wrote that "by common opinion he had never known woman.' His poems reveal that he knew them most intimately."[109] By "intimately" Domonkos obviously means "sexually." Some may assume, as the French humanist Muretus once said, that a poet who writes like Catullus is rarely like Cato in his morals,[110] but against this we can set Ianus' own statement in the epigram

---

[107] Birnbaum, 46.
[108] Birnbaum, 46.
[109] Domonkos, "Ecclesiastical Patrons as a Factor in the Hungarian Renaissance," 113, n. 35.
[110] "Quisquis versibus exprimit Catullum/Raro noribus exprimit Catonem."

Ad Petrum (1. 186; Kombol, 272):

> You who are a Fabricius[111] on the outside
> but an Apicius[112] within, please spare your
> strictures on my trifles. My morals and your
> words have something in common: you live
> the way I talk.

Ianus, moreover, is sure to have followed Guarino's often-repeated belief in the ancient doctrine of *proprietas*, enunciated, for example, in Catullus 16. 5-9: "It becomes a true poet to be personally chaste, but it isn't necessary that his verses should be so. In fact, the very thing that gives them zest and charm is that they may be just a little voluptuous and naughty, and able to arouse the flesh." Literary imitations were expected from students, and it so happened that Ianus chose above all to imitate Martial among the ancients and Antonio Beccadelli (1394-1471) among the moderns. The latter's *Hermaphroditus*, a two-volume collection of largely spicy epigrams, had appeared at Bologna in 1424. Guarino defended it fiercely in 1426, and although he was forced to write a partial retraction in 1434, he never changed his basic position that the personal morals of an author must not be confused with those of the characters he writes about.[113] It would be absurd, however, to suppose that Ianus had no sexual feelings. Birnbaum (p. 70-71),

---

[111] Gaius Fabricius Luscinus, Roman consul in 282 and 278 B.C., a military hero noted for his austerity and incorruptibility.

[112] Proverbial cognomen of several Roman gourmets, especially M. Gavius, who lived in the time of Augustus and Tiberius (Pliny, N.H. 10. 133). The cookbook. *De re coquinaria* ascribed to Caelius Apicius, probably belongs to the fourth century.

[113] His strongest statement of this doctrine, one of the pillars of his defense of teaching the pagan classics to Christians, comes in Guarino, *Epistolario* 2. Ep. 823, to Giovanni da Prato, a Minorite friar, who in his Easter sermon at Ferrara in 1450 had called for a burning of pagan books and their teachers.

claims that at least one poem (*Epigr.* 1. 332) has "definite autobiographical allusions". This we may believe of the lines:

My voice is thicker, all covered with desire,
my organ swells while caressing my young groins.
Just looking at a girl my heart is afire,
and burning dreams drench my sheet and my blanket.[114]

The remaining six lines, however, in which Ianus warns a "stinking pedagogue" not to open his pants, may simply reflect in a joking way a concern about morally dubious tutors, voiced in antiquity by Quintilian (1. 1. 4 and 23) and others, and frequently in the Renaissance by writers such as Maffeo Vegio, Enea Silvio Piccolomini, Vittorino, Guarino, and Lodovico Ariosto.[115] In an epigram (1. 127) addressed to Guarino, Ianus says:

When you happened to be reading my
little book (*libellum*), Guarino, you said

---

[114] *Epigr.* 1.332 (*De sua aetate*), 5-8. English translation in Birnbaum, 70-71.

[115] See, e.g., the strictures of Vegio, *De educatione puerorum et eorum claris moribus* 2. 4 and 5, and Piccolomini, *Tractatus de liberorum educatione* sec. 12 (in Garin, *L'Umanesimo*, 182 and 230, 232, respectively). The vice most feared was homosexuality. Francesco da Castiglione in his *Vita Victori Feltrensis* states Vittorino's position: *Abhorrebat precipue vitium soddomiticum. Si quem adulexcentum qui apud se erant illo infectum esse offendisset, nulla poterat vel magna in eum animadversione satiati* ("He particularly loathed sodomy. If he discovered any of the youths who were with him to be tainted with it, he could not be sated by any punishment, however great, meted out to him."). Guarino was likewise concerned when in 1426 Giacomo Zilioli, *referendarius* to Niccolò III d'Este, was considering hiring Antonio Beccadelli as tutor to Meliaduse d'Este. In *Epistolario* 1. Ep. 431 and 432 Guarino warned Zilioli of the moral danger to the young man; hiring Beccadelli (whom he does not actually name) would be "like throwing a lamb to a wolf." Most explicit is the statement of Ariosto, *Satire* 6. 25-27: "Pochi sono grammatici ed humanisti/Senza il peccato per cui Sabaot/Fece Gomorra e i suoi vicini tristi" ("There are few grammar teachers and humanists without the vice for which the Lord of Hosts devastated Gomorrah and its neighborhood.").

(so I'm told), "This isn't what I teach."
I admit, sir, it isn't what you teach, but
you do teach what makes it possible.

Birnbaum (p. 31) assumes that the *libellus* contained
epigrams of a "daring" nature, and that Guarino read them
"in perplexed disbelief," but "since Guarino was one of the
chief supporters of Beccadelli, there was little left for him to
say to the playful arrogance of his young favorite." There is
no evidence that what Guarino disapproved of was sexually-
explicit material. Even if it was, Guarino would not have
been "perplexed," since he well understood the doctrine of
proprietas, and the practice of *imitatio veterum* (imitation
of the ancients). The truth is that we can infer nothing
about Ianus' sexual experiences, or even that he had any,
from his poetry. We can probably infer, however, from such
epigrams as *Ad libros suos* ("To his books," 1. 293; Kombol,
204) and *In Iudaeum foeneratorem* ("To a Jewish money-
lender," 1. 294; Kombol, 204) that Ianus was often short of
cash. The epigram *Ad Mutinensem praesulem cum egebat*
("To the bishop of Modena, when he was short of money"
Kombol, 198) must refer to his financial embarrassment in
1451:

> I can't stay, and I can't leave, such com-
> mands summon me, such chains bind
> me. I'm in narrow straits. What am I
> to do? What gods am I to cry to? They
> exist, I think, but they are hard on the
> poor, and don't favor them, in my opin-
> ion. I implore your help, most gentle
> bishop of Modena, my glory and the first
> patron of my muses. I'm not asking for
> a cloak to fend off the blasts of Boreas
> (i.e. the north wind), or the soft flanks
> of your mule, or a bridle, a saddle, or
> anything like that. What, then? I owe

Guarino a coin or two, which I'm asking
you to stand surety for.

Another, *Ad Gallionem* (Kombol, 258), the addressee of
which was Guarino, with only a few letters of his name
changed, probably refers to the same incident:

If you don't care for personal I.O.U's on
a legal document, and you aren't im-
pressed with my good faith or the deities
I swear by, I'll arrange for a suitable
principal to provide your surety. Or do
you hesitate to trust even a bishop?

Hardly less tart is another epigram (Kombol, 288):

You commend and love my little book
(*libellum*) about you, which I sent to
you; but although you praise and love
the book, you'd rather have as many
coins (*monetam*) as it has verses.

If *libellus* here refers to the *Panegyricus*, which is also called
a *libellus* in the epigram, *Veronae commendat panegyricam
(sc. silvam) Guarinianam* ("He commends the panegyric
on Guarino to Verona"; Kombol, 240), we may date the
epigram to 1454. In any case, it is another wry comment
on Guarino's respect for money. In the *Panegyricus*, how-
ever, he praises Guarino's generosity (869-71). He must
have known that Guarino, who had a wife and twelve chil-
dren to support, was sometimes forced to extend credit to
students, especially those from distant parts, against the ar-
rival of money for their school fees and living expenses; he
had to be repaid, and sometimes he had to be insistent.[116]

---

[116] Once at least Guarino resorted to legal action to collect fees. Sab-

Overall a most attractive picture of Guarino emerges from the *Panegyricus*. Ianus depicts him as conspicuously moral (*Panegyricus* 382-85, 614-22, 701-02, 802-04), and a stern disciplinarian (831-33), who achieved obedience by kindness rather than force (382-90); as an excellent teacher, who encouraged the brighter students, without ignoring the slow learners (368-69); and as a man with a sense of humor (825-30), not prone to anger or spite (817-20), and not afraid to show emotion, when his heart-strings were plucked (839-46). Above all, according to Ianus (810), he was a religious man. This raises the matter of Ianus' own religious convictions.

Guarino gave no formal instruction in religion, this being left to the students' spiritual confessors, but he encouraged ordinary devotions, such as daily attendance at mass (585). Although he strenuously defended the pagan classics against the attacks of extremists like Giovanni da Prato, [117] he was careful to warn his students against heresies, and the incorrect theology of the ancients. "How often," says Carbone in his funeral speech on Guarino, "did this great Christian interrupt a lecture to refute the foolish ideas of the ancients about the immortal gods!" Carbone also says that Guarino "realized that we who are Christians must have a range of reading different from that of the pagans, who did not know God." Thus he included study of the

---

badini (Guarino, *Epistolario* 3.50-51) published a suit against Francesco and Niccolo Brenzon in 1420 for 100 ducats owed for the tuition and upkeep of Bartolomeo Brenzon. This was more than double his usual fee of 40 ducats a year (Guarino, *Epistolario* 1. Ep. 231.37). In the academic year 1448-49, he was forced four times to dun Mikolej Lasowski for his nephews' fees (Guarino, *Epistolario* 2. Ep. 817). Equally revealing is a letter of Zavissius Operowski (publ. in Guarino, *Epistolario* 3.416-417), complaining about Guarino's constant demands for money owed to him.

[117] See n. 113.

Church Fathers in his curriculum.[118] Imitation of the ancients required the introduction of "divine machinery," but this did not imply for Guarino rejection of the Christian revelation. He seems to have held the view that the pagan "gods" existed, but were actually demons.[119] Their names and myths were useful only as adornment or symbols in poetry. On the other hand, he was no ascetic or pietist. At Verona, he had warned his favorite pupil, Martino Rizzon, not to become a monk without consulting him first, hinting that there were more useful things for a scholar to do.[120] He also spoke with contempt of a religiosity, which "can be satisfied with nothing but tears, fasts, and psalms.[121] Such remarks, however, are not inconsistent with a faith in God. Distaste for what some Christians do is not the same thing as rejecting Christianity. Ianus, I believe, took his cue in religious matters from Guarino. He wrote a number of poems mocking the superstitious laity and corrupt churchmen, but Birnbaum goes too far, I think, in claiming that he identified religion itself with ignorance and hypocrisy.[122] I see no proof that he was ever an atheist,[123] and none that he

---

[118] See n. on *Panegyricus* 370-77.
[119] See n. on *Panegyricus* 71.
[120] Guarino, *Epistolario* 434. 35-50.
[121] Guarino, *Epistolario* 1. Ep. 346. 18-21: "Plus valet apud me conterranei mei vatis non illepidi auctoritas (ref. to Catullus 16.5-9) quam imperitorum clamor, quos nil nisi lacrimae ieunia psalmi delectare potest, immemores quod aliud in vita aliud in oratione spectari convenit."
[122] Birnbaum, 96: "Janus wrote no religious poetry, confessed no trust in God, and only had biting irony and sarcasm for the entire subject of religion which he consistently identified with ignorance and hypocrisy." This would be more accurate if she had written "irony and sarcasm for ignorant superstition and religious hypocrites." As for his failure to write devotional poetry, the answer surely is that it was simply not his *métier*.
[123] Birnbaum states (p. 96), "As a young student in Ferrara, however, she flaunted his atheism, using it to shock his readers and to exasperate his teachers," but she quotes no substantiating evidence.

eventually turned to Neoplatonism as a substitute for Christianity, as Birnbaum also suggests.[124] His poems contain "a plethora of gods," but this does not mean he believed in them. Similarly, his epigrams about sexual misbehavior at mass, or the ritual inspection of the Pope's testicles by the cardinals, or the greed of the Romans in Holy Year (1450) show only that Ianus had a naughty sense of humor and an eye for the truth. Birnbaum (p. 98) states, "In his own life, Janus's attitude is best expressed in his short poem "De sacrilego,' (*Epigr.* 1. 182): Taking a look at Jupiter, these were the words of a mortal: "The earth I want to have. Father, you may keep your heavens." She also claims (p. 105, n. 13) that Ianus presents "a similar view" in the epigram, *De Amore Deo* ("On the god, Love," 1. 183): "Love is a passion, not a god; it is human lust. It lays claim to an empty name as an excuse for its own vices."

I see no connection, as Birnbaum does, between these two poems, nor any statement in either about Ianus' attitude to life or to Christianity.[125] Likewise, I see no denial of the immortality of the soul in the epigram, *De Laurentio* (1. 370), on Lorenzo Valla, in which Ianus says that everyone must die, whether he follows Epicurus (who taught that the soul is material, and is dispersed at death) or Plato (who believed that the soul survives after the death of the body).

---

[124] She states (p. 168), "Having lost his belief in Christianity, perhaps Janus reached out to find a substitute religion for himself." But to lose faith is to imply that one once had it, and this would contradict Birnbaum's thesis that Ianus never had any. I would probably agree with her (p. 169) that "as a prelate he had more nonreligious than religious interests," but I cannot agree that he ever "challenged Christian doctrines," in the sense that he took an open, clear stance against any. It is by no means obvious that he was "only nominally a Christian."

[125] Both this epigram and 1. 182 seem innocuous; 1. 182 is no more than a bland imitation of the ancient joke about the shortcomings of the gods (especially Zeus), while *De Amore Deo* is a hit at people who will not call a spade a spade, and attempt to exalt their own derelictions.

The same may be said of the epigram, *De Valla* (1. 134; Kombol, 244): "So many centuries do the stag and crow live: Valla is dead before his time. Who would think that the gods exist?" Similarly, the epigram, *De Ludovico Carbone* 91. 94; Kombol, 274), already discussed, cannot be read as an anti-Christian comment. Birnbaum nevertheless quotes all of these poems to support her assertion (p. 99) that Ianus did not believe in the immortality of the soul, and that even by 1457, when Valla died, Ianus "had not changed his mind and come closer to God."

Those who deny any Christian faith to Ianus have concentrated mainly on the five epigrams (1. 315-319) against "Linus," a Franciscan preacher, and the six (1. 22, 247-251) on the Holy Year of 1450. Linus is depicted as an exorcist who uses his ceremonies as an excuse to consort with young men. In the last of the series (1. 319), he has dropped his religious pretense and is occupying his hands about the person of the young Troilus. Huszti was probably correct in suggesting that the subject matter was borrowed from Antonio Beccadelli's attack in the *Hermaphroditus* on his teacher, Mattia Lupi.[126] Attacks on corrupt Christians, however, are not necessarily attacks on the Church itself. It is clear, for example, that the epigram, *In Dionysium* (1. 129; Kombol, 212) contrasts "true religion" with the absurd belief of "Dionysius" that personal filth would somehow confer sanctity upon him, and here Birnbaum (p. 98) is surely right in saying that Ianus was probably not attacking any particular person, but asceticism itself.

The poems on the Holy Year (1450) show how bitterly Ianus felt about the profiteering of bankers, innkeepers, and even the Pope himself (as custodian of the wealth of the

---

[126] Huszti, *Janus Pannonius* 48-49.

Church) at the expense of pilgrims flocking from all parts of Europe to Rome. The most important of the epigrams is *Galeotti peregrinationem irridet* ("He mocks Galeotto's pilgrimage," 1. 22; Kombol, 316-18): "Why, I ask, are you, too, Galeotto–although you are a poet, albeit a deserter from the peak of Parnassus—going as a pilgrim with staff and knapsack to the Roman city? Leave this to the gullible riff–raff of foreigners, the common herd that is used to fearing ghosts, the crowds of hypocrites. Please believe what once the clever teacher of smart Euthlos thought, or Theodorus, who denied the gods, or that famous father of the dainty sect, who laid it down that pain is the greatest evil. But if blessed piety is what you fancy now, if you like walking with a twisted neck, [127] and want to believe all the caterwauling that's preached all day, every day, by Father Alberto, perched on high, and that chatterbox, Roberto, who delights in the wretched tears of poor old women, go on, then, say farewell to the beloved muses, break their sacred strings, and give the sweet poems of Phoebus to the lame smith of the gods. No one is both pietist and poet."

Gerézdi rightly says that in his poems on the Jubilee, Ianus was not attacking religion, but the abuses associated with it. Like Huszti, however, Gerézdi finds in the last line of the above poem, *nemo religiosus et poeta est*, a radical attack on religion itself. The very loose translation, "Believer or poet, you will have to choose," in Birnbaum's discussion (p. 97), misrepresents the meaning of *religiosus*, which does not mean a believer, as opposed to a non–believer, but rather "given to scrupulous religious observances." Hence,

---

[127] For the possible borrowing by Rabelais of "tor–coulx" and "torty-colly" from Ianus' "torticollis" in this poem, see L. Dorez, *Rabelesiana. Revue des Bibliothèques* 13–14 (1903), 140–144. The word, apparently a coinage by Ianus, conjures up a vivid picture of a religious hypocrite's posture.

I have translated it "pietist," since this seemed the closest to what Ianus meant. Ianus only means that Galeotto, as an educated man, should not be joining in the more hysterical manifestations of popular religion. Underlying these poems on the Holy Year may have been more than a mere resentment of pharisees and charlatans. János Hunyadi had received a special dispensation from the Pope, whereby pilgrimages made within Hungary in 1450 would be counted as equivalent to those made to Rome, any revenues so generated to be used for re-arming Hunyadi's armies against the Turks. Birnbaum (p. 96) doubts that Ianus knew about this, but I see no reason why he would not, since it was not a minor matter or a secret, and his own uncle must have been instrumental in arranging it. Ianus may therefore have been thinking about the loss of revenue for Hunyadi's crusade, when he burst forth against Slavs, Iberians, Gauls, and Teutons, who insisted on flocking to Rome,in *Epigr*. 1. 247. 3–4: Where are you rushing off to, you fools, to enrich the toll–booths of Latium? Can't anyone find salvation in his own country? In the *Panegyricus in Guarinum* and the *Elegia de morte Barbarae* Ianus shows respect for the Christian religion. A Christian outlook was probably something he took for granted, like Guarino, and the absence of confessions of faith does not mean that he had none. One must agree with Birnbaum (p. 103): "The largest body of his writings is, like those of his contemporaries, neither truly pagan nor Christian, but simply secular."

If Ianus had a god on earth, it was Guarino, whom he praised often and extravagantly. He wrote epithalamia for two of Guarino's daughters, Libera and Fiordimiglia, both of which include disproportionately long passages in praise

of their father.[128] In the *Panegyricus* 838–53 he praised
Battista Guarini at greater length than any of his father's
other students, picturing him like a young swan emulat-
ing the song of his moribund sire; and he does not omit
to say (836–37) that Guarino's other sons were strong in
mind, character, and religious devotion, just like their fa-
ther. The praises luxuriate in his comparison (661–57) of
Guarino's wife, Tadea, to "the Idaean Mother" (Cybele),
whose statue, with those of her twelve children, like the
twelve apostles, surrounds the golden image of Guarino,
who is gaudily depicted as a cross between Apollo the sun-
god and God–the–Father. When Tadea died, sometime be-
fore 1454, Ianus wrote an epitaph (*Epigr.* 1. 135; Kombol,
184): "Tadea, wife of the great Guarino, lies buried here.
Gladly she went before her husband, who will be late to
follow her. No marble will boast a greater name. She sur-
passed Pallas in the arts, Rhea in the number of her brood."
One gets the impression that Tadea's greatest claim to fame
was that she was Guarino's wife. The focus here is not
mainly on her, as it should be.

Ianus, however, was not always deferential to Guarino.
Aside from the poems in which he refers to the master's
stinginess, there is one in which he was downright rude to
Guarino. One of Guarino's sons had fathered an illegitimate

---

[128] *Epithalamium in Liberam Guarinam et Salomonem Sacratum*
(Kombol, 152–55), in which lines 5–10 and 43–52 of a total of 54
are devoted to Guarino; and *Epithalamium ad Gulielmum Calefinum
et Flordemiliam Guarinam*, lines 49–86 of the 90 extol Guarino. In
the one on Libera, Ianus says of Guarino (48–49), "Haud statui laudes
nunc memorare suas,/Seu quod, quo potui, prius illas carmine dixi,"
which Sabbadini (Guarino, *Epistolario* 3.434, n. 5) takes to refer to the
Panegyricus in Guarinum. Since he dated the *Panegyricus* to 1453, he
places Libera's wedding in that year. This seems to strain the evidence.
Even if Ianus was alluding to the *Panegyricus* (which is not necessarily
the case), it does not follow that the wedding, and hence the date of
this poem, was in the same year that the *Panegyricus* was written.

child on a servant, and Ianus offered this advice (*Epigr.* 1. 63; Kombol, 186): "Why, Guarino, most indulgent of fathers, don't you keep your sons away from shameful vices? Perhaps you don't know what one of them has just done? He managed to make you father–in–law to your own serving girl, and grandfather to a female slave. You are the talk of the town. Do you still not know of your own shame? Softest of papas, Guarino, why don't you, I repeat, keep your sons away from shameful vices? If *they* often get by with conduct like this with the servants, others, take my word for it, will have their way with your daughters." This may be, as Birnbaum says (p. 31), a reprimand in the style of Renaissance comedies, but it seems gratuitous and insensitive.

Much more respectful is an invitation, which Ianus wrote on behalf of himself and a group of senior students (Kombol, 296): "O learned Guarino, splendor and modern (*nova*) glory of our age, who are skilled in both languages, and under whose instruction we have lived so many years, please come now and be my guest for dinner. If you accept, you will do me the same honor that his Tirynthian guest did Evander."[129]

Guarino declined:

> Equals suit equals, and each age its own: as an older man, I shall be better off with old men. Smart young men-about–town shrink from nodding grey-beards, and fun and games fall flat in the presence of an oldster. So carry on,

---

[129] Evander, a legendary emigré from Greece, made a settlement called Pallanteum on what later became the Palatine Hill at Rome (Vergil, *Aen* 8.54). Hercules (the "Tirynthian") is said to have visited him, and to have slain the monster Cacus, in gratitude for which Evander established a cult of Hercules at the Ara Maxima (*Aen.* 8.158–275; Livy 1.7).

lads, bring on the laughs and merriment,
lest an unbending seriousness spoil your
rapid–fire jokes.[130]

Ianus, however, persisted (Kombol, 296):

> We are very partial to what you call "un-
> bending seriousness," and it won't suc-
> ceed in spoiling our fun. In fact, sir, your
> presence at our table would brighten it
> up no end. As for our fun getting out
> of hand, and the jokes too loose, the re-
> spect created by your majestic and seri-
> ous expression, and that body of yours
> that would do credit to a god, will take
> care of that. But don't think there's any
> harm in our swapping a youthful sally or
> two with you, even if you are an old man,
> because (as we have heard you say your-
> self) Tully himself was not averse, even
> in his later years, to racy humor. Who
> was ever more serious than Socrates,
> who was even holier? Yet quite often he
> had fun with the boys. In fact, the Stoic
> Cato himself was given to jesting at the
> festival of Flora. So heed the example
> of such stalwarts, and don't run away
> from what you so often endorse. Don't
> run away, but join the party, and never
> mind the age difference. And don't write
> me an answer: just come in person.

Guarino habitually held aloof from such student junketings,
but did not forbid them. His refusal to attend was good–
humored, but firm.

We do not know what Guarino thought of Ianus
as a person, but he certainly admired him as a
scholar. Guarino's first reference to him occurs in a

---

[130] Guarino, *Epistolario* 2. Ep. 836.

letter, dated August 16, 1452, to a certain Valerio Balbalio, [131] from which we gather that Balbalio had recently visited Guarino and made an excellent impression. Balbalio knew Ianus, or his poetry, because Guarino ends with the promise (lines 20–26): "I am sending Ianus' verses along with this letter. I would praise them, as coming very close to what we admire in the ancient poets, to show their high quality and the value of the gift, were it not that you are quite capable of making this judgement for yourself. Besides, a recommendation of Ianus from me might look like a recommendation of myself, which is something that the masters of life simply don't allow. Farewell. . . and let me know if the letter and its companions (i.e. the verses) arrive."

Even more laudatory is the second, and only other, reference to Ianus in Guarino's extant correspondence. Writing to Francesco Barbaro on February 5, 1453, Guarino says at the very end: "I recommend this Ianus to you, a student–boarder of mine, Pannonian by race, but Italian in manners, an admirable, indeed a stupendous scholar. Welcome him into your circle."[132] Since Ianus is not mentioned earlier in the letter, he seems to have hand–delivered it to Barbaro on a visit to Venice early in 1453. Barbaro had recently married, and had received from Ianus, whom he had never met, an epithalamium of 344 hexameters with a preface in iambic senarii. [133] Clearly, Ianus wanted to befriend him and other important men in Venice, because he would soon be enrolling as a law student at Padua. Guarino, who had been a friend of Barbaro for over fifty years, would not have

---

[131] Guarino, *Epistolario* 2. Ep. 858. Balbalio is otherwise unknown.
[132] Guarino, *Epistolario* 2. Ep. 870. 32–34.
[133] Published in E. Ábel, *Analecta* 108–119. In it Apollo panegyricizes Barbaro (lines 144–313), enumerating all the magistracies Barbaro had held.

recommended Ianus so highly, if he had not felt that Ianus could live up to it.

No doubt the *Panegyricus in Guarinum* was to some extent self–serving, since it proclaimed Ianus' credentials as much as Guarino's, but it was also, as Carlo Rosmini says, "il maggiore e il piu ricco tributo che della sua gratitudine possa dare un discepolo al suo maestro" ("The greatest and richest tribute of gratitude a pupil could give his teacher").[134]

Some readers may feel stifled by Ianus' recondite learning, and repelled by his exaggerations; but the *Panegyricus* must be read in terms of the literary imperatives that shaped it. Laudation and invective were characteristic humanist forms, because there was an intense competition for jobs: it made sense to praise friends, who might advance one's career, and damn enemies, who might be competitors. Realizing this, fewer and fewer readers took praise and blame seriously, and writers were forced to exaggerate more and more in an effort to compel belief. Panegyrics, moreover, had nothing to do with presenting a true picture, as Guarino had pointed out in a famous letter on historiography to Tobia dal Borgo.[135]

Most ancient poets, and the humanists who imitated them, made severe demands on the reader. They expected them to recognize reverberations of earlier poets, and to judge how skilfully these models had been adapted. Originality was not so much the production of new thoughts as the ability to present old ones in a new way. A reader had to recognize allusions to particular myths, and enough

---

[134] C. Rosmini, *Vita di Guarino Veronese e di'suoi discepoli* 3 (Brescia, 1808), 97.
[135] See my article, "Guarino's Views on History and Historiography," *Explorations in Renaissance Culture* 3 (1976) 49–69. The letter is translated into English on p. 58–63.

of the geography of the ancient world to enjoy the poetic associations of place–names. Certain writers, particularly those of the Silver Age, whom Ianus especially liked, cultivated obscurity of allusion and the use of recondite place-names, but a good poet like Ianus could use an epithet like "Philyrides" (the son of Philyra) not simply as a pompous equivalent for Chiron, but as a means of evoking ideas of tenderness and nurture. Thus "Phillyridis" as the first word of Ianus' *Praefatio* immediately strikes one of the keynotes of the poem. Examples cf Ianus' careful craftsmanship could be multiplied. For example, in *Panegyricus* 651–54, the Rivers Eridanus (Po) and Hister (Danube) are mentioned together, because the associations of the Italian river add dignity to the Pannonian one; the muses are called "daughters of Memory" to emphasize the importance of taking them to Hungary–Croatia, where Ianus will record the country's emerging greatness; the berries of Bacchus are called "Nysaean," because Nysa was a remote mountain where the infant Bacchus, god of ecstasy and inspiration in the arts, was reared, and the banks of the Danube are called "green," because humanism will be a fresh growth upon them.

Ianus used no single model for the *Panegyricus*. As Birnbaum says (p. 87), before Giulio Cesare della Scala (Scaliger) formulated "rules" for writing panegyric in his *Poetices libri septem* (1561), there were no rigid guidelines. His main models were Statius' *Achilleis*, Claudian's *De raptu Proserpinae* (On the Rape of Proserpine), and the Eclogues, Georgics, and Aeneid of Vergil. From reading them, and such panegyricists as Pliny the Younger and Velleius Paterculus, and no doubt also from Guarino's lectures, he had grasped that the most important ingredients in panegyric were unstinted praise of the individual, with corresponding denigration of his rivals or predecessors, and the

theme of restoration after a period of ruin. Hence Guarino
is said to be vastly superior to earlier teachers (*Panegyri-
cus* 325–26, 349–53, 361–67, 382–87, 443, 703–04, 760–72,
777–81, 799–801), and a paragon of every kind of virtue.
The theme of restoration appears in 114–15, 221–22, 277–
81, 296–97, 315–24, 425–31, 455–72, 753–59, 814–15, and
899–919, with Guarino bringing light out of the darkness
of medieval barbarism, and restoring the muses to their an-
cient haunts. The poem can be dated only from internal
evidence.[136] It seems to have been presented to Guarino
about May or June of 1454, which is probably also the date
we should assign to the epigram, *Veronae commendat pan-
egyricam Guarinianam* ("He commends the panegyric on
Guarino to Verona," Kombol, 240): "I commend to you,
Verona, the little book (*libelum*), which my Calliopea com-
posed for your Guarino. If you spurn the poem, the subject
at least should be honored; pages that ring with the sound
of his name deserve to be read by you. Though Ennius was
a beginner, he pleased the sons of Romulus, when he sang
of the fierce wars of the great son of Scipio."

Ianus probably worked on the *Panegyricus* for several
years before it was presented to Guarino. Lines 419–37
speak of Leonello as if he were still alive, and 714–24 re-
fer to the "recent" funeral of Leonello. One cannot, how-
ever, make too much of this, since the verbs in the passage
about Leonello can be taken as historical presents (like *ven-
eratur* in 795, referring to Vittorino, who died in 1446),
and *nuper* ("recently") could easily refer to an event of four
years before. Similarly, *pontificus ritu* in 671 might tempt
us to think it was added after 1459, when Ianus became a
bishop, but all Ianus actually says is that he will conduct

---

[136] See n. on *Panegyricus* 732 and 879.

the ceremonies in honor of Guarino "like a bishop," or "like a priest" (*pontifex* can mean either), and this fancy could easily have been in his mind in 1454. Huszti concedes that there is no firm evidence for revisions of the poem (in 1455 and 1469),[137] and I see no reason to believe that any were made.

Metrically, the poem is impeccable. In the hexameters Ianus most often uses a penthemimeral cesura (a strong break in the rhythm after the initial long syllable of the third metrical foot), but varies this in eighty of them with trithemimeral and hephthemimeral cesuras (weak breaks in second and fourth metrical feet of the same line). Lines with weak cesuras often occur in pairs or triplets.[138] Special effects are skillfully handled: for instance, the rhythm in 181–82, with its balanced distribution of dactyls (a long syllable followed by two shorts) and spondees (two long syllables), imitates the movement of a bee from flower to flower, with a brief pause on each bloom. As Ianus says in 773–74, such technical details do not come easily. His effects, however, are never labored.

The poem is well constructed. It begins with a *Praefatio* of eighteen elegiac couplets, each consisting of a hexameter followed by a pentameter. Ianus draws a parallel between the education of Achilles by Chiron and his own by Guarino. Chiron resembles Guarino in that both are superb teachers, gentle individuals, who are respected by their peers as ar-

---

[137] The evidence for a revision at Padua amounts to no more than lines 7–8 (iterumne Guarini/ludere vis ludum?) in the *Panegyricus ad Antonium Iacobum Marcellum Venetum*. But in these lines Ianus does not say he is working on a revision of the panegyric on Guarino; the whole context suggests that he was tired of old material and eager to start something new. It is true that in 1469 he was preparing his works for publication, but there is no evidence that he worked on the Guarino panegyric at that time.

[138] Lines 81–82, 190–91, 325–26, 385–87, 549–50, 826–27, 972–73.

biters in disputes (cf. *Praefatio* 23–24 and *Panegyricus* 787–90), hosts of the gods (cf. *Praefatio* 29–30 and *Panegyricus* 623–53, 838–53, where the students boarded by Guardino are not called gods, but it is implied that they will be immortal), good poets (cf. *Praefatio* 21–24 and *Panegyricus* 771–76), and healers (cf. *Praefatio* 1, 22 and *Panegyricus* 941, where Guarino is the healer of the diseases of ignorance). Both, too, are destined for immortality (cf. *Praefatio* 31–32 and *Panegyricus* 812–13 and 891–96). Achilles is like Ianus in that both have had a great teacher, are poets, come from a semi–barbarous country, and are destined for immortality. The parallels with Achilles are implied, rather than stated.

Lines 1–16 of the *Panegyricus* itself provide the justification for the poem: Guarino is like a god, to whom Ianus must offer the "first fruits" of his education as a sacrifice. *Pietas* (duty) demands it.

Lines 17–29 invoke Guarino himself as the inspiration of the poem, and touch upon his qualities as a teacher, a polymath, and a hard worker.

Lines 30–39 emphasize that Guarino did not succeed through divine inspiration, but by intense study.

Lines 40–57 sketch his early education, first with his mother and then under teachers, whom he soon surpassed. He rejects the established professions of law, medicine, and theology, and embraces humanism.

Lines 58–74 praise humanism as the most satisfying path to follow, and the source of a complete education, intellectually and morally.

Lines 75–87 revert to Guarino's education and give reasons why he decided to learn Greek.

Lines 88–121 contain a speech of Apollo, encouraging Guarino to learn Greek in the East and promising to protect him. Apollo cites examples of others, who traveled in search of knowledge. The contribution of Greek to Latin learning is emphasized.

Lines 122–144 describe Guarino's journey to Constantinople.

Lines 145–154 praise Manuel Chrysoloras as a polymath, and touch upon his career, ending with his death at Constance.

Lines 155–251 deal with Guarino's education in Constantinople, his total dedication to work under difficult and lonely conditions.

Lines 178–188 contain an elaborate "epic simile," comparing Guarino's industry to that of the bee which works all day to gather pollen before flying home with its riches.

Lines 252–324 describe the journey back to Italy, with an apostrophe to the winds (262–281), which forms a kind of internal *propemptikon* (poem wishing a traveler good fortune). Guarino is bringing home a priceless cargo, the whole wealth of Greek learning, necessary to dispel the darkness of ignorance in Italy. As Guarino approaches Delos, the oracle of Apollo again speaks (290–294), prophesying success and happiness for him, and charging him with the task of sharing his knowledge with others.

Lines 325–367 describe (fancifully) his joyous welcome in Italy, and the universal rush to his classroom. He is depicted as teaching Latin better than other masters, and the first to offer Greek to large numbers of students. There is another elaborate simile in lines 339–350, in which the scholars of Italy are compared to sheep which have starved through a long winter, but can graze on lush grass, when spring arrives. Masters and pupils alike are grateful for the new learning.

Lines 368–390 trace in general terms the tripartite scheme of education devised by Guarino, and praise him as a teacher of morals, and a disciplinarian who does not need the whip.

Lines 391–409 tell of the intense competition for Guarino's services as a teacher, and the cities where he has taught: Venice, Padua, Verona, Trent, Florence, Bologna, and Ferrara (the list is inaccurate and out of the proper order).

Lines 410–472 are a laudation of peaceful Ferrara, home of the arts, thanks to the civilizing presence of Guarino and the rulers, Niccolò and Leonello. Leonello is seen as a philosopher–king, earning the approval of Plato in the heavens. Ferrara under him is the centre of a new Golden Age, but Guarino is lauded as the real "founder of the city."

Lines 473–505 list the various foreign parts from which students come to study under Guarino: Dalmatia, Crete, Rhodes, Cyprus, France, Germany, Spain and Portugal, Poland, Britain, and Pannonia. From all quarters they come to hear Guarino, as if to the oracle of Apollo at Delphi, and receive enlightenment.

Lines 506–568 revert to Guarino's teaching methods and the curriculum. His thoroughness is emphasized, and his allegorical interpretations of ancient authors, particularly Vergil and Homer, are praised; many specific passages in the epics are alluded to, but no details of how Guarino interpreted them are given.

Lines 569–583 contain a simile, comparing Guarino's lecturing to the song of Arion as he rode the dolphin's back. Just as the sea creatures are fascinated by Arion's music, so Guarino's students are transported by his lectures.

Lines 584–612 return to the curriculum and sketch out a typical day in Guarino's life: morning prayers, a lecture on Vergil or Cicero at the public university, a tutoring session in the palace with Leonello's son, Niccolò, a frugal lunch, and then reading of Greek and Latin authors with the *contubernales* (student–boarders) until well into the evening. The students engage in set disputes, with Guarino acting as judge. Meanwhile his door is open to any non–boarder who wishes to consult him. His endless patience is stressed. Some students are so keen that they rise before dawn to study.

Lines 613–622 state that virtue is more important than mere learning, and cite the good effects of Guarino's protreptic personality: no quarreling, no lust, many examples of students who have reformed their wicked ways.

Lines 623–650 contain a list of Guarino's "notable" students, Italian and foreign, past and present.

Lines 651–674 picture Ianus returning home and erecting a temple to Guarino on the banks of the Danube. In it will be a golden statue of the master, surrounded by others of his family. The youth of Europe will pay homage, with Ianus officiating at the rites.

Lines 675–682 contain Ianus' promise one day to write an epic on the deeds of János Hunyadi.

Lines 683–702 touch upon Guarino's activities as a scholar at times when he could have been relaxing. Some of his works are alluded to.

Lines 703–724 mention his skill as an orator, particularly in a *prolusio* (inaugural lecture) on the liberal arts and in his funeral oration on Leonello d'Este. There is a "pathetic fallacy" in lines 716– 719, in which nature laments for Leonello, and a tasteless conceit in lines 720–721, in which the Po is said to be so swollen with the mourners' tears that it almost bursts its banks.

Lines 725–749 praise Guarino's knowlege of Greek, his past translations of Plutarch, and the translation of Strabo he has undertaken in old age.

Lines 750–785 point to the debt all other teachers and scholars owe him. All skills unite in him. Equally gifted in prose and verse, he gives his knowlege to the whole world. The past, present, and future are all in his debt.

Lines 786–801 allude to his admirers among fellow humanists.

Lines 802–837 mention some of his personal qualities: sterling moral fibre, restraint under attack, good humor, an ability to control his family.

Lines 838–853 are devoted to praise of his son and designated successor, Battista. The simile in 847–853, comparing Battista to a young swan, is perhaps the most beautiful in the poem.

Lines 854–873 point to examples of Guarino's generosity, but emphasize that the learning he imparts is worth far more than any amount of money.

Lines 874–896 praise his frugality in food and drink, his exuberant health, and command of all his faculties as he approaches eighty, and include a prayer (882–896) that he will live a very long life, and benefit the world as long as it lasts.

Lines 897–919 hail him as a benefactor of mankind, and the restorer of culture. He has done more for the world than such heroes as Romulus, Camillus, and Hercules.

Lines 920–941 contain a hymn to the sun (920–937) as the most remarkable thing in the universe, the eye of Jove, the mind of the world, etc. It is all gods in one, under whatever name it is worshipped. But it is not wholly beneficent, as Guarino is.

Lines 942–950 introduce the idea that divine providence was behind the birth of Guarino. As his mother goes into labor, the muse Clio prepares to address her eight sisters.

Lines 951–993 comprise Clio's speech. She complains that the world has lost interest in the arts, mankind is degenerating, and that the final conflagration must be approaching. The muses are being driven from their last refuges on earth, and are dishonored by men and fellow–deities alike. Testily, she threatens to shelter, together with her sisters, in the Underworld, if the situation does not improve soon.

Lines 994–1002 describe the sudden arrival of Mercury at Delphi, where he finds the muses disheartened and listless. He decides to cheer their spirits.

Lines 1003–1072 contain Mercury's good news. Moving between this and the next world, he has seen various
august spirits rejoicing over the coming restoration of
a Golden Age of culture on earth. The Fates have
performed a Dance of Destiny, symbolizing the shift
of culture from the Greek East to the Latin West.
They spin the thread of Fate and ratify the lots with
a song (1023–1030), urging a child to come to birth
as the saviour so long promised in prophecy, who will
lead the world out of darkness. Nature is depicted as
rejoicing at the happy event. Mercury reveals that he
will be born in Verona and surpass Catullus, Pliny,
and the Scaliger princes, not excepting Can Grande
himself. Guarino is identified as the wonder–child in
line 1062. Round his cradle are nymphs and Goat–
Pan, piping to dancing satyrs. He must quickly be
wrapped in a pink cloud and given to the Graces, to
save him from the dell–nymphs, who will try to steal
him. Already he is crawling towards the springs of the
nymphs, and attempting to cry in tune with Apollo's
song. The poem ends (1073) with the muses obeying
Mercury's order.

Mercury's speech, intended as a bravura climax, cannot
be judged a success. The idea of having the divine messenger announce the good news is ingenious, but in questionable taste, because of the obvious parallel with the announcement of Christ's birth in Luke 2. 10. It is also
suggested that Guarino was the child whose coming was
prophesied in Vergil's "Messianic" Fourth Eclogue. The
passage, moreover, contains a weird assortment of figures:
Life, Death, Genius, and the Fates sitting in solemn conclave; the muses striking different notes individually, while
Calliope mixes the harmony; springs gushing with ambrosia
and rivers with milk; mountains singing birthday odes; Mincius veiling his head with reeds and Benacus cavorting in his

glassy cave; Ilithyia suckling Guarino; the child in his cra-
dle, wrapped in a billowing pink cloud and surrounded by
woodland deities; and, finally, the infant Guarino crawling
towards the "Hyantean" waters of the muses, while crying
in harmony with Apollo's singing. Guarino might well have
said, "Haec ego non doceo" ("This isn't what I teach").
Even for panegyric, this must have seemed excessive. On
the other hand,the Dance of Destiny is original and power-
ful, and the figures of Goat–Pan, nymphs, and satyrs, with
the dell–nymphs lurking ominously in the hope of snatching
the baby away, effectively suggest the dangers of paganism
from which Guarino must be protected by the Graces.

    Ianus' faults in the poem are those of immature genius,
yet there are many fine passages, and overall it is a re-
markable achievement for a poet barely twenty years old.
Ianus wrote the *Panegyricus* for the same reason that Guar-
ino collected his *Chrysolorina*[139]: as an outward expression
of *pietas*, a Latin word for which there is no satisfactory
equivalent in English. It occurs in the first line of the *Pane-
gyricus* in its religious sense of dutiful conduct towards the
gods, suggesting that the whole poem will be a thanks-
offering to Guarino, an act of *pietas* toward the god–like
teacher. The word can also refer to the bond of mutual love
and respect that ideally exists between parent and child,
friend and friend, patron and protégé, pupil and teacher.
Plato's idea that the educational process (*paideia*) works
best between the noble *erastes* (lover) and the *eromenos*

---

[139] This collection, assembled in 1452, consisted of five old letters of his
own (Guarino, *Epistolario* 1. Epp. 7, 25, 27, 47, 54) and one by Poggio
(Guarino, *Epistolario* 1. Ep. 49), two *commentarioli* (brief notes) of his
own about Chrysoloras, Andrea Zulian's funeral speech on Chrysoloras,
four new letters of his own (Guarino, *Epistolario* 2. Ep. 893) and his
own sons Battista, Girolamo, and Manuel (Guarino, *Epistolario* 2. Epp.
863, 865, 866), and a poem of 82 lines (Guarino, *Epistolario*, 2. Ep.
867), solicited from Raffaele Zovenzoni.

(beloved) appealed to ancient educators such as Quintilian and Plutarch, and was developed during the Renaissance by teachers like Guarino and Vittorino. Nowhere, however, did it find more beautiful expression than in the lines from Juvenal, 7. 108–11, quoted by Lodovico Carbone in his funeral speech on Guarino:

> May the gods grant that the earth lie soft and light on the shades of our ancestors, may the sweet–scented crocus and eternal spring bloom over their ashes, who desired that their teacher should hold the place of a revered father.

Ianus, by his act of *pietas* towards Guarino, justly merits such a prayer.

IANI PANNONII
PANEGYRICUS
IN GUARINUM VERONENSEM

RAEFATIO

THE PANEGYRIC OF
IANUS PANNONIUS
ON GUARINUS VERONENSIS

ROLOGUE

Phillyridae monitis cum profecisset Achilles
Edoctus pariter gramina tela chelyn,
Non labyrintheos relegentem Thesea flexus
Ante nec Alcidae monstra perempta manu
Nec saevum Oebalio prostratum Bebryca caestu   5
Nec matris fertur concinuisse toros
Semiferi laudes quam praelusisse magistri:
Illa fuit tenerae prima Camena lyrae.
Vixdum fila levi tentarat tinnula plectro,
Aspiceres placidas accelerare feras: 10

Phillyridae: Matronymic for the centaur, Chiron, said by Pindar
(*Pyth.* 4. 115) to be the son of Kronos (Latin, Saturnus). His mother
was the nymph, Philyra (Pindar, *Pyth.* 4. 181; Ovid, *Ars Amatoria* 1.
11; Vergil, *Geo.* 3. 550, Phillyrides Chiron). The spelling *Phillyrides*
is *metri gratia*. Unlike others of his kind, Chiron was just and refined,
with special skills in music and healing. He was the tutor of Actaeon,
Jason, Asclepius, and Achilles. *Achilles*: Son of Peleus, king of the
Myrmidons of Phthiotis in Thessaly, and the Nereid, Thetis; foremost
hero of the Greeks in the Trojan War.
    2. *gramina tela chelyn*: For this special training of Achilles, see
Statius, *Achilleis* 2. 159-62, 131-36. 156-58. His general education
under Chiron is described in 2. 96-167. *chelyn*: Greek word meaning
"tortoise," it is often used metaphorically to mean "lyre," which was
thought to have been first invented by Hermes out of an empty tortoise
shell. Pure Latin is *testudo*, but Statius, whom Ianus imitates, uses
chelys regularly.
    3-6: Cf. Statius, *Achilleis* 1. 188-94, where these themes of
Achilles' song to Thetis are listed.
    3. *Thesea*: The most notable feat of Theseus, the great legendary
hero of Athens, was the killing of the Cretan minotaur, half-bull, half-
man, that devoured a yearly tribute from Athens of seven youths and
seven maidens, and lived in a dark labyrinth. By unwinding a ball of
twine given to him by King Minos' daughter, Ariadne, Theseus was able

When Achilles had profited from the teachings of Phillyrides, and was thoroughly trained in herbs, weapons, and the lyre, he is said not to have sung of Theseus threading his way back through the winding labyrinth, nor of the monsters slain by Alcides, nor of the savage Bebrycian laid low by the Oebalian cestus, nor yet of his mother's wedding, before first singing the praises of his part-beast master: that was the first inspiration of his tender lyre. Scarcely had he essayed its tuneful strings with the light plectrum, when wild beasts could be seen placidly hurrying towards him:

to retrace his way out of the labyrinth. References to this myth are frequent in classical authors (e.g., Vergil, *Aen.* 6. 27-30; Ovid, *Met.* 8. 173-74).

4. *Alcidae*: "Descendant of Alceus," i.e., Hercules, whose putative father was the mortal, Amphitryon, son of Alceus. When it became apparent that his real father was Zeus (Jupiter), he is said to have dropped the style Alcides. The line is an echo of Claudian, *De raptu Proserpinae* 2. Praef. 30, *Herculis et forti monstra subacta manu*.

5. *Oebalio*: Poeticism for "Spartan." Oebalus was a king of Sparta, father of Tyndareus, who was the husband of Leda and stepfather of the boxer, Pollux (Greek, Polydeuces), and the racer, Castor. *Bebryca*: During the voyage of the Argonauts (see n. on *Iason*, 243), Amycus, king of the Bebryces, a people of Bithynia, lost a boxing match to Pollux.

6. *matris ...toros*: The wedding of the Nereid, Thetis, to the mortal, Peleus, was a great event to which all the deities were invited, except Eris (Discord), who by throwing a golden apple inscribed "to the fairest" among the goddesses started a squabble among Athena, Hera, and Aphrodite. It was resolved by Paris, prince of Troy, in favor of Aphrodite, and this led ultimately to the Trojan War. The wedding as a popular literary theme, treated, e.g., in Catullus 64.

8. *Camena*: The *camenae* were water spirits with the gift of prophecy in the old Roman religion, but became identified with the Greek *mousai*, goddesses of inspiration in the arts. There was no muse specifically assigned to panegyric, but Ianus may have been thinking of Thalia, whose province was the lighter one of comedy and pastoral.

Iuncti gryphes equis, lepores venere Molossis,
Contulit accipitri blanda columba latus,
Non tigrim cervus tremuit, non damma leonem,
Sedit et hirsutis agna propinqua lupis.
Mobilis Oetaeo de vertice silva cucurrit,   15
Nuper ad Herculeos silva recisa rogos,
Nudus Athos mutila Lemnon non attigit umbra,
Repsit ad auditos Pindus et Ossa modos,
Constitit Eurotas et non nebulosus Anaurus,
Peneum supra nec Titaresus iit.   20
Carmen erat pueri, cithara quantum ille valeret,
Quam bene Paeonia pelleret arte malum,
Nosset ut iratos dictis lenire bimembres
Impia tranquilla proelia pace domans:
"Te non Ixion fallaci nube creavit,   25
Saturnus fratrem sed dedit ipse Iovi;

9–20: An echo of Claudian, *De raptu Proserpinae* 2. Praef. 16-28.
10. *placidas ...feras*: The submission of wild nature to the power
of fine music was a commonplace; cf. Vergil, *Ecl.* 2. 3; *Panegyricus*
570-73.
11. *gryphes*: Legendary beasts with the body and paws of a lion,
and the head and wings of an eagle. Horses were regarded as their
natural enemies: cf. Vergil, *Ecl.* 8. 27, and for other unlikely pairs,
Ecl. 4. 22. Ianus may also have had in mind the famous passage in
Isaiah 11. 6. *Molossis*: *Molossi* (sc. *canes*) were a famous breed of
dogs from Molossia in the interior of Epirus.
15. *Oetaeo*: Refers to Oeta or Oete, a mountain range in southern
Thessaly, where Hercules built his own funeral pyre. For the response of
inanimate nature to music, cf. Vergil, *Ecl.* 6. 28; 8. 4 (rivers halting).
17. *Athos*: Easternmost of three peninsulas in Chalcidice in north-
east Greece; also (as here) the mountain on the Strymonian Gulf, facing
the island of Lemnos, about fifty miles southwest.

griffins came with horses, hares with Molossian hounds; the gentle dove sidled up to the hawk; the stag did not tremble at the tiger, nor the doe at the lion; and the lamb settled down close to the hairy wolf. The rustling wood, recently shorn to make a funeral pyre for Hercules, hastened down from the upper slopes of Oeta, and Athos, stripped bare, did not reach towards Lemnos with its docked shadow. Pindus and Ossa moved in response to the notes they heard. Eurotas and unclouded Anaurus halted, and Titaresus did not flow above Peneus. The boy's song told of Chiron's great skill on the cithara, how well he drove sickness away with Paean's art, and his ability to soothe with words the angry creatures with two sets of limbs, taming impious battle with unruffled peace: "Ixion did not create you out of a deceptive cloud, but Saturn himself gave you as a brother to Jupiter.

18. *Pindus ... Ossa*: Mountain ridges in western and eastern Thessaly, respectively.
19. *Eurotas*: Not the better known river in Laconia, but a tributary of the Peneus in Thessaly (see note on 20). *Anaurus*: Small river in Magnesia, in Thessaly, which flows past Iolkos into the Pagasaean Gulf, notable as the stream in which Jason lost a sandal on his way to reclaim the throne of Iolkos.
20. *Peneum*: According to Herodotus 7, 129, one of the five main rivers of Thessaly. It rises in northwest Thessaly, and flows through the vale of Tempe to the sea. Except at the end of its course, it is shallow and sluggish.
Titaresus: Properly, Titaresius, the main tributary of the Peneus. It rises in Mt. Titarus and joins the Peneus from the north between Larissa and the Vale of Tempe. According to Homer, *Il.* 2. 753-54, its waters floated on top of those of the Peneus like oil over water, so that it was thought to be a branch of the Styx that flowed in the Underworld. Pliny, *N.H.* 48. 31 repeats the story. Homer calls the Peneus *argyrodines* (silver-eddying), a poetical exaggeration perhaps inspired by the whitish hue caused by earth suspended in its waters. Strabo (9. 5. 20),

Non convivali tibi frangere pocula rixa
Nubentes studium nec violare nurus.
Tu Phoebi nutris subolem, tu sedulus hospes
Accipis aeternos curva sub antra deos.   30
Pro quibus alta manet meriti te regia caeli,
Contrahit et caudam Scorpios ecce tibi."
Haec pius Aeacides. Mihi pro Chironc Guarinus;
Hunc sibi praescribet pagina nostra ducem.
Imbuat ille meae, fas est, exordia Musae,   35
Pierium vati qui reseravit iter.

misinterpreting Homer, says the Peneus is clear, the Titaresius oily; but
the reverse is true. Ianus seems unaware that the Titaresius and what
he calls the Eurotas (19) were the same river.

21. *cithara*: A stringed instrument more complicated than the lyre.
The choice of this word here is intended as a compliment to emphasize
Chiron's professional superiority over Achilles (and by extension, Guar-
ino's over Ianus).

22. *Paeonia*: Referring to Paean, i.e., Apollo, in his capacity as
the god of healing.

23. Chiron persuaded his fellow centaurs not to kill his grandson
Peleus when he wandered onto Mt. Pelion, their special haunt. See
Apollodorus 3. 13. 3. *bimembres*: Centaurs were half-horse, half-
human.

25. *Ixion*: King of Thessaly who attempted to rape Hera. She
complained to her husband Zeus, who made a cloud with Hera's image
on it. Ixion lay with the image and fathered the monster Centaurus,
human in form, who mated with the mares on Mt. Pelion, thus siring
all the centaurs except Chiron (see n. on 1).

26. *fratrem*: Saturn (Gk. Kronos) was father of Jupiter; hence
Chiron was Jupiter's half-brother (see n. on 1 and 25).

27-28. Ixion's son, Pirithous, was king of the Thessalian tribe of
Lapiths. At his wedding to Hippodamia, the centaurs got drunk, and
true to their rowdy and lecherous nature, tried to rape the bride and
other Lapith women. They were routed by Theseus and Pirithous, and
expelled from Mt. Pelion. On this occasion, Chiron's persuasiveness

You had no urge to smash cups quarreling with fellow-guests or to rape daughters-in-law at their wedding. You rear the son of Phoebus, and like the attentive host you are, you welcome the everlasting gods into your arching cave. For this, a lofty mansion awaits you in the heaven you deserve; see, the Scorpion is drawing in his tail for you." Such was the song of dutiful Aeacides. Guarino has been my Chiron; my poem will bear his name written at the top, as the one who guided me. It is right that he who opened the poet's way to Pieria should christen the first efforts of my muse.

counted for nothing (cf. n. on 23). The story was well known: see, e.g., Ovid, *Met.* 12. 210 ff; Horace, *Od.* 1. 18. 7; 2. 12. 5; Vergil, *Geo.* 2. 455. Cf. also Statius, *Achilleis* 1. 40, where Thetis surmises that Achilles will be singing of the battle of the Lapiths and Centaurs.

29. *subolem*: i.e., Asclepius, son of Apollo. Ianus, as a poet, would also see himself as a "son of Apollo."

30. *deos*: The gods welcomed into his home by Chiron are paralleled by the fine students boarded and educated by Guarino (see *Panegyricus* 623-53, 838-53). Ianus does not call these students gods, but implies that their works will be immortal. *curva ... antra*: Cf. Statius, *Achilleis* 1. 106-07.

32. *Scorpios*: A constellation in the southern hemisphere, next to Sagittarius on its "tail" side, and to Libra and Lupus on its "claws" side. Centaurus is just beyond Libra and Lupus. The line is imitated from Vergil, *Geo.* 1. 34-35, where the Scorpion is drawing in its claws (*bracchia*) to accommodate the emperor Augustus. Ianus' mythology is sound when he talks of Chiron's translation to the heavens as the constellation Centaurus (see Servius, *ad Geo.* 3, 91; 5. 550; 4. 270), but his knowledge of the position of Centaurus is incorrect.

(Sagittarius, however, is sometimes represented as a centaur. *The Oxford Classical Dictionary* (under "Centaur") cites pseudo-Eratosthenes: "Most men call him a Centaur. Others dispute this, because he does not appear to have four legs, but stands upright and shoots with his bow. But none of the centaurs used a bow. This figure, though a

PANEGYRICUS

ustica si pietas consuevit rite quotannis
Flaventes Cereri spicas,/
nova musta Lyaeo,
Arbuta Pomonae,/
bacas offerre Minervae,
Veris opes Florae, cuivis sua munera divum,
Iure, Guarine, tibi nos carmina nostra dicamus   5
Fontibus hausta tuis. Mea nec lyra dignius ullum
Ante sonet, quam quo didicit crepitare magistro.
Verum ego, si totum docili simul ore bibissem,
Quicquid tu invidia nil subducente fluebas,
Tantarum haud possem fastigia tangere laudum.   10

man, has horse's feet, and, like the Satyrs, a tail." Could Ianus have
been equating Sagittarius with Centaurus?)

33. *Aeacides*: "Descendant of Aeacus," i.e., Achilles. *Mihi ... Gua-
rinus*: Ianus intends us to see that he resembles Achilles in having a
remarkable teacher, a superb education, poetic skill, a semi-barbarian
origin and sure future fame. Guarino is like Chiron in his teaching skills,
his poetic ability (cf. 771-76), his good nature, his reception of famous
students, and his impending immortality (see 655-72; 688; 695; 812;
891,96).

34. Cf. Vergil, Ecl. 6. 12.

35. *exordia*: Some of Ianus' epigrams and elegies, probably a pan-
egyric to Lodovico Gonazga (see Birnbaum, 82), a *carmen pro pacanda
Italia* to the Emperor Frederick III, a panegyric on René d'Anjou, and
a long poem, *Eranemos* (Birnbaum, 29-30; Huszti, 71-76) were written
before the *Panegyricus* was completed (1453), so we cannot take him
literally here. He means that the *Panegyricus* is his first serious work
as a poet beyond the stage of doing exercises (cf. 731, where he calls
Guarino's early translations of Plutarch *praeludia*).

THE PANEGYRIC

If it is the custom of rustic devotion to make yearly offerings of yellow ears of corn to Ceres, of new wine to Lyaeus, of fruits to Pomona, of berries to Minerva, and the riches of spring to Flora, to each of the deities their own gifts, it is right that I dedicate my poem to you, Guarino; it was drawn from your fountains. Nor could my lyre sound a nobler theme than that of the master from whom it learned to speak. But even if I had drunk in and learned all your unstinted plenty, I could not attain such heights of praise.

36. *Pierium*: Referring to Pieria, in southeast Macedonia, a haunt of the muses.

FOOTNOTES TO THE PANEGYRIC 1-6. The Greeks, and to a greater extent, the Romans, offered the first fruits of the season to the gods: see, e.g., Ovid, *Fasti* 2. 520 and *Met.* 8. 274. Metaphorical first-fruits occur frequently in the classical writers, e.g., Vergil, *Aen.* 11. 156. The phrase *primitiae et quasi libamenta ingenuarum artium* in Aulus Gellius' Preface was frequently imitated by Guarino; e.g., in offering his first known translation (of Isocrates' *Ad Demonicum*) to Floro Valerio in 1450, he concludes: " Mearum igitur lucubrationum primitias habe." (Guarino, *Epistolario* 1. 4. 17).

2. *Cereri*: Ceres (Gk. Demeter) was goddess of the growth of crops, particularly cereals. *Lyaeo*: Lyaeus (also Bromius) was one of the cult titles of Bacchus (Gk. Dionysos).

3. *Pomonae*: Pomona was a minor Roman deity of fruits, especially those on trees. Minervae. Minerva (identified with Gk. Athena) was originally an Italian goddess of handicrafts. Her connection with berries arises from their use in dyeing cloth.

4. *Florae*: Flora was an Italian goddess of flowering and blossoming plants.

Nunc, cum parva tuae nobis sit portio venae,
Quid plus proficiam, nisi quod fortasse videbor
Susceptorum abs te non immemor esse bonorum,
Quanquam non alias similem sperare favorem
Thespiadum nobis liceat, nec iustius illae   15
Affuerint ulli quam te, Guarine, canenti?
  Sed de Parnasi cur nunc ego vertice Musas Sollicitem?
Coeptis tantum ipse audacibus adsis,
Aspirasse simul Bromium et Paeana putabo.
Nam te haud exiguum gestare in pectore numen   20
Certa fides. Quod si divinae vatibus haustum
Mentis et insanis prisci tribuere Sibyllis,
Hae ventura vident, illi, quod carmina pangunt,

11 tua *A*

9. *nil subducente*: Cf. 294; 521; 611-12.
15. *Thespiadum*: The muses were called *Thespiades*, because Thespiae, an old town in Boeotia, is situated at the foot of their haunt, Mt. Helicon.
17. *Parnasi*: Parnassus is a mountain in Phocis with twin peaks, sacred to Apollo and the muses. Delphi, site of the greatest oracle of Apollo, is on its slopes.
18. *adsis*: Cf. Vergil, *Geo.* 1. 40, "audacibus adnue coeptis," and the entire passage (24-40), where Augustus is invoked (as Guarino is here) as virtually a god.
22. *Sibyllis*: Generic name for prophetesses, possibly deriving from an original proper name, Sibylla. There were many sibyls at different times and in different places in the ancient world. Poets and prophetesses were thought to be inspired by the gods.
24. *Quid ... licet*: Cf. Vergil, *Geo.* 1. 104.

But I do have a tiny portion of your talent, so what better could I do than to seem, perhaps, not unmindful of the blessings I received from you, even if at any other time I could not expect such a favor from the muses, and they never came with more justice to anyone than to him who sings of you, Guarino. But why should I now rouse the muses from the summit of Parnassus? Only be present yourself as I boldly begin, and I shall think that Bromius and Paean together have breathed upon me; for I am sure that you carry no small divinity in your breast. But if the ancients granted a draught of divine itelligence to poets and crazed sibyls, because the former make poems, and the latter see into the future,

24-25. *totius ...tenes*: Cf. 501, and 493-505, where Guarino is compared to the augur Apollo.

26. *numeros*: Sabbadini prints samples of Guarino's poetry in *La scuola e gli studi di Guarino* 225-30.

27. *tot ...poetas*: Cf. the statement made of Publius Valerius Cato, the teacher of Cinna, Ticida, Furius Bibaculus, and possibly Catullus: "solus legit ac facit poetas" (Suetonius, *De grammaticis* 11).

30. *Hesiodum*: Cf. Hesiod, *Theogony* 22-35, which tells how as Hesiod tended sheep on Mt. Helicon the muses called upon him to sing of the gods. See also Vergil, *Ecl.* 6. 63-64.

33. *Castalio*: The Castalian spring, sacred to Apollo, is at Delphi, at the beginning of the Sacred Way leading to the god's precinct.

34. *Ennium*: Quintus Ennius (239-169 B.C.) was the author of tragedies, comedies, *saturae* (mixed verse), and miscellaneous other poems, a prose work called *Euhemerus*, and *Annales* , an epic in eighteen books arranged on the historical pattern of consular years. Like his other works, this last survives only in fragments. The *Annales* opens with the description of a dream in which the ghost of Homer tells Ennius that he was his reincarnation.

Quid de te censere licet, qui totius aevi
Acta animo comprensa tenes nec cudere solum   25
Ipse potes numeros, magni sed Apollinis instar
Hoc aliis praebes et tot facis esse poetas?
Dos tamen ista tibi facili non indita casu,
Sed per difficiles accessit parta labores.
    Hesiodum gelidae pascentem in vallibus Ascrae   30
Obvia nescio quae dominarum turba disertum
Effecit propere, cum porrexisset edendam
Laurum et Castalio potum de fonte dedisset.
Ennius in viridi carpens Helicone soporem
Vidit Maeoniam subito vitalibus umbram   35
Irrepsisse suis, ac pulsa nocte resurgens
Dictare annales et condere proelia coepit.
Te nec somnus iners pecudum nec pabula, frondes,
Sed propria erudiit sollerti industria cura.
    Vix tua reddebat graciles infantia voces,   40
Cum tibi non vano paribus contendere lusu
Tantus amor quantus tabula chartave notatos
Balbutire apices et laetae ostendere matri
Discreta inter se variis elementa figuris.

40-47. For other comments on Guarino's early promise, see n. on
79-83. Ianus says much the same about himself in his *Elegia de morte
Barbarae* 101–102 (Kombol, p. 16): "Imbiberam tenerae vix prima
elementa Minervae/Nec mala venturi iam documenta dabam." He also
praises (88–100) Barbara's encouragement in these early years.

what is one to think of you, who hold the whole course of the
past in your mind, and can not only forge rhythms yourself,
but like great Apollo impart this skill to others and make
poets of so many. But that gift was not given to you easily
and by chance; it was acquired by hard work.
When Hesiod was feeding his flock in the glens of cool
Ascra, a strange group of ladies met him and of a sudden
made him eloquent, after handing him laurel to eat and
giving him a drink from the Castalian spring. As Ennius
was catching a nap on green Helicon, he saw the ghost of
Maeonides suddenly slipping into his vitals, and when the
night was over, he got up again and began to compose his
Annals and sing of battles. No shiftless slumber nor leafy
animal fodder made you a scholar, but your own application,
sustained by skill and care.
You were scarcely speaking in the thin accents of early
childhood, when you loved to compete with your peers in
earnest play, and you were just as fond of lisping out the
sounds of letters, following their outlines marked on a slate
or a piece of paper, and of showing your delighted mother
the individual letters with their different shapes.

43. *matri*: Libera di Zanino, who, like Ianus' mother, was left a
widow when her gifted son was still a boy. Guarino (*Epistolario* 2. Ep.
904. 15-32) says she gave him love and encouragement, a love of honor
and respect for his family name.
49. *Aeolides*: A rare patronymic for Ulysses. There was a story that
Ulysses was the son of Anticleia not by Laertes, but by the notorious
sinner, Sisyphus, son of Aeolus: cf. Ovid, *Met.* 13. 31f. *lituo ... armis*:
Cf. Statius, *Achilleis* 1. 5-6.

Iam tum gaudebas digitis in pulvere ductas   45
Pingere litterulas et passim forte iacentes
Nondum intellectos tamen attrectare libellos.
Femineo quondam celatum syrmate Achillem
Callidus Aeolides lituo deprendit et armis:
Te si virgineo genitrix velasset amictu,   50
Oblato actutum potuisses codice nosci.
Post, ubi creverunt sensus crescentibus annis,
Non medicina tibi, scitu pulcherrima quanquam,
Actu foeda tamen, logicae aut placuere protervae
Iurgia inexplicitos frustra nectentia griphos   55
Nec verbosarum discors concordia legum.

52. *crescentibus annis*: It is not known when or how Guarino embraced humanism. His early education (probably under Marzagaia of Verona) was medieval in character, as he himself admitted in later life (*Epistolario* 2. Ep. 862. 1-11, 21-31, 93-106). It is often said (e.g., by Birnbaum, p. 24) that he studied under Giovanni di Conversino da Ravenna, a teacher of rhetoric with humanistic leanings who taught at Padua 1392-1408. But this was merely a guess by Sabbadini in *La Scuola e gli studi di Guarino* 5 and *Vita di Guarino* cap. 3-4, which has passed into biographical dogma. In fact, we know nothing about Guarino after his childhood in Verona, except that his name appears as one of the witnesses to a Venetian document dated 21 August, 1403 (E. Bertanza and G. della Santa, *Maestri, scuole, e scolari in Venezia fino al 1500* in *Documenti per la storia della cultura in Venezia* 1. (1907) 245). Leonardo Giustinian makes the statement (Guarino, *Epistolario* 2. Ep. 755. 26-28), "We think of you (Guarino) as more Venetian than Veronese, because you laid the first foundations of your life, learning, and character among us," but the most we may surmise from it is that if he was in Venice for any length of time before 1403, he could have met such men as Pier Paolo Vergerio, Giovanni da Ravenna, Paolo Veneto, and perhaps also Manuel Chrysoloras, who was in Lombardy 1400-03.

Already you enjoyed tracing tiny letters in the dust with your fingers, and handling books that happened to be lying around, even if you did not yet understand them. The cunning Aeolides once used weapons and a clarion to detect Achilles, dressed as a female: if your mother had put you into a girl's dress, you would have been recognized immediately by having a book handed to you.
Later, as your sensibilities deepened with the passage of years, you showed no interest in medicine, very fine in theory but disgusting in practice, nor in the exchanges of pert logic that vainly weave tangled monstrosities, nor in the discordant concord of the wordy laws.

53-56. *medicina ...logicae ...legum*: The three established professions were those of law, medicine, and theology, for all of which a university doctorate was required. Guarino does not seem to have had a university degree, but he may have been qualified as a notary: in the *Libri Commemoriali della Reppublica di Venezia* 3, Bk. 10, n. 16, recording a legal agreement of 1406 between Paolo Zane and the Byzantine emperor, he is referred to as Zane's "notary and secretary." He had no interest in scholastic philosophy, but he respected law and medicine, and had many friends in these professions (cf. *Panegyricus* 444). The advice he gave his favorite pupil, Martino Rizzon, in 1427 (*Epistolario 1. Ep.* 387. 40-55) was that if he did not want to teach, he should consider law or medicine, since both were highly prestigious careers, but warned him that the returns were slow, the fees poor, and the fruits uncertain. The best career, he advises, would be that of Apostolic secretary.
55. *griphos*: A very rare, post-classical word, meaning "nets," hence "puzzles." The phrase "griphos dissolvere" occurs in Aulus Gellius 1. 4. 4.
63. *ingenuae ...quattuor artes*: i.e., the medieval *quadrivium*, consisting of arithmetic, astronomy, geometry, and music (both theoretical and practical). The *trivium* consisted of grammar, rhetoric, and logic. Completion of study in the "Seven Liberal Arts" conferred the degree of

Rhetoras et vates studio complecteris omni,
Quos si quis novit, nil ignorare probatur.
Inde carens vitio sermonis regula surgit,
Inde fluit cultae dulcis facundia linguae,   60
Hinc dissertandi subtile paratur acumen,
Hinc rerum scitur series et forma locorum.
Nec minus ingenuae discuntur quattuor artes,
Quae numeros voces mensuras sidera tractant.
Adde tot humanae praecepta salubria vitae   65
Dogmate mulifido pugnantibus edita sectis:
Iunge etiam semper patientis semper agentis
Materiae fluxus et fata regentia mundum.

63 ingenue *J*

Magister Artium (Master of Arts). Some universities offered a doctorate in Arts, but the usual pattern was to take an M. A. before studying for a doctorate in Law, Medicine, or Theology.

65. *praecepta*: No doubt Guarino knew the major tenets of the ancient philosophers (see 170, 172,77), but his conception of philosophy was that of a set of well-rounded moral maxims. Such material as did not square with his own stance as a Christian would be ignored or dismissed, as Carbone tells us in the funeral speech: "The standard that governed all Guarino's lectures, all his exemplary anecdotes, and all his teaching, was that of the good and blessed life. How often would this great Christian interrupt a lecture to refute the foolish beliefs of the ancients ...for he realized that we who are Christians must have a range of reading different from that of the ancients, who did not know God." It is noteworthy, however, that in a letter of 1459 to his son Battista, whom he had educated, he advised him to find a really adequate teacher of "philosophy or dialectic" (*Epistolario* 2. Ep. 911, postscript), thus seeming to admit that his own instruction had been insufficient in these areas.

You embrace the poets and orators with all your heart. If a man knows them, it stamps him as a scholar. From them arises grammatically faultless speech, from them flows the sweet eloquence of a refined tongue, from them is obtained subtlety in debate and a knowledge of history and geography, and from them also are learned the four liberal arts that deal with numbers, sounds, measurements, and the stars. Add to that the many precepts beneficial to human life taught by sects warring with many different doctrines, and the flux of matter as it constantly acts and is acted upon, and the fates that rule the universe.

68. *fata*: That Ianus was interested in astrology is evident from other poems also: e.g., *Elegia* 3. 38-52 (Kombol) and *Elegia* 4 (Kombol), in the second of which all but five of its one hundred and forty-six lines are concerned with the effect of the moon on human affairs. It is dangerous; however, to assume from this, and his later contacts with astronomers like Gazulus, Regiomontanus, and Ilkusch (for which, see Birnbaum, 170-71), that he had any real knowledge of the heavenly bodies, or any developed belief in astrology. Huszti, in "Janus Pannonius asztrológiai álláspontja," *Minerva* (1927) 43-58, is probably right in classing Ianus (and János Vitéz) among those who knew very little about either astronomy or astrology, but did not hesitate to use terminology and ideas current in both. Birnbaum acutely observes (p. 171), "Since Janus absorbed and amalgamated all his experiences into his poetry, the findings of astronomy and the divinations of astrology became unseparably (*sic*) interwoven in his oeuvre. They turned into poetic images, tropes, and conventionalized symbols which can be followed along Janus's entire poetical career." It seems to me likely that whatever interest in astrology Ianus had was initiated by Galeotto Marzio at Ferrara, because Guarino, from whom he took so much else on trust, appears to have been totally uninterested in it. In the whole of Guarino's voluminous writings, I have found only one direct reference to astrology, in a letter of 1452 to his son Niccolò: "In the meanwhile, Mercury, as the poets or astrologers (*astrologi*) would say, but to speak more truly on the basis of Christian faith, the

Invenies illic, memorem ne singula, quicquid
Tradidit Aegypto Babylon, Aegyptus Athenis,   70
Qui superi et manes, quid agant post corpora mentes,
Quis deus, unde ingens causarum pendeat ordo.
Ergo nil illis ornatu pulchrius unquam,
Nil usu melius donarunt numina terris.
Hos tu praecipuos auctorum ex agmine tanto   75
Deligis et nunquam fecunda volumina cessas
Nocturna versare manu, versare diurna.
Aequaevis mixtus rauca inter pulpita ephebis
Mox praeceptorum non tantum dicta tuorum
Percipis et retines, meliora sed ipse potenti   80
Ingenio profers ac te iam consulit omnis
Turba et discipulus doctori incognita monstras.

78 Acquaevis *A*

Lord God who created Mercury ...sent Manuel Chrysoloras to us."
(*Epistolario* 2. Ep. 862. 42;45). For Guarino's distrust in divination,
see n. on 71.
    70. *Aegypto ...Athenis*: Cf. Macrobius, *In Somnium Scipionis* 1.
19. 2, perhaps the source used by Ianus, But many authors say the
same thing: see, e.g., the passages cited in *The Didascalicon of Hugh of
St. Victor*. Translated ...with an Introduction and Notes by Jerome
Taylor (New York and London, 1961) 210-11 (notes 34-36).
    71. *superi*: This word usually means the Gods in general, but
since Ianus uses *deus* in 72 as if it were a separate and superior cate-
gory of divinity, he may here mean by *superi* the superterrestrial spirits
called *daimones* by Plato in *Symposium* 202 D-E and *Republic* 620
D-E. In the Neoplatonic and Christian traditions, *daimones* were some-
times good (these often being equated with angels in the Christian
writers) and sometimes bad. Guarino may have believed that the pa-
gan gods were actually demons in the Christian understanding of that

In brief there you will find all that Babylon passed on to Egypt, and Egypt to Athens; the nature of spirits above and below the earth; what souls do when they leave the body; and who God is, the source on which depends the mighty chain of causation. The gods, then, have endowed the earth with no fairer ornament, with nothing better than those writers. From such a vast throng of authors, it is these you pick out as the most important, and you constantly handle their fertile volumes day and night. Then, as you mingle with young men of your own age amid the noisy benches, you not only understand and remember what your teachers say, but produce from your powerful mind better material of your own. The whole class now looks to you for advice, and, as a student, you show the teacher things he does not know.

term, and that demons were responsible for much of the "divine" phenomena of antiquity. There is a marginal annotation, in his own handwriting, in a Strabo codex, once the property of Ciriaco d'Ancona, where Guarino added to Ciriaco's index *thauma theou Pythiou*, "wonder of the Pythian god," the words *mallon de tōn daim onōn*, "but rather of the demons" (See p. 117 of Diller's *The Textual Tradition of Strabo's Geography*, cited in n. on 732-33). *quid ...mentes*: Probably Ianus had in mind the purification of souls described in Vergil, *Aen.* 6. 703-52
    72. *deus ...ordo*: This is Stoic terminology. By *deus* the Stoics meant the divine Spirit or Mind or Wisdom or Providence or Creative Fire that infuses itself through the universe and is responsible for the creation and orderly maintenance of everything in it (Vergil, *Aen.* 6. 724-34 and *Geo.* 4. 218-226; Cicero, *De natura deorum* 2. 20. 58, 2. 22. 57, etc.). The "mighty chain of causation" is likewise the Stoic *hormos aitiōn* (in Latin, *series causarum*), a concept that denies free will and postulates a deterministic universe (Cicero, *Academica* 1. 29). Ianus does not tell us how Guarino interpreted Stoic

Multa tamen suberant libris obscura vetustis
Praesertim externam nostrae admiscentia linguam,
Quae cupidam certum penitus pernoscere verum   85
Mentem obturbabant et desperare iubebant,
Cum tuus ambiguum sic te est affatus Apollo:
"Parce tuo, iuvenis, nimium diffidere voto
Praemia nec pigeat parituri magna laboris.
Nil non posse tibi pater annuit: omnia disces,   90
Omnia tu veterum monumenta docebis avorum.
Sed non in patria dabitur, Romane, quod optas:
Longinqua emenso lustranda est Graecia ponto,
Ut tibi succedat perfecta scientia rerum.
Multi hanc extremum vestigavere per orbem.   95
Sic Plato Memphitas, Samius sic quaesiit exul
Assyrios, sic, quos vocitant Brachmanas, adivit
Multivagus Tyaneus, Indi mirator Iarchae.
Tu nunquam, per quae reptasti, tecta relinques?

doctrine as he encountered it in ancient authors, but we may be sure
that his interpretations would not contravene ordinary Christian belief
and teaching.

75. *praecipuos*: Like all humanists, Guarino regarded the ancient
poets, orators, and historians as the prime repositories of all useful
knowledge. He recognized, however, the need for certain specialized
texts (see n. on 370-77), such as the commentary by the Paduan math-
ematician and astronomer, Prosdocimo di Belmondo, on John of Holy-
wood's *Sphaera*, which he was searching for in 1428 (*Epistolario* Ep.
570. 20-21).

77. Borrowed from Horace, *Ars Poetica* 269.

79-83: Carbone in the funeral oration on Guarino testifies to signs
of good character and an intellectual brilliance beyond his teachers'
range in the young Guarino. Similar praise is found in the speech of the

There were, however, many obscure passages in ancient books, especially where there was a mixture of our language with a foreign one. To a mind bent on getting the whole truth, this was disturbing and an invitation to despair; but then your Apollo spoke to you in your quandary. "Have some confidence, young man, in your aspirations, and do not resent the hard work that will produce great rewards. The Father has granted you all kinds of ability; you will learn everything, you will teach all the works left by the ancients. But what you wish for, Roman, will not be granted in your native land. To acquire perfect knowledge, you must cross the sea and seek out distant Greece. Many have searched for this knowledge to the ends of the earth. Thus Plato went to Memphis, and the Samian exile to Assyria. Thus did the much-traveled man of Tyana, the admirer of Indian Iarchas, visit those whom men call Brahmans.

so-called Anonymous Veronese, a pupil who in 1424 wrote a spirited defence of Guarino. Sabbadini published the Latin text in *Atti e Memorie, Accademia d'agricoltura, scienze e lettere di Verona* (1916-17) 232-242.
    83-87: Intellectual curiosity was certainly one reason why Guarino learned Greek, but it cannot have been the only one. He had been excited by the presence in Italy of Manuel Chrysoloras, first as a teacher of Greek at Florence 1397-1400, then as a diplomat in Lombardy until the spring of 1403, although there is no record of the two men meeting at this time. Probably sensing that a command of Greek would give him an advantage among the *avant garde* enthusiasts for the new learning, and open up a better career for him, he welcomed the offer of the Venetian merchant prince, Paolo Zane, to take him to Constantinople and pay for his instruction at the school of Manuel and his nephew, John Chrysoloras. In a letter of 1453 to Marco Zane, Guarino gives the impression that Paolo Zane's motives were purely altruistic (*Epistolario* 2. Ep. 873. 14-19), but doubtless a business

Anne est turpe tibi, quod foedum Varro negavit,   100
Quod Cato, iam grandem puerilis prima Minervae
Orsa sequi et veteris notulas agnoscere Cadmi?
Vel te forte movet solitus ridere loquaces
Inachidas Marius, qui plus cum Marte Lyaeum,
Quam me cum Musis coluit? Prudentior illo   105
Arpinas alius, cui copia vocis Achivae
Praestitit eloquio cunctos superare Quirites.
Graiis ingenium, Graiis dedit ore rotundo
Musa loqui: Ausoniis quicquid spectabile chartis
Actaei fudere senes et origine prisca   110
Vester ab Aeoliis descendit sermo Pelasgis.
Nec modo Romanas aliud magis obruit artes
Quam quod Cecropidum studia intermissa Latinis.
Quare, age, tu saltem Danaas post longa Camenas
Saecula redde tuis, tantae primordia laudis   115
Praeripe nec dubita praeclarum exemplar haberi,

man like Zane saw the advantages of having a trained speaker and writer
of Greek on his staff. We know he was working for Zane in 1406 (see n.
on 53-56).

92. *Romane*: This word emphasizes that Guarino could as yet
command only Latin, and evokes the oracular tone of Vergil, *Aen.* 6.
851 and its surrounding verses.

96. *Memphitas*: After the execution of Socrates in 399 B. C., Plato
traveled extensively for the next twelve years. Egypt may have been
one of the countries he visited. *Samius ... exul*: i.e., Pythagoras, who
emigrated from his native Samos about 531 B. C., perhaps to escape
the tyranny of Polycrates. He is said to have traveled in the Near East.

97-98. *Brachmanas ... Tyaneus*: Apollonius of Tyana, a Neopy-
thagorean sage who was born about the beginning of the Christian era
and lived until the reign of Nerva, is said to have visited India, in par-
ticular the Brahmins, the learned caste of the Hindus: see Pliny, *N.H.*
6. 17. 21.

Will you never leave the house you crawled through as a child, and recognize the letters of ancient Cadmus? Or perhaps you are influenced by Marius, who used to make fun of the talkative descendants of Inachus and was more devoted to Lyaeus and Mars than to me and the muses? Another man of Arpinum, more sensible than he, had an abundant knowledge of Greek and surpassed all the Quirites in eloquence. The muse gave the Greeks genius and the power to speak in rounded tones. The Actaean elders poured into the writings of Ausonia all that is admirable in them, and your language takes its ancient origin from the Pelasgi of Aeolia. Nothing has damaged Roman arts more than the cessation of Greek studies among the Latins. After long centuries, then, restore the Danaan muses to your countrymen. Take first credit for this, and do not hesitate to be thought a model

99: Perhaps an echo of the first four lines of a short Poem by Claudian (Loeb ed., ed. M. Platnauer, 2. Poem 20) on a Veronese who had never left home: "Felix qui propriis aevum transegit in arvis,/ipsa domus puerum quem videt, ipsa senem,/qui baculo nitens in qua reptavit harena/ unius numerat saecula longa casae." This Veronese, however, never travels abroad or engages in worldly affairs; he is the very opposite of Guarino.

100: *Varro*: Marcus Terentius Varro (116-27 B. C.) was the greatest scholar among the Romans, and a proponent of Greek studies.

101. *Cato*: Marcus Porcius Cato the Censor (234-149 B. C.), though an enemy of Greek culture most of his life, learned Greek in his old age (Plutarch, *Cato Maior* 2; Cicero, *De Senectute* 3).

102. *Cadmi*: Cadmus, son of Agenor and Telephassa of Tyre, was sent to find Europa after her abduction by Zeus. In his wanderings, he is said to have founded Thebes and to have introduced writing into Greece. The Greek alphabet is derived from the Phoenician.

Quod mox multorum virtus accensa sequatur.
Neve iter ignotum, medium neu terreat aequor,
Salvum ego te ducam salvumque, Guarine, reducam
Veronae ad muros et fama nominis alti   120
Oceanum tranare dabo, contingere caelum."
His motus stimulis vento caput et maris undae
Credis et Hadriacos Veneta legis arbore fluctus.
Laeva monticolae Carni linquuntur et Histri,
Necnon Illyriis passim gens mixta Liburni,   125
Tum plaga Dalmatiae, tum Pyrrhi nobile regnum,
His adversa iacens tellus Oenotria dextra.
Porro inter Pelopis terras et litora vectus
Sicaniae Dictaea Iovis cunabula visis
Nec petis oppositas sine re modo nomen Athenas,   130
Plena sed Aegaeo committens vela patenti
Transis dispositas in magnum Cyclades orbem
Ac Sporadum nullo sparsas fugis ordine cautes.

124 monticulae A

104. *Inachidas*: Properly, "descendants of Inachus" (Inachus was the first king of Argos), but here used generically to mean the Greeks, as in Statius, *Thebais* 3. 365.

Marius: Gaius Marius (c. 157-86 B. C.), the Roman general and politician, was born near Arpinum in the Apennines. For his scorn of Greeks, see Plutarch, *Marius* 2; for his heavy drinking, *Marius* 45.

106. *Arpinas*: i.e., Marcus Tullius Cicero, a native of Arpinum. Like most cultivated Romans, Cicero spoke Greek fluently; see Plutarch, *Cicero* 4. 4-5.

108-09: *Graiis ...loqui*: Borrowed from Horace, *Ars Poetica* 333-34.

109. Ausoniis: Ausonia is a poetical name for Italy.

quicquid spectabile: The idea that Latin literature did not begin to flourish until after Greek learning spread to Rome is a commonplace

for many other talented and enthusiastic scholars to follow. And do not let the unknown path and the open sea terrify you. I shall lead you safely, Guarino, and bring you safely back to the walls of Verona. I shall grant you the power to swim across the ocean and to touch the sky, through the fame of a great reputation."
Thus encouraged, you entrust your life to the wind and waves of the sea, and skim the billows of the Adriatic in a Venetian ship. Left behind on the left are the hill dwellers of Carnus and Hister; the Liburnians, a race mixed in places with the Illyrians; then the expanse of Dalmatia and the noble kingdom of Pyrrhus. Opposite them on the right lies the land of Oenotria. Next you sail between the land of Pelops and the coast of Sicania, and visit the cradle of Jupiter on Dicte. You do not go to Athens, lying opposite, a mere name without substance, but entrusting full sails to the open Aegean you pass over to the Cyclades, arranged in a huge circle, and shun the scattered rocks of the Sporades.

among classical Latin writers, e.g., Cicero, *De oratore* 1. 11. Similarly, Guarino often insisted (e.g., in *Epistolario* 2. Ep. 861. 45-49) that a proper understanding of Latin was impossible without a knowledge of Greek. Battista Guarino says the same, with illustrative examples, in *De modo et ordine docendi ac scribendi* (Woodward, *Vittorino* 166-67). In particular he states (Vittorino, 167): "But I turn to the authority of the great Latins themselves, to Cicero, Quintilian, Cato, and Horace: they are unanimous in proclaiming the close dependence of the Roman speech and Roman literature upon the Greek."
    110. *Actaei*: "Attic," here used generically to mean "Greek."
    110-11. *origine ...Pelasgis*: The Pelasgi, or original inhabitants of Greece, were also spread over Asia Minor (*Aeoliis* = Aelian), Crete, Etruria, and Latium (Servius, *ad Aen.* 2. 83; 8. 600; Pomponius Mela 1. 16 and 19; Pliny, *N.H.* 3. 5. 8). Hence, there arose an idea that Latin was originally derived from the Pelasgian language.

Mox hinc Lemnon, at hinc abscondis Lesbon et alta
Prospicis Iliacas Tenedi de rupe ruinas.   135
Excipit artatum terris propioribus aequor,
Qua nitido effusam flevit vectore sororem
Phrixus et infelix flevit Leandria virgo
Funera, qua iunctam vix credens Seston Abydo
Cantat adhuc Medos nautarum fabula pontes.   140
Fusior inde tua sulcatur nave Propontis,
Donec in Odrysios cecidit gravis ancora portus,
Aemula Romuleis tollens ubi moenia muris
Thracius Euxinas angustat Bosporus undas.

136 arctatum A

113. *Cecropidum*: "descendants of Cecrops." In myth, Cecrops was the first king of Athens.
114. *Danaas*: Another generic word for "Greek." In myth, Danaus was the son of Belus, (great-grandson of Zeus through his union with Io, and brother of Agenor of Tyre). When Aegyptus wanted his sons to marry Danaus' daughters, Danaus fled to Argos with them, where they claimed help and shelter.
123. *Veneta...arbore*: Manuel Chrysoloras and the Byzantine emperor, Manuel Palaeologus, set sail for Greece from Venice at the beginning of April, 1403 (See G. Cammelli, *I dotti bizantini e le origini dell' umanesimo* 1; *Manuele Crisolora* [Florence, 1941] 129). Sabbadini in *La scuola e gli studi di Guarino* 10-11; *Vita di Guarino* cap. 21; and Guarino, *Epistolario* 3. 5 says that Guarino went with them. Cammelli (p. 133) doubts this, with good reason: Guarino himself says, "redeuntem in patriam Chrysoloram subsecutus sum" (*Epistolario* 2. Ep. 862. 79-80), and there is documentary evidence (see n. on 52) that he was still in Venice in August, 1403. He must therefore have left Venice with Paolo Zane sometime after that.

From there you see Lemnos sinking in your wake, then Lesbos, and from the high steep of Tenedos you see in the distance the ruins of Ilium. A sea bounded by closer shores now welcomes you, where Phrixus wept for his sister when she was thrown off her shining carrier, and another unhappy girl wept for the death of Leander, and where sailors still sing chanties about the Persian bridge, hardly believing that Abydos was joined to Sestos. From there your ship ploughs through the wider waters of the Propontis, until its heavy anchor falls in the Odrysian harbor, where the Thracian Bosporus, lifting up ramparts to rival the walls of Romulus, hems in the Euxine waves.

124. *Carni*: An Alpine tribe inhabiting the mountains separating Venetia from Noricum extending from Rhaetia on the west to the confines of Istria on the east. Strabo confines them to the mountains, regarding the plain about Aquileia as part of Venetia, but Pliny calls the district round Aquileia (which Ianus has in mind) "the region of the Carni." A ship leaving Venice would pass Aquileia on the left.

Histri: The inhabitants of Histria (or Istria), a roughly triangular peninsula near the head of the Adriatic Sea between the modern Trieste and Pola. Its name was derived from the common but mistaken belief of the ancients that a branch of the Danube (*Hister* or *Ister*) flowed into the Adriatic at this point.

125. *Liburni*: An Illyrian people on the east coast of the Adriatic, who once occupied a large part of the Illyrian litoral (Strabo 6. 2. 4), but in Roman times were confined to an area between the modern River Raša to the west of Istria and the border of Dalmatia.

126. *Pyrrhi...regnum*: i.e., Epirus.

127. *tellus Oenotria*: The name given by Greeks in early times to the southern part of Italy, then applied by the poets to Italy in general. Aristotle (*Politics* 7. 9. 2) relates a myth that a king of the Oenotrians called Italus gave his name to the whole country.

128. *Pelopis terras*: The Peloponnesus.

129. *Sicaniae*: i.e., of Sicily.

Vir fuit hic patrio Chrysoloras nomine dictus,   145
Candida Mercurio quem Calliopea crearat,
Nutrierat Pallas; nec solis ille parentum
Clarus erat studiis, sed rerum protinus omnem
Naturam magna complexus mente tenebat.

Dictaea Iovis cunabula: In myth, Zeus was reared in a cave on Mt. Dicte in Crete, and there fed by the honey of bees (see n. on 634) and the milk of the goat Amalthea. It is unlikely that Guarino went to Mt. Dicte, but he probably landed in Crete, which was on the regular Venetian trading route to the East.

130. *Athenas*: Athens was not on the regular sea route from Venice to Constantinople. By 1403 it was an insignificant town. Guarino (*Epistolario* 2. Ep. 861. 24-27) talks of its fallen walls and ruinous state, but there is no evidence that he ever visited it.

132-33. *Cyclades...Sporades*: Island groups in the Aegean.

134. *Lemnon...Lesbon*: Guarino's ship probably did not call at these islands but made straight for Tenedos (see n. on 135).

135. *Tenedi*: Tenedos, a small island with an excellent harbor, lies off the Troad in Asia Minor, about twelve miles from Cape Sigeum. In his note on Vergil, *Aeneid* 2. 23, R. D. Williams observes that Vergil's description of Tenedos as "now just a curve of the coastline and a treacherous landfall for ships" is not to be read (as it often is) as a comment by Vergil, but as a statement of Aeneas referring to the deterioration of the famous harbor during the Trojan War. The convenience of Tenedos was recognised in the sixth century by the Emperor Justinian, who constructed granaries there to receive the regular corn shipments from Alexandria to Constantinople. In the fifteenth century, it was a Venetian base, so there is every likelihood that Paola Zane's ship put in there. Guarino may have descried some old Roman buildings on the distant mainland, but they could not have been the ruins of ancient Troy, which had not yet been excavated, nor even securely located. The line, however, is highly evocative and a fine poetic touch.

136. *artatum...aequor*: i.e., the Hellespont (or Dardanelles), a long strait about three miles broad, leading from the Aegean Sea into the Propontis.

137 *Phrixus*: Son of Athamas and Nephele, and stepson of Ino, who plotted to have him sacrificed to Zeus. Nephele, however, rescued him and his sister Helle by putting them on the ram with the golden fleece,

There was a man whose family name was Chrysoloras, the offspring of Mercury and shining Calliope, and the nursling of Pallas. He was not only distinguished in the studies of his ancestors, but he had a grasp of the whole range of nature in his great mind.

which flew away. Between Sigeum and the Chersonesus, Helle fell off into the sea which was thereafter called the Hellespont. This legend is frequently referred to by the later Roman poets, e.g., Ovid, *Heroides* 18. 117, 137; Propertius 1. 20. 19; Lucan 5. 56.

138. *Leandria virgo*: Hero, the priestess of Aphrodite in Sestos, to visit whom Leander swam every night across the Hellspont from Abydos. One night he drowned, and the grieving Hero threw herself into the sea.

140. *pontes*: In the second Persian War (480 B. C.), King Xerxes moved his army from Asia to Europe by building two bridges of boats from the neighborhood of Abydos to the coast between Sestos and Madytus (Herodotus 7. 36).

142. *Odrysios...portus*: i.e., the harbor of Constantinople, at the southern end of the Bosporus connecting the Propontis and the Euxine (Black) Sea. *Odrysios* is poetical for "Thracian."

143. *aemula*: The triple walls of Constantinople were of enormous size, and much stronger than those of Rome had ever been. The city itself was often referred to as "the new Rome," or simply "Rome," e.g., by the Turks, "Rum" being an Arabic echo of "Rome." The Byzantine emperors regularly styled themselves emperors of the Romans and could legitimately claim this title, since the last emperor in the West was deposed in A. D. 476, while the eastern Roman empire continued to exist. Comparisons between the "old" and "new" Rome were inevitably made, e.g., by Manuel Chrysoloras in his Greek treatise *Comparatio veteris et novae Romae*.

145. *Chrysoloras*: Manuel Chrysoloras (ca. 1357-1415) was a Byzantine scholar and diplomat of knightly rank, and undoubtedly the greatest influence on Guarino's life, as Guarino was on Ianus'. He first came to Italy in 1394 as a diplomat seeking aid for the empire aginst the Turks. In 1395 he received an invitation to teach Greek in Florence, which he accepted, and taught there 1397-1400. Among his pupils were Leonardo Bruni, Pier Paolo Vergerio, Palla Strozzi, and Roberto Rossi. He spent the period 1400-03 in Lombardy trying to raise financial and military support for the empire, while the emperor himself toured the courts of Europe on the same mission. Both men failed and returned

Postmodo sacrilegae rabies quem perfida gentis,   150
Errori quod se socium pius ipse negabat,
Sedibus eiectum Latio transmisit avitis.
Sancta nec ossa viri tumulis iacuere suorum,
Sed procul Arctoo rigat haec Constantia Rheno.
Hunc petis et miris tot pulchra ornatibus unum   155
Quaeris in urbe virum. Non tantum verba docentis

home in March or April, 1403. Chrysoloras returned to Italy in January, 1406, and was back in Constantinople by the end of the year. He converted to Latin Christianity in 1406 and moved to the West permanently in 1407, but continued to represent the cause of the empire. From 1409-10 he visited London and was at the Council of Constance 1414-15, where he died in 1415. Although he was nominally head of a school in Constantinople, his nephew, John Chrysoloras was the *de facto* principal. (Guarino could only have been taught by Manuel in the years 1403-end of 1405.) For the position that his real mission was always that of a diplomat, see I. Thomson, "Manuel Chrysoloras and the early Italian Renaissance," *Greek, Roman, and Byzantine Studies* 7. No. 1 (1966) 63-82. The only full-length biography of Chrysoloras is by Cammelli (see n. on 123). 146-47. *Mercurios...Calliopea...Pallas*: Mercury was god of eloquence; Calliopea (or Calliope) was chief of the nine muses, goddess of epic poetry, and sometimes in the poets, of every other kind of poetry; and Pallas Athena was goddess of wisdom.

148-49. *rerum...tenebat*: Guarino testifies (*Epistolario* 1. Ep. 25. 26, 43-45, 49-50) to Chrysoloras' grasp of science and philosophy. Humanists in general regarded the combination of literary and "scientific" skills (by which, however, they usually mean philosophical speculation about the physical universe) as desirable and sanctioned by such passages as Vergil, Ecl. 6. 31-40 and *Aen.* 1. 740-46 (based on Orpheus' song in Appollonius of Rhodes I. 496f), in the second of which the poet Iopas sings of eclipses, the origin of human and animal life, the causes of thunder, etc. In *Geo.* 2. 475-92, Vergil seems to imply that the ideal poet would be a combination of himself and a philosopher like Lucretius.

150-52: These lines refer to Chrysoloras' conversion to the Latin rite, which I see as an act of political expediency rather than the sincere submission to Rome that Ianus suggests it was. In 1395, the Sultan

In later years the mad treachery of a sacrilegious race cast him out of his ancestral home and sent him over to Latium, because he was a pious man and would not be party to their error; and the man's sacred bones do not lie among the graves of his own people, but are washed, far away, by the arctic Rhine, at Constance. In a city beautiful with so many adornments you seek out this one man, and in order not to come as a stranger to hear him teaching, but to see and

Bayezid laid siege to Constantinople, desisting only to defeat a half-hearted crusade at Nicopolis in September of that year. The empire had to find armed support or perish, but a stumbling block was the schism that had existed between the Eastern Church and Rome since 1054. Pope Gregory XII swore to end it in an oath written out by Leonardo Bruni and taken by Gregory in December, 1406. The price of reconciliation, however, was total submission to the Roman rite, and a number of such "political" conversions resulted (see F. Heer, *The Medieval World* [Mentor Books, 1962] 128-30), including, as I believe, that of Chrysoloras. Hans Baron, *Political and Humanistic Literature in Florence and Venice* (Cambridge, Mass., 1955) 111 cites a letter by Vergerio in 1406 in which Chrysoloras is mentioned as "wanting to become a Latin" (*"cum cupiat esse Latinus"*). Baron shows that at the end of 1405 Chrysoloras had applied to the Pope for permission to take holy orders in the Western Church. His "conversion" took place the next year, but he was not, as Ianus claims, expelled for that. He chose to live as a "Latin" only to increase his effectiveness as a diplomat.

155. *Constantia*: Chrysoloras died April 15, 1415, while attending the Council of Constance. Guarino wrote a magnificent *consolatio* to John Chrysoloras (*Epistolario* 1. Ep. 25). Pier Paolo Vergerio wrote to Niccolò Leonardì, suggesting that Guarino should write some formal *commemoratio* on behalf of all the great master's pupils, but Guarino referred the task to Vergerio (G., *Epistolario* 1. Ep. 27. 19-76). Vergerio wrote only the epitaph still preserved in Constance: "Ante aram situs es dominus Manuel Chrissolora, miles Constantinopolitanus, ex vetusto genere Romanorum, qui cum Constantino imperatore migrarant: vir doctissimus prudentissimus optimus, qui tempore generalis"

Advena captares, sed proximus intima vitae
Arbiter inspiceres, famulus colis atria docti
Hospitis et mixto geris auditore ministrum.
Tam cito non rapuit Neoclides Persida vocem,   160
Barbara dum victi sedet ad praetoria regis,
Quam cito tu sectam quino discrimine linguam
Hausisti Crasso longe distinctius ipso.
Nec quisquam Hesperiis natum dixisset in oris,
Cum tua Mopsopiam sonuissent ora loquelam.   165
Quod plane assiduus fandi tibi contulit usus
Ac declamandi totiens nec more sinistro
Pythagorea annis servata silentia quinis.

"concilii Constantiensis diem obiit ea existimatione ut ab omnibus
summo sacerdotio dignus haberetur. XVI Kalendas maias conditus est
anno Incarnati Verbi MCCCCXV." Guarino quoted the epitaph in a let-
ter to Giacomo dei Fabbri (*Epistolario* 1. Ep. 54. 77-84), substituting
the more classical expression *Chrysoloras eques* for the more medieval
term and spelling used by Vergerio. Particularly interesting is the sug-
gestion that Chrysoloras was in the running for election as Pope. The
lack of a worthwhile literary monument to Chrysoloras weighed heavily
on Guarino's conscience, but it was only in 1452 (*Epistolario* 2. Ep.
861) that he launched an appeal for contributions to a commemorative
miscellany to be called *Chrysolorina*. Its nucleus was five old letters of
his own (*Epistolario* 1. Epp. 7, 25, 27, 47, 54) and one by Poggio (Id.,
Ep. 49), two *commentarioli* (notes) of his own, and the funeral oration
by Andrea Zulian (extant in many codices). To these he added four
new letters of his own, and four solicited from Poggio, and his own sons
Battista, Girolamo, and Manuel (*Epistolario* 2. Epp. 861, 862, 864,
892, 893, 863, 865, 866). There was also a poem of 82 lines from Raf-
faele Zovenzoni (G., *Epistolario* 2. Ep. 867. Excluded as a contributor,
Ianus perhaps included his verses on Chrysoloras in the *Panegyricus* in
the hope that they would find their way into the *Chrysolorina*.
157. *advena*: Possibly an echo of Job 19. 27.

judge his life at close quarters, you live as a menial in the halls of your scholarly host as both his servant and pupil. Neoclides, sitting at the court of the vanquished king, did not grasp the Persian tongue as quickly as you drank in the five-part language, with more brilliance than Crassus himself. When your lips uttered the speech of Mopsopia, no one would have called you a native of Hesperia. This was the result of constant practice in conversation and declamation, not of Pythagorean silences perversely held for five years.

158. *famulus*: The story that Guarino worked as a menial in Chrysoloras' house is accepted by Sabbadini in his *Vita di Guarino* cap. 22, but rejected in his *La scuola e gli studi di Guarino* 11, where he points out that the Anonymous Veronese (the ultimate source of the tale) simply says that Chrysoloras took Guarino into his home ("hunc domi suscepit"), and Ianus "un po' troppo poeticamente" made Guarino into a *famulus*. Actually, the Anonymous Veronese merely says that Chrysoloras received Guarino in his home (*domi*), not into his home. Certainly, Guarino was familiar with the house with its "hanging garden" and cool cypresses, but he nowhere states that he was a servant in it. In fact, he specifically says in *Epistolario* 2. Ep. 873. 16-18 that he was honorably supported by Paolo Zane and thus permitted to quench his thirst for Greek. (For Zane's motives, see n. on 83-87).

162. *quino discrimine*: Referring to the Stoic classification of the Greek language into five parts: *onoma* (noun), *rhema* (verb), *syndesmos* (conjunction), *arthron* (article), and a fifth, which in Chrysippus, "On the Five Cases" *(Stoicorum Veterum Fragmenta* ed. E. Von Arnim 2. 45, was almost certainly the adverb. See *Oxford Classical Dictionary* 2nd ed., under "Grammar, Grammarians," sec. 5.

163. *Crasso*: Lucius Licinius Crassus (140-91 B. C.) was an outstanding orator, idealized by Cicero in *De oratore*, in which he is the chief speaker.

164. *Hesperiis*: "Western," but also "Italian," as in Vergil, *Aen.* 2. 731, because Italy is west of Troy.

Scire loqui haud satis est, penitus sed nosse laboras,
Historici quicquid, quicquid scripsere sophistae,   170
Quicquid divini tegit alma poesis Homeri.
Inde alias, post inde alias transcendis ad artes,
Singula degustans vel quae rigidissima firmat
Porticus incertis vel contra sensibus edit
Helleboro tardam purganda Academia bilem   175
Vel si quid melius spatiantum interserit ordo
Quive individuis e partibus omnia fingunt.
Non secus ac flavi stipatrix Daedala mellis

167 declamatum *A*
171 divine *A*
173 quae vel *A*

165. *Mopsopiam*: Adjective from *Mopsopia*, an old name for At-
tica. Ianus probably means no more than "Greek," but no doubt Guar-
ino imagined that in addition to the spoken demotic he picked up nat-
urally he was also learning classical Attic Greek from Chrysoloras, who
was a leading figure in an Attic revival at Constantinople.
    168. *Pythagorea...quinis*: The philosopher Pythagoras is said to
have enjoined a five year silence on new students. This ran counter
to Guarino's idea (see Battista Guarino's remarks in *Vittorino* 168)
that constant *viva voce* exercises are necessary to test knowledge of the
inflexions in Greek.
    171. *tegit*: Guarino interpreted both Homer and Vergil allegori-
cally. See n. on 535, 562.
    174. *Porticus*: i.e., the Stoic school of philosophy founded by
Zeno, a Semite of Citium in Cyprus, who went to Athens in 311 B.
C. and ten years later began to teach in the Painted Stoa (Porch).
Stoicism was more dogmatic than earlier philosophies. It aimed at self-
sufficiency and taught less by an appeal to reason than by authoritarian
utterance. Zeno claimed that sense perceptions which come with irre-
sistible strength can be accepted as truth. In physics, he postulated that

Not content with knowing how to speak the language, you
labor for a complete knowledge of all the writings of the
historians and philosophers, all the divine content hidden
in the nourishing poetry of Homer. Thence you pass to
other, and yet other arts, getting a thorough taste of all that
the totally inflexible Porch asserts, or the Academy (which
needs to be cleansed of its dull madness with hellebore)
teaches in rebuttal about the unreliability of the senses, or
any better idea that the order of Peripatetics, or those who
fancy the universe is made up of indivisible particles, put
between the two. As the stippled packer of golden honey

everything is material, including God and the soul. God maintains the
physical and moral perfection of the world, and everything in nature is
rational and good. In ethics, he believed that virtue means conforming
to nature; even bad things are intended to educate us, and are therefore
for our ultimate good. The supreme good is happiness, achieved by
conforming to the natural laws, which are just and rational.

175. *Academia*: The school of philosophy originally founded by
Plato, possibly as early as 385 B.C. It survived, with many changes in
doctrine, until the fifth century A.D. Under Arcesilaus and Carneades
in the third and second centuries B.C., it was the chief centre of skeptic
thought, which accepted the outward appearances of things, but denied
that real knowledge was possible. By stating that they should take
hellebore, a purgative much used in the ancient world as a remedy for
mental illness, Ianus signifies his disapproval of skepticism.

176. *spatiantum...ordo*: The Aristotelian school called the Peri-
patetics because, according to a legend related in Diogenes Laertius 5.
2, Aristotle walked while lecturing. Often called the Lyceum, this school
acquired permanent buildings under Aristotle's successor, Theophras-
tus. In the early period it conducted systematic research into almost
every branch of learning, but later turned to literary criticism, discur-
sive biography, and trivial moralizing. There was a revival under An-
dronicus of Rhodes in the first century B.C., but in doctrine there was

Florentem primis subiit cum roribus hortum,
Omnia odorati populatur germina veris,   180
Nunc casiam, nunc illa thymum, nunc lene papaver
Delibans, nunc fila croci redolentia parvo
Crure legens, donec sero iam vespere notas
Pulsat onusta fores et cerea tecta revisit:
Sic Chrysolorei cupide tu pectoris omnes   185
Carpis divitias et corde recondis in imo
Sedulus ac nullam consumis inaniter horam
Obsequiisve vacans domini monitisve magistri.

little to choose between them and the Stoics and Academicians. In the first two centuries A.D., Aristotle's logic and natural philosophy were much studied, but after that the school passed into obscurity, as Neoplatonists took over the task of writing commentaries on Aristotle.

177. *quive...fingunt*: The Epicurean philosophy, which opposed all others. Founded by Epicurus of Samos at Athens in 306 B.C., it taught materialism, starting from Democritus' doctrine that everything in the universe, including the soul, is composed of atoms that recombine into other forms when animals die or objects disintegrate. Gods exist, but take no interest in human affairs. Since death ends all, there is no need to fear a future life. The supreme good is *ataraxia*, i.e., freedom from pain, physical or mental. It was not a hedonistic but a quietest philosophy, advocating withdrawal from worldly ambitions and the kind of life that would bring most peace of mind and bodily comfort, as dictated by common sense. Virtue and moderation are the true keys to happiness. Inaccurately, Epicureans became identified in the popular mind with coarse pleasures, gluttony, and selfish indulgences of all kinds.

178-188: This "epic simile" is compounded from Vergil, *Geo.* 4. 180-83 (bees going out in the morning, sipping plants, and coming home laden); 4. 51-66 ("spangled" bees going in search of honey); and short phrases from *Geo.* 4. 216 ("stipantque frequentes") and 4. 163-64 ("mella stipant").

enters a garden blooming in the first dews and plunders all the plants of sweet-smelling spring, now sipping mezereon, now thyme, now the supple poppy, now skimming the filaments of the crocus with her tiny leg, until, laden, she knocks in the late evening at the familiar door, and returns to her waxen home; so you eagerly pluck all the riches from Chrysoloras' mind and carefully stow them away in your innermost heart, and pass no idle hour, with time for nothing but your master's orders or your teacher's instructions.

183. *crure legens:* Cf. Vergil, *Geo.* 4. 181. Bees carry pollen in balls in a hollow of their hind legs.
188. See note on 158.
192. *Veneris...expers:* Cf. Vergil, *Geo.* 4. 198-99, "(the bees) do not indulge in sex nor loosen their bodies in idle lust."
193. *Argus:* The giant set by Hera (Juno) to guard Io, whom Zeus had changed into a heifer. One or more of his hundred eyes were always awake. To rescue Io, Zeus sent Hermes, who used his magic staff (*caduceus*) to close all Argus' eyes, and then killed him. Ianus is suggesting that only Hermes (god of eloquence) can put Guarino to sleep as he pores over his books.
201. *Symplegade ...Sirmio:* The Symplegades were two islands near the entrance to the Hellespont, which were fabled to clash together when anything passed through them. The Argo was the only ship to succeed in sailing through, after which the rocks became fixed. Sirmio is a small promontory on the south shore of Lake Garda near Verona.
202. *Pangaeis Alpes:* The Pangaean mountain ridge is in Thrace. The Alpes are in Switzerland and extend into northern Italy.
(202) *Athesis ...Hebro:* The Athesis is the modern River Adige, flowing through Verona. The Hebrus (the modern Maritza) is the principal river of Thrace.

Si quid ab his reliqui superest tibi temporis unquam,
Vel scribis vel scripta legis vel lecta reponis,   190
Multa ferens multa et faciens, sudoris et algi
Nunquam expers, vini ac Veneris sed iugiter expers,
Nec magis indulgens somno quam pervigil Argus
Aut Colchus Libycusve anguis vel inhospita Gorgon.
Nam, cum te ardenti tandem indormire lucernae   195
Impulerat totis urgens sopor invidus alis,
Tu fessos acri stimulabas vulnere sensus
Eduros teneris immergens artubus ungues:
Tantus amor veri, tantae sapientia curae.
Macte animi, qui tam procul a natalibus arvis,   200

182 fida *A*

206. *Aonidum*: i.e. the muses, so called because Mt. Helicon and
the fountain Aganippe were in Aonia (poetical name for Boeotia).
207. *qui*: i.e. the Athenian orator, Demosthenes (384-322 B.C.),
who vigorously opposed the expansionist policies of Philip of Macedon.
Plutarch (Demosthenes 7.3) recounts that Demosthenes built an un-
derground room, where he would remain for two or three months at a
time, practising his rhetorical delivery. To avoid the temptation to go
outside, he shaved his head on one side only.
210. An exaggeration. While in the East, Guarino wrote letters to
Floro Valerio, Giovanni Quirino, and Francesco Barbaro (G., *Epistolario*
1. Epp. 3, 4, 5.) Doubtless he wrote other letters which have not
survived.
211. *Euclides*: Aulus Gellius 6. 10 recounts an episode during the
Peloponnesian War, in which Euclides, a Megarian disciple of Socrates,
was forbidden to enter Athens under a decree banning entry to all men
from Megara. He therefore disguised himself as a woman and visited
his master by night.

If you ever have any time to yourself after these tasks, you read or write or store away what you have read, with many burdens to bear and much to do, never free from cold and sweat, but strictly abstaining from wine and Venus, and yielding to sleep no more than did the ever-wakeful Argus, or the serpents of Colchis or Libya, or the inhospitable Gorgon. For as often as slumber, pressing on you with all its squadrons, drove you to slump at last over the burning lamp, you would rouse your tired senses with a sharp nip, sinking your hardened nails into your tender flesh: such was your love of truth, so much did you care for wisdom. What wonderful courage! As far away from your native soil

213. *Democritus*: Democritus of Abdera (ca. 460-357 B.C.) is said to have travelled extensively in search of learning. When he returned, he divided the family property, keeping only a small sum of money for himself, which he spent on books and further travel (Diogenes Laertius 9.34-35).

214. *Cleanthes*: According to Diogenes Laertius 6. 169, the philosopher Cleanthes was so poor that he had to draw water in gardens at night to pay for his attendance at the lectures of Zeno the Stoic. No ancient authority says that he owned a well.

215. *Chrysippi secreta*: i.e. Stoic philosophy. Chrysippus (ca. 280-207 B.C.) was converted by Cleanthes, and succeeded him in 232 B.C. as head of the school founded by Zeno.

217. *Anaxagoras*: According to Diogenes Laertius 2. 7, the philosopher Anaxagoras (500-428 B.C.) was accused by relatives of neglecting his property. He therefore transferred it to them, and retired to a life of learning.

229. *Vellera*: Cf. Vergil, *Geo.* 2. 121. The ancients believed that both cotton and silk were vegetable products gathered by combing them from leaves.

Instabili quantum Symplegade Sirmio, quantum
Pangaeis Alpes, Athesis diducitur Hebro,
Talia quaerendis persudas otia Musis.
Quae satis aequa tuo reddam praeconia facto
Quemve unquam simili flagrasse cupidine dicam   205
Aonidum? Caeco latuit male tonsus in antro
Bellacem orando fregit qui paene Philippum:
Tu te non propriae subter penetralia cellae
Clausisti, sed tam longe studiosus abisti,
Unde tuis de te nunquam vel fama rediret.   210
Induit Euclides muliebria tegmina membris:
Dorica pro Latio tu sumpsti pallia cultu.
Democritus contempsit opes, sed parte retenta:
Tu nil servasti. Putei mercede Cleanthes
Chrysippi secreta bibit: tu mille subisti   215
Iussa cliens doctoris heri. Dimisit avitos
Fortis Anaxagoras late sterilescere fundos:
Tu, cor ut excoleres, sulcis tibi corpus arasti.
    Scilicet haud unquam leviter pretiosa parantur
Nec nisi difficili surgunt ingentia nisu.   220
Nimirum illa rudes mundo abstersura tenebras
Ornatura novos illustratura vetustos

202 deducitur A

•

230. *Hyperboreas:* The Hyperboreans were an imaginary people in
the extreme north, blessed by good fortune. See, e.g., Pindar, *Pyth.* 10.
29-48.

as Sirmio from the restless Symplegades, as the Alps from the Pangaean ridge, as the Athesis from the Hebrus, yet you spend your spare time laboring in pursuit of the muses. What praise shall I give you that could match your achievement, or which of the daughters of Aonia shall I say ever burned with a passion like yours? He who with his oratory almost broke the power of warlike Phillip lay hidden and unshaven in a dark cave: you did not closet yourself in the depths of a private cell, but went so far away to study that word about you did not even get back to your people. Euclides put on woman's clothing: you put on the Dorian cloak in place of the fashions of Latium. Democritus despised his wealth, but kept some of it: you kept nothing. Cleanthes drank the secrets of Chrysippus, paying for them with a well: you carried out a thousand orders in the service of a master who was also your teacher. Brave Anaxagoras let his ancestral estates go barren far and wide: to cultivate your mind, you ploughed your body with furrows.

In truth, things of value are never obtained with little effort, nor do great achievements arise without a hard struggle. No wonder the knowledge that was to banish gross darkness from the world, to adorn the moderns and throw light on the ancients,

232. *Erythraea ...concha*: i.e. the oysters from which pearls were gathered in the Red Sea.
233-35: Cf. Ovid, *Met*. 1. 138–140.
239–240: The Zephyr is the West wind, the Auster the South wind. The usual legend about Perseus is that he was given winged sandals by Athena, which enabled him to fly on his mission to kill the Gorgon,

Per magnos cumulanda fuit doctrina labores.
Nec te aerumnarum pigeat, Guarine, tuorum:
Sudasti haud frustra, suus haec incommoda fructus 225
Obruit et longe cedunt dispendia lucro.
  Hic licet Eos currens ignotus ad Indos
Barrorum dentes Arabumve reportet odores
Paxave lanigeris fulgentia vellera silvis,
Alter Hyperboreas timide rimatus arenas   230
Eruat innumero servatos gryphe smaragdos
Aut, Erythraea, legat, quos celat concha, lapillos,
Ille metalliferi scrutatus viscera montis
Palleat et Stygiis quam caelo admotior umbris
Effodiat, curet quam protinus abdere massam: 235
Non tamen has aequabit opes. Haec gaza Sabaeas
Exuperat species ebur aurum Serica gemmas.
  Quid, quod inutilius quidam haud leviora tulerunt?
Perseus et Zephyrum pennis lustravit et Austrum,
Tolleret ut domiti pretium Cepheida monstri;   240
Occidui Alcides solis devexa secutus,
Fulva Phoroneos ut poma referret ad Argos;
Trunca puppe audax Colchos ingressus Iason
Serpentum excubias taurorum incendia pugnas

231 in numero *A*
238 quidam leviora *A*

Medusa. On his way home, he rescued Andromeda, daughter of King
Cepheus, who was to be sacrificed to a sea monster. In all accounts,
the location of these exploits is vague, but the rescue of Andromeda
is always in the Levant, and the slaying of Medusa somewhere to the
north.

had to be amassed with much labor And do not regret your pains, Guarino: you have not sweated in vain, the gain outweighs the loss, and the expense is far less than the profit. Some unknown fellow may run to the East Indies and bring back elephants' tusks or the perfumes of Arabia or gleaming fleeces combed from wool-bearing forests; another may timidly sift Hyperborean sands and dig up emeralds guarded by a host of dragons, or harvest the tiny stones that the Erythraean shell conceals; another may grow pale from searching the innards of a metal-bearing mountain, and, nearer the Stygian shades than heaven, dig up a mass he is immediately at pains to hide: but none of them will match the wealth you have. This treasure is above ivory, gold, silk, gems, and the splendors of Sheba.

Some have done things just as difficult, but to less advantage. Perseus crossed the Zephyr and Auster on wings to carry off the daughter of Cepheus as his reward for defeating a monster; Alcides followed the slanting rays of the sunset to bring golden apples to Phoronean Argos; Jason boldly went to Colchis in his lopped ship, and shuddered at the guardian serpents, the bulls' fire,

242. *Phoroneos*: So called because Phoroneus was the legendary founder of Argos, to which Hercules on his eleventh Labor brought back the apples of the Hesperides.

243. *trunca puppe*: The stern of the Argo was shorn off as the Symplegades (see n. on 201) clashed together for the last time.

243-45: In order to claim the throne of Iolkos, Jason had to fetch the golden fleece from Colchis, a country bounded on the west by the Euxine Sea, on the north by the Caucasus, on the east by Iberia. King Aeetes would not let him take the fleece until he had yoked a pair of brazen-hoofed, fire-breathing bulls, then used them to plough a field

Horruit anguigenum. Quae tantis digna periclis   245
Praemia? Flaventi nempe illita lana metallo.
Tu revehis victor, quod non modo vile nitenti
Pellicula et malis Libycis et virgine fusca
Non mutare velim, sed pro quo cuncta recusem,
Quae Mida convertit, quae pollens divite regno   250
Lydorum aurifluis collegit Croesus in undis.
Altera perfecto celebrabat Olympia lustro
Elis et Alpheus terrae per operta volutus
Visa recensebat Siculis sollemnia Nymphis,
Cum te iam Graio plenum praecordia Phoebo   255
Admonuit patriae leviter deus aure prehensa.

and sow it with the teeth from the dragon once slain by Cadmus at Thebes. From the teeth sprang armed men, whom Jason managed to kill off by throwing a stone among them and starting a fight. The fleece itself was guarded by a dragon, which Medea drugged. The story is recounted in Ovid, *Met.* 7. 100-158.

250. *Mida*: Bacchus, having received hospitality from King Midas (alternative form, Mida), granted him the boon of turning anything to gold at a touch. Since even his food and drink turned to gold, Midas implored the god's aid. Bacchus told him to bathe in the River Pactolus, the sands of which were afterwards flecked with gold.

251. *Croesus*: King of Lydia 560-46 B.C., famous for his wealth, which was said to come from gold mined in Mt. Tmolus and gathered from the Rivers Pactolus (see n. on 250) and Hermus (for which cf. Vergil, *Geo.* 2. 137, "auro turbidus Hermus").

252-56: Sabbadini insists (Guarino, *Epistolario* 3. 5-6) that *lustro* here means a period of five years, citing in support Ianus' *Epigrammata* 1. p. 246. 2, and concludes that since Guarino left Venice in 1403, he departed from Constantinople in 1408. We can arrive at the same

and the battles of the dragon's offspring. What prizes were worth such great dangers? Just wool smeared with yellow metal. You bring back as victor something that I would not wish to trade for the tawdry glitter of a paltry fleece, for Libyan apples or a dusky maiden, but something for which I would even refuse all that Midas turned to gold, all that Croesus, powerful in his rich kingdom of Lydia, gathered in his gold-rolling waters.
Elis had completed a lustrum, and was celebrating another Olympic festival, and Alpheus, after winding his underground course, was again viewing the sights sacred to the Sicilian nymphs, when the deity took you gently by the ear, and, now that your heart was full of Greek Apollo, reminded you of home.

conclusion, however, taking *lustro* to refer to a four-year period, as it clearly does in *Panegyricus* 879. If each *lustrum* corresponds to each official four-year Olympiad (not to any given four-year period), and since Guarino left Venice in 1403, he would have arrived in Constantinople in the last year of the 544th Olympiad. The next Olympiad did not begin until high summer (roughly, August) of 1404. The start of the 546th Olympiad would take Guarino into late summer, 1408. He seems to have left before November of that year (see n. on 279).

253. *Alpheus*: Chief river of the Peloponnesus, flowing through Arcadia and Elis, not far from Olympia, where the Games were held, and into the Ionian Sea. Part of its course is underground: hence the myth that the river god Alpheus pursued the nymph Arethusa, who fled into the sea, but passed through it without harm, coming up near Syracuse in Sicily as the fountain Arethusa.

256. *leviter ...prehensa*: Cf. Vergil, *Ecl.* 6. 3,4, "Cynthius aurem/vellit et admonuit." The ancients regarded the ear as the seat of memory; hence, witnesses in law-court cases were summoned by touching their ears. (Pliny, *N.H.* 11. 103).

Ergo recedenti Byzantia Roma recedit
Nec minus adversam condunt Calchedona nubes,
Mollis laeva Asiae, dextra de parte ferocis
Vicina Europae tellus fugit et vice iusta   260
Lata bis angusto succedunt caerula ponto.
Vos o cyaneo volitantes aere venti,
Iustitiae fratres, divae omniparentis alumni,
Qui quatitis terras et ab imo Nerea fundo
Eruitis, per quos caeli variatur imago,   265
Ut modo caliget nebulis polus et modo late

259. *mollis*: A derogatory epithet hardly applicable to the Asian
Turks in 1408, when they were rapidly conquering what was left of the
Byzantine empire in "fierce" Europe. It would be even less appropriate
in 1453, when Constantinople finally fell to Mehemmed the Conqueror.
In the *Panegyricus* Ianus makes only one reference (976-78) to the Turk-
ish aggression.

261. *bis angusto*: The sea is twice narrowed, by the Bosporus
and the Hellespont, giving out to the Propontis and the Aegean Sea
respectively.

262-81: Embedded here is what would technically be called a *pro-
pemptikon* (Cf. Statius, *Silvae* 3. 2.) if it were a poem on its own. Such
poems (e.g., Horace, *Od.* 1. 3) were intended to speed a voyager on
his way. Note the wordiness of Ianus' treatment of the winds as against
Horace's classic economy (*Od.* 1.3.4, "obstrictis aliis praeter Iapyga").

262. *cyaneo ... venti*: i.e., the winds off the Bosporus, at the Black
Sea end of which stood the Cyaneae ("Dark Rocks," so called from their
dark greenish hue caused by the presence of copper). Herodotus 4.85
identifies them with the Symplegades.

263: A reminiscence of Ovid, *Met.* 14. 545-46, where the winds are
called *Astraei fratres* ("the Astraean brothers"), and the *alma parens*
("nurturing mother") is Cybele, the Phrygian Great Mother. The par-
ents of the winds were the Titan Astraeus and Eos (Aurora, Dawn),
according to Hesiod, *Theogony* 378, but Ianus obviously took *Astraei
fratres* to mean "the brothers of Astraea," she being the child of Zeus
and Themis, and goddess of Justice.

So Byzantine Rome recedes as you depart, and the clouds
hide Chalcedon opposite; soft Asia on the left, and its neigh-
boring land of fierce Europe on the right, flee into the dis-
tance, and by a fair exchange the twice narrowed ocean gives
way to a broad expanse of blue sea.

You winds that blow around the Cyaneae, brothers of
Justice and nurslings of the divine Mother of all who shake
the earth and uproot Nereus from the lowest depths, by
whose agency the face of heaven changes, so that now the
sky is dark with clouds, now the

264. *Nerea*: Nereus, son of Pontus and Doris, was (like Proteus
and Triton) one of the "old men of the sea" in myth, with the gift of
prophecy and the power to change shape at will. He was father of the
40 Nereids, including Thetis and Galatea (see n. on 577).

270. *Hippotades*: "Son of Hippotes," i.e., Aeolus, god of the winds.

271: Cf. Vergil, *Aen.* 1. 124-41, where Neptune rebukes the East
and West winds for stirring up the sea.

272. *parcite*: Juhász' *percite*, "rouse" would require *navem* or
ratem understood ("stir up the ship with your blasts"), or *flabra* in-
stead of *flabris* ("Stir up your blasts.") Ianus is asking the winds to
blow gently, not wildly.

274. *turpes thalamos*: Literally, "shameful bed-chambers." The
image is one of a luxurious pleasure-craft such as a "debauched" Turk
might sail in.

275. *Phari*: Pharos, a small island off Alexandria, on which the
famous lighthouse was built, symbolizes the unnamed debaucheries of
Egypt and the East generally.

276-77. *meliore ... Mercurio*: Mercury, as god of the market place,
had his bad side as patron of thieves, and his better as god of honest
merchants and of eloquence.

278. *facundia bina*: i.e. eloquence in both Latin and Greek.
The claim, often made, that Guarino had a large number of Greek
manuscripts with him should be laid to rest: see I. Thomson, "Some
Notes on the Contents of Guarino's Library," *Renaissance Quarterly*
24. 2 (1976) 169-77.

Rideat optati facies tranquilla sereni,
Unde vices anni nec non et frigora et imbres,
Unde graves tonitrus et hiulci fulminis irae,
Sic vos Hippotades leni moderamine frenet   270
Nec ferus eversum Neptunus vindicet aequor,
Paulisper cohibete minas et parcite flabris,
Dum ratis haec Italas contingit sospes arenas.
Non turpes thalamos piratarumve cohortem,
Delicias non illa Phari peregrinave nostrae   275
Luxuriae fomenta gerit, meliore coemptas
Mercurio sed ducit opes. Hac tota vetustas,
Hac una vehitur facundia bina carina.
Quae nisi Orionias evadat salva procellas,
Fandi ubi cultus erit, divina ubi carmina vatum,   280
Ingenia Hesperiae quanta sub nocte iacebunt?
Audimur. Spirant Euri post terga secundi
Nec deest pollicitis proles Latonia, Paean.
Ille etiam, Ortygien cum iam tua prora subisset,
Fatidicas in te laurus commovit et ultro   285
Delia sortilegi patuere oracula templi
Nulla nec optavit compleri numine Phoebas,
Dum servire suos gaudet tibi laeta furores.

272 percite *J*

279. *Orionias*: The setting of Orion at the beginning of November is associated with the onset of storms and rain. If Ianus is to be believed, Guarino set sail just before November.
282. *Hesperiae*: Hesperia ("the western places") was a name given to Italy by Greeks, because it lay west of Greece.
284. *Ortygien*: "Quail Island." It cannot be identified with certainty, but in the Homeric hymn to Apollo, it was the birthplace of

calm face of the fair weather we have prayed for smiles far and wide, you upon whom depend the seasons of the year, the cold spells, the downpours, the heavy thunderclaps, and the furious blasts of gaping lightning, so may Hippotades hold you gently in check, and wild Neptune not take revenge for his uptorn waters, restrain your threats for a little; and spare your blasts, until this ship touches the sands of Italy in safety. She does not carry a foul harem, or a gang of pirates, or the delights of Pharos, or strange fomentations for our luxury, but riches bought under the better Mercury. On this one ship sails the whole of antiquity, the eloquence of both languages. If she does not safely escape Orion's storms, where will the study of eloquence be, or the divine songs of the poets? Beneath what vast night will the great minds of Hesperia lie? We are heard. The east winds blow favorably from behind, and Paean, the son of Latona, lives up to his promises. As your prow approached Ortygia he even stirred his prophetic laurels in your direction and the Delian oracles in the temple of prophecy opened out of their own accord. There was not a priestess of Phoebus but longed to be filled with the god, while rejoicing that her inspiration was at your service.

Artemis. In other accounts it is clearly another name for Delos, where there was an oracle of Apollo in historical times.

290. *felix*: A very strong word in Latin, with a double signification: "happy" in the sense of "blessed with good fortune" (as in Vergil, *Geo.* 2. 490), and "fertile" or "productive," as in *Geo.* 1. 1.

290. *placido cum funere*: Guarino died on Dec. 4, 1460. (Muratori, *Rerum Italicarum Scriptores* 28. 1096). His son, Manuele, records that his death was peaceful: "Septimum ac octuagesimum agens annum indigna ac invida pleuresis correptus infirmitate, cum profusis omnium

Tum sic ex imis cortina remugiit antris:
"O felix, longam placido cum funere vitam   290
Cui tribuit pater et decus indelebile clari
Nominis et centum numerosa e prole nepotes,
Id tantum, Guarine, cave, tua ne bona solus
Possideas unive tuus tibi luceat ignis."
    Edita nec caeca te fors ambage fefellit.   295
Illico sensisti tua te impertire iuberi
Omnibus et sacros doctrinae effundere rivos.
Inde futurorum iam certior aequora rursus
Mensa remetiris nec longum tempus et urbem
Ingrederis Venetam spoliis Orientis onustus   300
Non Mavorte fero, placida sed pace paratis.
    Laus fuit haec veterum patrias traducere ad oras,
Si quid in orbe alio pulchrum rarumve notassent.
Transeo te, regum victor Luculle duorum,
Ornasti Latios Scythicis qui fructibus hortos;   305
Nobiliora sequar. Populo monstravit hianti
Mummius eversa viventia signa Corintho,
Persei Scaurus dedit ossa immania ceti,
Regulus immensi transmisit terga draconis,
Hic primus media discurrere fecit arena   310

lacrymis et moerore publico caelestem immaculatus ad patriam emi-
grasti" (publ. in C. Rosmini, *Vita e disciplina di Guarino Veronese* 2.
190). Carbone in the funeral oration also mentions the pneumonia and
the peaceful death.
    292. *centum ... proles*: He means Guarino's many pupils. *Centum*
in Latin can mean an indeterminately large number.
    295: Cf. Vergil, *Aen.* 6, 691.
    297: Cf. 512-13.

Then did the tripod thus bellow back from the depths of the cave: "O happy man to whom the Father has granted a long life with a peaceful death, the indestructible glory of a famous name, and a hundred descendants from numerous offspring. Beware, Guarino, of only one thing, that you do not keep your talents to yourself, and that your fire does not give light to you alone."

The oracle thus proclaimed did not deceive you with its blind double meaning. You understood immediately that you were bidden to share what you had with everyone, and to pour forth the sacred streams of learning. Hence you travel seas once crossed before, now surer of what the future holds, and soon you enter the city of Venice, laden with spoils of the East, acquired not through savage Mars, but in peace and quiet.

The ancients were praised for bringing to their native shores anything they had noticed as rare or beautiful in another land. I omit you, Lucullus, conqueror of two kings, who adorned the gardens of Latium with Scythian fruits; I shall seek nobler examples. After the sack of Corinth, Mummius displayed living statues to a gaping populace; Scaurus gave them the gigantic bones of Perseus' sea-monster; and Regulus sent home the backbone of a huge serpent, and was the first

298: That Guarino was impoverished and anxious about his future in 1408 is evident from G. *Epistolario* 1. Ep. 4. 117-18, in which he asks Francesco Barbaro for help on his return to Italy.

299. *nec longum tempus*: Guarino may actually have taken many months to reach Italy. A letter written in 1410 to Guarino (*Epistolario*

Spectatas non ante feras Italisve volucres
Ignotas lucis a Nilo aut Phaside duxit,
Ille novum lapidem Phrygia Libyave petitum
Mirave longinquae portavit robora silvae:
Tu Latio cunctis infers maiora triumphis,   315
Quae nec magnanimi dives victoria Pauli
Aequarit, Cypro nec quod Cato vexit opima.
Troius Aeneas raptos ex hoste penates
Attulit et matrem torva cum Pallade Vestam:

2. Ep. 930 A) by Isidore, later Bishop of Monembasia, lists the places
Guarino was reported to have visited within the previous two years,
among them Chios and Rhodes. The Anonymous Veronese says that
Guarino held a magistracy "with conspicuous success" on Chios, and
confirmation is provided by G., *Epistolario* 1. Ep, 121. 23, which proves
that he was familiar with the governor's house there. Chios was then a
Genoese possession under the Racanelli, but it was common for *externi*
(citizens from another state) to exercise short-term offices, usually of six
months or a year. We know Guarino was in Rhodes from an inscription
in his own *Souda*, proving that he bought it there (Sabbadini, *Scoperte
dei codici latini e greci* [1905] 45, n.4), but Rhodes may simply have
been a port of call. Even so, it is possible that he did not reach Venice
until 1409. The first we hear of him in Italy is October 10, 1409, when
he delivered a valediction to the out-going podestà and welcomed his
successor in Verona: the speech is published by Sabbadini, *La scuola e
gli studi di Guarino* 170-72.
   304. *Luculle*: Lucius Licinius Lucullus, the Roman general, invaded
Pontus and forced its king, Mithridates, to flee to Armenia. Lucullus
then invaded Armenia and in 69 B.C. occupied its capital. Thus he
conquered both Mithridates of Pontus and Tigres of Armenia, although
modern historians see these exploits as temporary successes only in an
inconclusive war. After 59 B.C. Lucullus retired to a life of luxury and
dissipation, for which his name became proverbial.
   307. *Mummius*: The Roman general Lucius Mummius Achaicus,
who as consul in 146 B.C. crushed the Achaean League and sacked
Corinth, the treasures of which he shipped back to Rome.
   308. *Persei*: the legendary hero of Argos, who on his way back from
slaying the Gorgon slew a sea–monster to which Andromeda, daughter
of Cepheus of Tyre, had been offered as a sacrifice.

to make wild beasts never before seen run around in the
arena, and to bring from the Nile or Phasis birds unknown
to Italian groves, while Scaurus transported new stone got in
Phrygia or Libya, or wondrous timber from woods far away:
you bring to Latium things greater than all the triumphs in
the world, things not matched by the rich victory of great
hearted Paulus, or by what Cato brought from lush Cyprus.
Trojan Aeneas brought the household gods he rescued from
the enemy, and Mother Vesta, and grim Pallas:

Scaurus: Probably Marcus Aemilius Scaurus, who as aedile in 58
B.C. gave lavish public games. According to J. Pearson, *Arena* 118–
20, Curius in 275 B.C. had elephants at his triumph after his defeat of
Pyrrhus; by the second century B.C. *venationes* (hunts in the arena)
were already in vogue; and M. Scaurus brought the first hippopotami
and crocodiles to Rome.

309. *Regulus*: Marcus Attilius Regulus, the Roman general who
was taken prisoner by the Carthaginians in the First Punic War. Pliny,
N.H. 3. 8. 37 records that he killed a serpent or dragon 120 feet
long, using ordinance and catapults, and brought it back from the River
Bagradas in Africa to Rome, where its jaws and skin remained in a
temple until the Numantine War.

312. *Phaside*: The Phasis (modern Rion) was the chief river of
Colchis at the north-eastern end of the Black Sea, *Phasiani* (pheasants)
were first brought from its banks to Rome: see Statius, *Silvae* 4. 6. 8.

314: An evocative line, and an example of what Dryden called a
"golden" hexameter, in which a verb in the middle is balanced by an
adjective and noun combination on both sides.

316. *victoria Pauli*: Lucius Aemilius Paulus, consul in 182 and
168 B.C., defeated Perseus, king of Macedon, near Pydna in his second
term, and gave his troops seventy cities in Epirus to be pillaged.

317. *Cato*: Marcus Porcius Cato Uticensis (95-46 B.C.) was in
58 B.C. compelled by Clodius to annex Cyprus, from which enormous
booty was taken: see Plutarch, *Cato* 36-39.

318-19: Cf. Vergil, *Aen.* 2. 293. Among the talismans said to have
been brought by Aeneas to Italy was a wooden statue called the Palla-
dium, which was either one of Athena herself or one carved by her in
the likeness of a maiden, Pallas, whom she was remorseful over slaying.

Tu divos Itala dudum tellure fugatos   320
Restituis; tecum virgo Tritonia, tecum
Somnifera insignis virga Cyllenius ales,
Tecum deserto remeant Helicone Camenae,
Tu Bacchi thyrsos et Phoebi plectra reducis.
Vix tactum bene litus erat, vix ianua ludi   325
Mandatis adaperta dei, vagus omnia rumor
Gymnasia Italiae centeno murmure complet
Affulsisse virum, gemina qui Pallade solus
Polleat et duplicem praestet sitientibus haustum.
Curritur ad bifidi suavissima flumina fontis   330
Atria nec capiunt studiosas ampla catervas.
Mirantur cuncti melius vel nostra docentem

Vesta (identified with the Greek Hestia) was a Roman goddess of the
hearth. Athena is also called Tritonia (321) from her early upbringing
near Lake Tritonis.
     322. *Cyllenius*: Hermes (Latin, Mercurius), said to have been born
on Mt. Cyllene.
     324. *thyrsos*: The cone-shaped wands or phallic symbols carried by
the maenads, worshipers of Bacchus (Dionysus), god of the vital force in
nature and patron of the Greek theatre. Ianus' coupling of inspiration
with disciplined art, symbolized by Apollo, is effective.
     325-29: Ianus, if he knew about them, says nothing of Guarino's
difficulties in finding employment after his return from the East (see n.
on 299). In *Epistolario* 1. Ep. 6. 4-5 Guarino talks of the recent spell
of leisure he had had to take, against his will. He had gone to Verona,
where in 1409 he translated Plutarch's *Flamininus* and Isocrates' *Laus
Helenae* in an attempt to attract a patron. But no one had much use
for a Greek scholar: at this early stage of the Revival of Learning the
subject was more honored in the breach than the observance, an inter-
esting bagatelle for wealthy amateurs or self-indulgent humanists like
Leonardo Bruni, who made their living from their skill in Latin. In
February, 1410 Guarino was at Bologna, where the papal curia was in
residence, but no one wanted his services. Bruni, however, was sympa-
thetic, and wrote two letters recommending him as both a Latinist and

you restore the gods long since put to flight from Italian soil; with you return the virgin Tritonia, and the winged Cyllenian, famous for his staff that induces sleep, and the muses, deserting Helicon; and you bring back the thyrsus of Bacchus and the plectrum of Apollo. Scarcely had the shore been firmly touched, scarcely had the school door been opened, as the god had commanded, when a rumor went round and filled all the higher schools of Italy with the murmur of a hundred voices, that a man had shone forth, who alone was strong in both sides of Pallas, and who was offering a double draught to the thirsty. People rush to the sweet streams of the fountain with its twin jets, and the large halls cannot hold the crowds of students. All marvel at a man who teaches our language

Hellenist to the Florentine bibliophile, Niccolò Niccoli (*Leonardi Bruni Aretini Epistolarum Libri VIII* ed. L. Mehus [Florentiae, 1741] 1. Lib. 3. Epp. 4 and 15). He spent about two years as a factotum for Niccoli, against whom he launched in 1413 or 1414 the only bitter invective he ever wrote (*Epistolario* 1. Ep. 17). He had a happier association with Antonio Corbinelli (*Epistolario* 1. Ep. 327. 20-25), to whose brother Angelo he dedicated a translation of pseudo-Plutarch, *De puerorum educatione* in 1411 (*Epistolario* 1. Ep. 5), again in an attempt to find a patron who appreciated his skill in Greek. Finally, he was appointed in October, 1413, to teach Greek at the University of Florence, but there is no evidence that he attracted many students. In 1414 he accepted Francesco Barbaro's suggestion that he try his luck in Venice, but there his students were few, and his success moderate (see n. on 331).

331. *catervas*: Guarino's first lodging in Venice was with the Barbaro family, and his first pupils were Francesco and Zaccaria Barbaro, and Leonardo Giustinian. He opened his first *contubernium* in 1415 or 1416, but in the latter year plague struck in the early summer and dispersed his students. He fled to Verona, then to Padua, where he complained of having saved no money, and perhaps sought relief from his

Vel nova Erechtheae promentem nomina linguae.
Mirantur caecis tandem prodire latebris
Sensa tot auctorum mille indeprensa per annos   335
Nec prius auditos puduit risisse magistros.
Verborum pars nulla perit, sed cuncta citatis
Excipiunt calamis et longa in saecla recondunt.
Ceu cum depastis late fenilibus aegrum
Lenta gregem tenuavit hiems et debile languet   340
Ieiuna pecus omne fame, si figore pulso
Afflavit tepidos Zephyri clementia campos,
Ocius erumpunt stabulis armenta reclusis
Ac primum virgas et quaelibet omnia tondent;
Quod si maturas iamdudum vallis apricae   345
Planities ostendit opes, huc agmine facto
Irrevocata ruunt et laeto vere fruuntur
(Pastorum tacitas pertentant gaudia mentes):
Ad tua sic avidi contendunt limina coetus,
Ut meliora novae decerpant dona Minervae.   350
Ast aliis deserta vacant subsellia nec iam
Ipse manet cathedra, modo qui dictabat ab alta,
Sed se discipulis comitem properantibus addit.
Omnis condicio, sexus simul omnis et aetas

339 agrum A

worries in dalliance with the local whores, whose blandishments he de-
scribed in detail (*Epistolario* 1. Ep. 59. 42-43 and 91-103.) On the
whores, see my article, "Two Unpublished Items from Toledo MS 100.
42," *Traditio* 25 [1969] 414-16). In January, 1418, he was still dissatisfied
with teaching as a livelihood, and wrote dejectedly to Antonio Corbinelli
that a post he had hoped to get in the Roman curia (probably with

better or brings forth new words in the Erechthean tongue. They marvel at how the meanings of so many authors, undetected for a thousand years, are finally emerging from their dark hiding-places, and they are not abashed to laugh at their former teachers. None of your words is lost, but with pens flying they take everything down and store it away for long centuries to come. As when haylofts have been used up far and wide, and a slow winter has made the flock thin and sick, and all are faint and feeble with starvation, if the cold departs, and a kindly zephyr blows over the plains and warms them up, the animals burst out of their fold the moment it is opened, and immediately graze on shoots and anything they find; but if the level floor of a sunny valley displays its long-ripened abundance, they crowd together, rush to it, and cannot be called back, and enjoy the fertile spring, while the shepherds' quiet hearts thrill with delight: even so do eager throngs crowd your door, to pluck the better gifts of the new Minerva. The benches of other teachers are empty and deserted, and the teacher himself, who but lately was dictating from his lofty chair, joins his students in their hasty exit. Every condition, every age and sex together

Cardinal Zabarella, who died September 26, 1417) was no longer open, and that he was "teaching one or two students, and, as they say, passing my life away" (*Epistolario* 1. Ep. 89. 38-41). Only after he moved to Verona in 1419 did his fortunes improve. By 1427 he was able to boast, "There is such a throng of students around me everywhere that when we have to go out walking one would say that sparrows or locusts were migrating in swarms." (*Epistolario* 1. Ep. 419. 18-20).

Accelerant. Plebi stipatur curia; mixti   355
Primaevis cani, maribus sedere puellae.
Multi, quos vitae ratio diversa tenebat,
Iam Musas ac plectra volunt. Mercator avara
Prosilit a mensa. Neglecto durus aratro
Rusticus et posita festinat cuspide miles.   360
Nec reliquis pretium manet artibus: ars tua cunctis
Praefertur studiis. Radio geometra relicto
Te petit. Assuetus rerum disquirere causas
Se tibi submittit sapiens. Tua tecta frequentant
Morborum curas et legum scita professi.   365
Patribus in primis summi pia gloria voti
Erudienda tuae committere pignora curae.

333. *Erechtheae*: i.e. Athenian, from Erechtheus, a legendary king of Athens.

338. *excipiunt*: Before the advent of printing, text books were hard to come by, so teachers dictated (see 352, *dictabat*) traditional commentaries or commentaries of their own during the formal lecture. Individualized tuition, often the business of a *repetitor* (assistant master), took place outside class. Battista Guarini recommended (Woodward, *Vittorino* 173) that class notes be written up as carefully as material for publication, since this leads to accurate construing, ready composition, and exact recall of information; such notes, duly ordered, would form a commonplace book for use in original writing later in life. R. R. Bolgar rightly notes in *The Classical Heritage and its Beneficiaries* (Cambridge, 1954) 258 that this technique, introduced into Italy by Chrysoloras, contributed to the rapid spread of humanist skills and marked the essential difference between the age of Petrarch and that of Guarino. See also n. on 370-77.

339-48: An over-elaborate simile that compares poorly with its obvious inspiration, Vergil, *Geo.* 2. 322 and 30.

350. *novae Minervae*: Minerva (identified with Athena, goddess of wisdom) is often used in Latin to signify wit and learning (e.g. in

hurry to you. The hall is packed; a mixed crowd is seated, young with old, males with females. Many whose lives were different before now crave the muses and the plectrum. The greedy merchant rises from his table. The hardy farmer, abandoning the plough, and the soldier, laying down his spear, hasten to you. Nor do the other arts retain their currency: your art is preferred to them all. The geometer, leaving his rod behind, seeks you. The philosopher, used to investigating the causes of things, submits himself to you. Professors of law and medicine crowd your household. The paternal boast and dearest wish of the city fathers is to send their children to you to be educated.

phrases like *pingui Minerva*). Here it means humanism, and Greek studies in particular.

355. *stipatur*: For the images of bees this suggests, see n. on 178.

356. *puellae*: There is no other evidence that Guarino accepted female students. He is unlikely to have taken any into his household, but there was nothing to stop them attending public lectures. Humanists, following the lead of Plato and Aristotle, were not averse to women receiving an education, and several treatises were written on the subject, e.g. Leonardo Bruni's *De studiis et litteris* (edited by Hans Baron in *L. B. Aretino. Humanistisch-philosophische Schriften mit einer Chronologie seiner Werke und Briefe* [Leipzig-Berlin, 1928] 5-19, reprinted in Garin, *L'Umanesimo* 146-69 with facing Italian translation. English version in Woodward, *Vittorino* 123-33), which Woodward dates ca. 1405, but Baron more convincingly places between 1422 and 1429. Isotta Nogarola of Verona, who was tutored by Guarino's pupil, Martino Rizzon, dared to challenge the male humanists by writing letters for public dissemination (see E. Abel, *Isotae Nogarolae Opera* I-II [Vindobonae, 1886]), and was bitterly attacked. Guarino had praised her in 1436 (G., *Epistolario* 2. Ep. 697. 39-75; Ep. 698. 38-46) and comforted her in 1437 (*Epistolario* 2. Ep. 705), but her career foundered several years later.

Nam quis te melior vel provexisse volentem
Vel contra ignavo discendi subdere calcar?
Principio recte das fundamenta loquendi   370
Recte scribendi compendia tradere callens,
Ne lingua accentu, calamo ne dextera peccet.
Mox argumento formatur epistola ficto.
Proxima volvendis annalibus otia dantur.
Declamare dehinc et carmina fingere monstras,   375
Dum matura suam facundia crescat in arcem

358. *avara*: An example of hypallage, i.e. transfer of an adjective
from the noun one would normally expect it to qualify to another noun:
cf. *solos*, 685.

368-69: Cf.   611-12, and Battista Guarini's recommendation
(Woodward, *Vittorino* 163): "In the case of elder boys, emulation and
the sense of shame, which shrinks from the discredit of failure, must be
relied on. I advise also that boys ...work two together with a view to
encouraging a healthy spirit of rivalry between them."

370-77: Refer to the tripartite scheme of education (277, *certos
...gradus*) which Guarino adapted from Quintilian 1. 4. 1 and 1. 4.
9. Battista Guarini describes it in *De modo et ordine* (Woodward,
Vittorino 163-72). In the elementary course covering the first part of
"grammar" correct pronunciation is insisted upon, as conducive to an
exact recall of forms in the "inner ear." Nouns and verbs are then
learned by oral drills, written tests, and the correction of erroneous
forms purposely introduced (a practice which most modern education-
alists would reject). *Methodice* (defined as the rules that govern the
parts of speech) is to be taught from Guarino's own *Regulae* (see n. on
371) or some similar book, with oral and written testing. Oral compo-
sition promotes fluency, so classes should be conducted in Latin. Good
texts are to be used as models of style. The rules of quantity and
metre are now introduced, a useful book for this being Alexander de
Villa-Dei's *Doctrinale* (a medieval text containing the rules of syntax
in hexameters), which is to be learned by heart, together with all the
works of Vergil. The first metres to be mastered will be hexameters and
elegiacs; more complex ones can be progressively absorbed later. Greek

For who is better than you at bringing on the willing
student or spurring the slow learner? First, you give the
basic rules of good speech, cleverly summarizing those of
good writing also, lest the tongue err in accent, or the hand
with the pen. Then a letter is composed on some fictive
theme. Next, the student's time is given to history. After
that, you show him how to declaim and to write poetry,
until his mature eloquence, raised through definite

is now started, as vital to understanding Latin language and literature
(Neither Battista nor Guarino ever spoke of it as worthy of study for
its own sake). The text will be Chrysoloras' *Erotemata* or Guarino's
abridgement of it. Regular Greek verbs must be mastered by learn-
ing paradigms, then irregular forms are to be taught. Simple narrative
prose is now introduced, with emphasis on vocabulary and grammati-
cal structure. Homer will be the first Greek poet studied, followed by
other epic poets and the dramatists. Notes are to be taken and me-
thodically arranged (see n. on 338). The Greek accents are now taught.
All along, there must be regular exercises in simple Greek composition,
and translation of Latin prose passages into Greek. Meanwhile, Latin
has continued to be studied, but students should by now be ready for
the fuller rules contained in Priscian's grammar. Cicero's Letters are
to be committed to memory, but other good stylists can also be used
as models. In the stage known as *historice* (the second in the overall
scheme, consisting of "advanced grammar") continuous prose authors,
especially historians, are to be studied. Justinus and Valerius Maximus
provide a basic introduction to the events of the Roman past and, more
importantly, a stock of moral *exempla*. The other historians are then
read in chronological order (It is not clear whether this means the order
in which their lives occurred, or refers to the order of events with which
their works deal). Students should also learn the manners, laws, and
institutions of nations other than the Romans. During study of the
historians, poets should not be neglected, and in both kinds of litera-
ture the emphasis will be upon the underlying moral meanings (see n.
on 535). Vergil is the supreme poet followed by Statius in his *Thebais*
and Ovid in his *Metamorphoses* and *Fasti*. The last two are regarded
as the richest source of myths, but other works of Ovid are best omitted.

Per certos evecta gradus. Nec scripta recenses
Omnia, sed tantum recipit quae fida vetustas.
Quod si quem imbutum non pura fruge notasti,
Agricolae ritu filicem prius eruis arvo,   380
Semina deinde iacis fructus latura metendos.
Par morum doctrina tibi. Quis Zeno, quis unquam
Sic potuit Crantor vitiis avertere mentes
Ac teneram dextro pubem deducere ramo,
Angustum qua surgit iter? Non cera figuras   385
Tam digito subigente rapit, quam mollis ephebus
Te ducit figente virum. Nec verbere torvo
Aut ferula insanis, sed maiestate potenti
Tranquillus delicta premis, cessante flagello
Obiurgata tuis paret lascivia frenis.   390

Seneca's tragedies, Terence's comedies. and Juvenal's satires yield a co-
pious and elastic vocabulary. The sexually explicit passages in Juvenal
should not be omitted, since they occur in a context of denunciation:
the anger of the reader should be directed against the vices, not the
author who merely reports them. Plautus can be read for his elegance
and wit. Horace's *Ars Poetica* and *Satires* deserve study, but Persius is
best avoided because of his difficulty. Other poets such as Lucan can be
read later. The reading of poets is best accompanied by occasional pe-
rusal of writers on astronomy and geography, such as Pomponius Mela,
Solinus, and Strabo. Ptolemaic geography is to be learned. The third
stage is *rhetorice*, beginning with the pseudo-Ciceronian *Rhetorica ad
Herennium*, followed by Cicero's *De Oratore*, *Orator*, and *Brutus*. The
rhetorical theory they contain is now to be examined by reference to
his speeches. Quintilian may also be read. Logic is to be studied, as
well as Aristotle's *Ethics* and Plato's Dialogues. Battista Guarini indi-
cates a predilection for Ciero's *De Officiis* and Tusculan Disputations.
Some knowledge of Roman law is desirable. Important in Guarino's
teaching was a set of "learning precepts" which he ascribes to Manuel
Chrysoloras in a letter of 1434 to Leonello d'Este (*Epistolario* 2. Ep.
679. 86-137): (1) Pronounce words clearly and avoid mumbling into

stages, grows to its natural zenith. Nor do you go over the whole of literature, but only what was acceptable to trusty antiquity. But if you notice anyone who has tasted bad fruit, like a farmer you first pluck the fern from the field, then sow seeds that will bear a crop fit for harvesting. Morality is just as important to you as learning. What Zeno, what Crantor could ever turn minds away from vice as you do, or lead tender youth by the right branch, where rises the narrow way? Wax is not more yielding to the thumb than the soft teenager who develops into a man under your moulding. Nor do you rage with the brutal strap or rod, but calmly curb bad behavior with your powerful and majestic presence. Wildness is reproved and obeys your bridle without the whip.

the teeth. (Both he and Battista believed that sounds impinging on the ear set thoughts in motion: the clearer the sound, the clearer the thought. Following Plutarch and the elder Pliny, they also maintained that using the voice aids digestion); (2) Try to form a mental picture of the structure of a sentence as it is read. If words and meaning do not rise together instantly, go over the sentence as a whole until they do. (This suggests that sentences were to be comprehended, so far as possible, in their Latin or Greek order, rather than dissected piecemeal in the Italian order of subject, verb, object, with the modifiers fitted in after that); (3) At the end of a passage mull over its contents and master them before moving on. (This was basic to humanist method. Its best treatment was by Erasmus in his *De ratione studii* and *De conscribendis epis-tulis*: see W.H. Woodward, *Desiderius Erasmus Concerning the Aim and Method of Study* (Columbia U.P., New York, 1964) 173-76, 223-26; (4) Note down striking phrases and important facts. (See n. on 338); (5) At the end of every month review what has been learned. (Battista recommends a nightly review also, a practice of the Pythagoreans); (6) Find some kindred spirit with whom to discuss your work. (For Ianus' use of this precept, see n. on 637).

Nil igitur mirum, si te mercedibus amplis
Tot sibi certatim populi petiere magistrum.
Nec vero tu te prius una in sede locasti,
Quam sparsa innumeras tibi disciplina per oras.
Sic genitus Celeo Siculae nova semina matris   395
Non Pandioniis tantummodo condidit arvis,
Sed procul aerio vectus per inania curru
Chaonias late iussit vilescere glandes,

371. *compendia*: i.e. Guarino's *Regulae Grammaticales*, first men-
tioned in *Epistolario* 1. Ep. 98 of January, 1418. It is a plain exposition
of Latin grammar, with definitions of all technical terms first. Then fol-
low impersonal verbs; constructions involving the idea of place; supines;
gerunds and gerundives; participles; the uses of prolepsis, syllepsis,
zeugma, synthesis, antiptosis, evocatio, appositio, and synecdoche;
patronymics; incohative, desiderative, conative, and frequentative
verbs; relative pronouns; *quis* and *uter* and their compounds; hete-
roclite nouns, with a selection of mnemonics; and an exposition of the
verbs *solvere*, *nubere*, and *latere*. See Sabbadini, *La scuola e gli studi di
Guarino* 38-47, esp. 43, where Sabbadini suggests that in his elemen-
tary course Guarino used not the medieval *Donatus minor* but a similar
work known as the *Ianua* ("Door"), so called from its opening motto:
*Ianua sum rudibus primam cupientibus artem/Nec sine me quisquam
rite peritus erit* ("I am the door for those who want the basic art, and
without me no one will be properly educated").
    373. *epistula*: Battista Guarini says nothing about writing fictive
letters (see n. on 370-77), but Guarino refers to the practice in a let-
ter (*Epistolario* 1. Ep. 421) to his pupil, Lodovico Brenzon. He is to
propose some written exercise (*thema*) to himself, and cast it in the
form of a letter to Guarino, keeping before him a mnemonic (22-24) for
the commonplaces of praise and blame: *Quattuor ista solent augere ne-
gotia cuncta:/Utile, iucundum, laudes, iungetur honestas* ("These four
elements usually provide amplifications for all subjects: the useful, the
pleasant, praises, and add respectability"). Guarino would send such
letters back, with corrections (see *Epistolario* I. Ep. 166. 17-21).

It is not therefore surprising that so many communities have vied to have you as a teacher, at considerable salaries. But you did not want to settle in one place before spreading your learning in countless others. Thus did the son of Celeus bury the new seeds of his Sicilian mother not only in Pandonian fields, but traveling far away through the void in his airbourn chariot, he bade Chaonian acorns become common far and wide,

380: An echo of Plato, *Euthyphron* 2 C-D?
382 *morum*: Good moral conduct was always the major aim of the best humanist education. It is explicit in the title of the first humanist tract on education, Pier Paolo Vergerio's *De ingenuis moribus et liberalibus studiis adulescentiae* (1404), the standard edition of which is that by A. Gnesotto in *Atti e Memorie dell'Accademia di Scienze e Lettere* 34 (Padua, 1918) 75-156.
Zeno: See n. on 174.
383. *Crantor*: Crantor of Soli in Cilicia (c. 335-c. 275 B.C.) was a pupil of Xenocrates and the friend of Arcesilaus, whom he persuaded to leave the Peripatetics to join the Academy (Diogenes Laertius 4. 22; 24; 25; 29). He wrote a commentary on Plato's *Timaeus* and a work *On Grief*, but does not seem to have been an original thinker so much as a respected stylist.
384. *dextro*: Cf. Vergil, *Aen.* 6. 540-43, where the right hand path leads to Elysium, the left to the realms of Dis. Guarino is like the sibyl: he leads the human soul, as she leads Aeneas, but his direction is the path to salvation.
387-88. *verbere ...ferula*: Discipline had been generally harsh in medieval schools, but humanist educators avoided corporal punishment wherever possible. Guarino's ideas on the subject had no doubt been confirmed, if not formed, by Plutarch's *De liberis educandis* 12, 8F-9A, his translation of which was: *omitto enim ea magis servos decere quam liberos ...liberalibus autem pueris maiorem laudes ac vituperia quam verbera commoditatem afferunt.* (Quoted in Garin, *L'Umanesimo* 206). Battista Guarini echoes this (Woodward, *Vittorino* 163). Guarino's own remarks are much the same in a letter (*Epistolario* 1. Ep. 340) he wrote in 1425 to help his pupil, Martino Rizzon, control the

Emeritos donec taciturni conscia sacri
Orbe peragrato colubros disiunxit Eleusis   400
Tu mare frenantes Venetos, tu Antenoris alti
Instituis cives, tua te Verona legentem
Finis et Italiae stupuit, sublime Tridentum,
Nec iam flumineum referens Florentia nomen
Ac Phoebo quondam, nunc sacra Bononia Marti   405
Tandem mansurum placida statione recepit
Pacis et aligeri, Ferraria, mater Amoris,
Qua Padus in geminos iterum se dividit amnes
Luget et ambustum fratrem pia silva sororum.
Hic tum Nicoleos rerum retinebat habenas,   410
Stirpis Atestinae clarum decus. Ille, venustis
Artibus ut natum simul exornaret et urbem,
Te Phaethonteos Musis sacrare colonos,
Te Leonelleae voluit superesse iuventae.

sons of Giovanni Tegiaci. He emphasizes the need for *pietas* (mutual love and respect) between master and student. Since children are imitative, Rizzon must set a good example, and above all avoid angry threats, foul language, and flogging as a means of enforcing discipline. Guarino, however, was not permissive (cf, *Panegyricus* 830-35), as we may see from G., *Epistolario* 2. Ep. 831A. 18-21, which describes how a student in one of his classes called the poet Antonio Beccadelli (Panormita) "non Siculus, sed suculus" (not a Sicilian, but a little porker). Prone to such punning himself, and admitting to being inwardly convulsed with laughter, Guarino could not let this insult to a fellow scholar pass, so he turned a grim look (*torvum vultum*) on the class, and the laughter died away. But he never lost sight of the need for gentleness. In *Epistolario* 1. Ep. 231. 21-24 he ascribes to Chrysoloras the thought that just as some people are ready to devote infinite care and patience to training their pets, so teachers should exercise as much care and sympathy in shaping young minds.

until Eleusis that knows the silent rite unyoked the serpents, now retired after traversing the earth. You teach the Venetians, who tame the sea, and the citizens of high Antenor; your own Verona, and Trent, high up at the end of Italy, have been dazzled by your lectures, as have Florence, which no longer reminds one of the name of its river, and Bologna, once sacred to Phoebus, but now to Mars. At last Ferrara, the mother of Peace and winged Love, welcomed you to stay in her quiet haven, where the Po divides for the second time into two streams, and the forest of sisters dutifully mourns their burnt brother. Here at that time Niccolò, a bright adornment of the House of Este, held the reins of state. To grace both his son and the city with the fine arts, he desired you to consecrate Phaethon's yeomen to the muses, and to supervise the young Leonello.

390-92: These lines are best understood in the context of Guarino's difficulties over his salary after Borso's accession. As early as April, 1432, Verona had tried to lure Guarino back, but he refused (*Epistolario* 2. Ep. 599) in a poem of 56 lines extolling the generosity of the Este family. The next year he turned down another offer from Verona, this time for 200 ducats (*Epistolario* 2. Ep. 615). Unquestionably, he saw a more lucrative future ahead for him in Ferrara, where his salary was 350 ducats (Ep. 615. 20-21, which is confirmed by an entry dated May 11, 1435 in Archivio di Stato di Modena. Registro dei mandati 1434-1435 f. 103v). Additionally, he received gifts from time to time, for example, the subsidies of grain from Leonello on June 23 and 23 October, 1434 (Archivio di Stato di Modena. Registro dei mandati. 1434-1435. f. 38v and 58v), and a grant towards the purchase of his house in 1437 (see n. on 591). When he became Public Professor of Rhetoric in 1436 his salary was fixed by a decree of March 29 (published in Cittadella, *I Guarini* 24) at 150 ducats, plus 100 lire marchesane to cover the rent of his house. This was raised the next year to 400 lire, plus the 100 lire rent subsidy. According to Sabbadini (G., *Epistolario*

Oppida nam fieri Plato si felicia dixit,   415
Purpura cum sapiat vel cum sapientia regnet,
Divinum hic quiddam tum duxit iure futurum,
Si rector doctam moderetur rectior aulam.
Nec frustrata virum sua spes. Videt ecce suprema
Aetheris e specula quod tota mente petebat,   420

410 cum A

3. 298), 400 lire marchesane equalled 250 ducats. If so, then the to-
tal of 500 lire works out at just over 312 ducats. He would, of course,
have made a profit from his student boarders. It is difficult to guess
how much was involved in boarding each, or how much the fees were
at Ferrara, but we do know that in 1423 he was charging 40 ducats
(*Epistolario* 1. Ep. 231. 37, "nec me aurei XL movent"). It therefore
upset him greatly when one of Borso's first acts on his accession was to
cut Guarino's salary before the beginning of the academic year 1450-51
to 75 lire marchesane (F.G. Borsetti, *Historia almi Ferrariae gymnasii*
[Ferrara, 1735] 1. 56). Borso, who was often phenomenally generous,
has often been blamed for penny-pinching in his early dealings with
the university, and the humanists in particular, but he may have been
driven to severe economies. As Gundersheimer points out in *Ferrara:
The Style of a Renaissance Despotism* (Princeton, 1973) 101-102, the
university had grown considerably since 1441, and most of the profes-
sors' salaries came from the communal treasury, sometimes augmented
by grants from the marquis. Borso changed this almost immediately,
and paid the university faculty from the ducal treasury. Taking advan-
tage of Guarino's malaise, the Council of Verona voted in December,
1451 to offer him a public professorship at a salary of 200 ducats, which
was augmented in January, 1452 to 250 (documents published in Carlo
Rosmini, *La vita e disciplina di Guarino Veronese e de' suoi discepoli*
[Brescia, 1805-06] 1. 104-106). A poem was sent from Verona (G.,
Epistolario 2. Ep. 857) as well as a letter (*Epistolario* 2. Ep. 855)
dated January 8, 1452, urging hin to accept. Guarino replied with a
poem (*Epistolario* 2. Ep. 856) acknowledging the higher offer and stat-
ing that he was ready to come. His state of mind about this time is
reflected in five letters from Giorgio Valagussa, his student from 1448

For if Plato said that towns find happiness when those who wear the purple are philosophers, or when philosophers are kings, he was also right in thinking that something divine would happen, if a learned court were governed by an even more learned ruler. And he has not been disappointed. Lo, from his watchtower in the highest heaven he witnesses what he wanted with all his heart;

to 1455, to Antonio da Pesaro, extracts of which were published by Sabbadini in G., *Epistolario* 3. 456-58: (1) "The departure of Guarino seems to me ...like a weight heavier than Etna, since I have to go, too; don't ever think that if Guarino goes, Ferrara could hold Giorgio ...I don't know what day Guarino is leaving, but I know his things are being packed right now. I imagine that as soon as he can knock his money out of the prince, he'll say goodbye to this city and take off for Verona ...(2) Guarino hasn't yet decided on what day he'll be moving camp. He's frantically chasing the money for his salary, because if he doesn't get it while he's here, it will be hard to get it when he isn't ...How I wish, as you say in your letter, that this idea of his would vanish, and he were just content to live in this place where he has spent twenty years in great honor and more than ordinary glory, and amassed a fair amount of money ...(3) Recently I took a walk with Guarino to a certain pleasure garden he bought on the outskirts of town. I started asking this kindest of men to confide to me his thoughts about leaving. He answered that he had every intention of going to Verona, that he wanted to give the rest of his life to his native city ...He said he hadn't been able to do it before because of Prince Leonello, and that when he had been Leonello's tutor he had never been able to bring permission to leave from him ...What prince ever loved and respected scholars more, and paid them better? ...Tears began welling from Guarino's eyes and down his cheeks at the memory ...But after the cruel Fates cut short ...Leonello's life, Guarino made an absolute decision to go to Verona ...so I fear he needs must be off and away within a few days. (4) You write that nothing can make you believe that Guarino is going to Verona, because it would be to his loss and the prince's shame. I shall say nothing of the prince, but ...the departure of this man will

Nam cultam studiis Leonellus cultior alma
Sic in pace regit patriam, sic iure quieto
Temperat, ut, reliquis late cum ferrea volvat
Urbibus, huic uni vehat aurea saecula Titan.

do more good for Verona than it will for Ferrara. The Veronese envoys
are here with dispatches promising two hundred gold ducats a year to
Guarino for life, whether he lectures or not; they just want to enjoy
having him there. But if he does lecture, he will get in addition the
profits from his private students ...the envoys haunt the court daily
and keep badgering Duke Borso, to snatch the man from his jaws, but
Borso is temporizing and foxing them with words. Guarino is fuming. I
think the departure of such a great man would count against the duke, as
you say in your letter. So everything's in the balance, and it's not clear
what's going to happen. But Guarino has already put his house up for
sale. He's asking 3,000 ducats, and there have been many prospective
buyers ...(5) When the nobles and civic leaders of Ferrara heard that
Guarino was leaving, they came in force to the palace, demanding that
the prince not allow such a monstrous thing to happen, which would
be no small loss to Ferrara and a huge blot on his name. They made
the prince waver. Time is being wasted, and the envoys are going off
the idea of hiring Guarino, because they see that the marquis is lying
to them daily. But Guarino is pressing, and trying hard to get his way
...I'm afraid his efforts will come to nothing. If the prince doesn't want
him to go, he'll just have to make his home in Ferrara, and that would
suit both you and me ..." In the end, Borso took the university under his
wing, although as Gundersheimer points out (Ferrara, 162-63) he was
always more interested in law and medicine than in humanism. This
did not prevent Battista Guarini from flattering him in his *prolusio*
in 1453 (see n. on 842). By 1454 Guarino's salary had been raised
to 300 lire marchesane (Archivio di Stato di Modena. Memor. Cam.
duc. 1454 AA f. 86), which probably represented a substantial raise,
because in 1452 Borso introduced golden lire to replace the old silver
ones (Gundersheimer, *Ferrara* 161). The Veronese made one last motion
to repatriate him, but it was defeated in a vote of the Council on July
26, 1454 (G. Giuliari in *Propugnatore* [1873] Pt. 2. 118).
    394. *innumeras oras*: See n. on 401-05.
    395. *genitus Celeo*: i.e. Triptolemus, son of Celeus, king of Eleusis,
and Metaneira. The myth has it that as one of her favors to Eleu-
sis, where she found hospitality during her search for Proserpine, Ceres

for Leonello, the most cultivated in a land refined by scholarship, rules it in such gracious peace, and controls it with
such quiet justice, that while Titan brings round the iron
age to all other cities, to this one alone he brings a golden
age.

(Greek, Demeter, called the Sicilian mother because Proserpine had
been abducted in Sicily) restored the fertility of their soil and sent Triptolemus to carry corn seeds and the art of sowing to lands unacquainted
with them.
     396. *Pandioniis*: i.e. Athenian, fron Pandion, a legendary king
of Athens. Isocrates 4. 28 records the traditional Athenian boast that
they had been the first to get corn seeds from Triptolemus.
     398. *Chaonias*: i.e. of Dodona: cf. Vergil, *Geo*. 1. 8.
     399. *sacri*: The Eleusinian mysteries, said to be silent because the
rites were kept secret.
     400. *colubros*: Triptolemus is said to have traversed the earth in a
magical chariot drawn by two winged serpents or dragons, which Ceres
had given him. See Ovid, *Metamorphoses* 5. 645 ff; *Fasti* 4. 507 ff
and Servius, *ad Geo*. 1. 19, where Triptolemus is named rather than
Demophoon.
     401-405: Guarino's stays in Venice (1414-late 1419), Verona (1419-
29), and Florence (1411-early 1414) are well documented, but there is
no evidence that he taught at Padua (401, the city of Antenor, the legendary Trojan founder). In 1424 he left Verona to escape the plague,
going eventually to Trent (403, Tridentum; see G., *Epistolario* L. Epp.
269, 270, 279, 280) and a village called Perzen (Italian, Pergine; see
Epistolario 1. 276). We know that he learned some German on this
visit (See Sabbadini, "Documenti Guariniani" in *Alti della Accademia
di Agricoltura di Verona* 18 [1916] 242-45), but his correspondence shows
that he did not teach there. In 1424 he had offers of employment from
Venice and Bologna (*Epistolario* 1, Ep. 281), which he declined. Rosmini. *Vita e disciplina di Guarino* 1. 17, claims that Guarino taught
at Bologna (405, Bononia), but his authority is this passage of Ianus,
and there is no other. Guarino's name does not appear in Mazzetti's
Repertorio dei professori bolognesi (Bologna 1847).
     404: Guarino was popular at Florence, but hardly as famous there
as Ianus claims. He disliked the city profoundly: see, e.g. *Epistolario*
1. Ep. 245. 22-24, in which he tells Girolamo Gualdo, "I call God and

An non Saturni sunt illic saecula patris,   425
Bella ubi nulla fremunt, nisi quae descripta leguntur,
Semper ubi laetas populo plaudente choreas
Intus festa sonant et picta palatia surgunt,
Arva foris gravido locupletat Copia cornu?
Fortunati ambo: plebs praeside, plebe tyrannus,   430
Ambobus sed tu, tantorum causa bonorum.

His holy angels to witness that hardly a day dawned ... when I was not
harassed by some slanging-match or squabble or exchange of words."
    408: *geminos amnes*: In 1152 the main stream of the Po, which
then flowed south of Ferrara, changed its course just above Ferrara and
has since flowed about three miles north of the city. The attenuated
southern branch is called the Po di Primaro.
    409: *fratrem*: i.e. Phaethon, son of Helius and Clymene, who
wrung permission from his father to drive the chariot of the Sun. He
could not control it, the horses bolted, and the earth was in danger of
being burnt up. Earth appealed to Jupiter (Zeus), who slew Phaethon
with a thunderbolt. Phaethon fell into the Eridanus (Po), and his sis-
ters wept for him until they turned into poplar trees, from which the
gum known to us as amber distils. The fullest account is in Ovid,
Metamorphoses 1. 750-2. 366.
    410: *Nicoleos*: The marquis Niccolò III d'Este (1383-1441), an
equestrian statue of whom stands today, with another of Duke Borso,
outside the main gate of the Corte Vecchia in Ferrara, was a feudal-
type despot, careful to court popular opinion. He came to power as
a minor in 1493. He adored the trappings of chivalry, never more
than when the Emperor Sigismund on his way back from his corona-
tion in Rome stayed for a week at Ferrara and conferred knighthood
on Niccolò's favorite sons, Leonello, Borso, Ercole, Folco, and Sigis-
mondo (G., *Epistolario* 2. Ep. 640). His court was colorful. Guar-
ino refers, for example, to a vast mythological pageant written and di-
rected by the Sicilian poet, Giovanni Marrasio (*Epistolario* 2. Ep. 611).

Are these not the times of Father Saturn, where no wars rage, except those that are described and read about, where festivity sounds within, as the people applaud joyful dances, where painted palaces are rising, and where Plenty enriches the surrounding fields from her laden horn? Both are fortunate: the people in their prince, the prince in his people; but you, the source of such great blessings, are fortunate in both.

Loyal to friends, considerate of his subjects, and affectionate towards his mistresses and many bastards, he was not without culture, having studied in his youth under Donato degli Albanzani, the friend of Petrarch and Boccaccio. The inventory of his books in 1436, published by Adriano Cappelli, "La Biblioteca Estense nella prima metà del secolo XI," *Giornale storico della letteratura italiana* 14 (Torino, 1886) 12-30, shows 279 manuscripts, including nearly 200 in Latin, 23 in Italian, and 58 in French, most of them romances. He avoided armed conflict whenever possible and acted often as an arbitrator in disputes between individuals and states. But he could erupt in impulsive savagery, as in 1425 when he executed without proper trial his wife Parisina and her stepson Ugo for adultery, and in 1434 when he ordered the strangulation of his *referendarius*, Giacomo Zilioli. Nowhere was his statesmanship more acute than in his policy of attracting to Ferrara a nucleus of artists and scholars, particularly humanists. His reign is well treated in W. Gundersheimer, *Ferrara* 66-91. Guarino wrote a long funeral oration on him, dated January 6, 1442, and published as Ep. 777 to Leonello d'Este in G., *Epistolario* 2.

    413: *Phaethonteos*: See n. on 409.
    414: *superesse*: Both Ianus and Carbone say that Guarino came to Ferrara to tutor Leonello, but Niccolò seems to have wanted him initially as a court secretary when he arrived in December, 1429. In *Epistolario* 2. Ep. 577. 1-3 (April 28, 1430) Guarino mentions the piles of correspondence and other official documents he was required to write or dictate daily. It is nowhere recorded when he became Leonello's tutor, but it was probably about May, 1430, the date of Ep. 579, written by Guarino to Cardinal Orsini on Leonello's behalf, to request a copy of the Codex Ursinianus of Plautus.

Per te belligeris praelatus fratribus alto
Ille sedet solio monitis et se inde fatetur
Profecisse tuis, quod te complectitur omni
Parte sui et seris mandare nepotibus optat   435
Nec secreta tibi Larium negat ulla suorum
Formandam pariter credens cum coniuge prolem.

418. *rector*: Charles Trinckhaus points out in *Journal of the History of Ideas* (June, 1956) 431: "Northern Italian humanists remained true to the despotic outlook of their own particular enviromment." The superiority of a monarchy over a republic is emphasized in Giovanni di Conversino da Ravenna's *Dragmalogia de eligibili vite genere* ed. and trans. by Helen L. Eaker with introduction and notes by Benjamin G. Kohl (Associated University Presses: Cranbury, N.J., 1980) 107-141. Guarino was no exception to this tendency. Carbone in his funeral oration states: "(Guarino) thought it better to live in the kind of city which was neither oppressed by the power of the few nor bedeviled by the rule of the mob. Time and again he had read in the poets, philosophers, orators, and all writers that the best rule is that of a single man, which the Greeks call monarchy." Guarino's most eloquent expression of this belief came in 1435, when he engaged in a controversy with Poggio over the relative merits of Caesar (representing monarchy) and Scipio (representing republicanism), for which see n. on 794.

doctam: Still useful as studies of Ferrarese court culture are G. Bertoni, *Guarino fra letterati e cortigiani a Ferrara 1429-1460* (Geneva, 1921) and E. G. Gardner, *Dukes and Poets in Ferrara* (New York, 1903). The best modern account is Gundersheimer's *Ferrara: The Style of a Renaissance Despotism.*

422: *pace ... iure quieto*: Cf. the Anonymous *Diario Ferrarese* 33: "Li populi suoi in pace con grande sapientia guverno."

424: *Titan*: i.e., the sun.

425: *Saturni ... saecula*: The legendary Golden Age, when Saturn, son of Uranus, ruled. See Vergil, *Ecl.* 6. 41 and *Geo.* 2. 538.

426. *nisi ... leguntur*: Cf. G., *Epistolario* 2. Ep. 904. in which he tells how his father was captured in a battle lost by the Veronese (probably Brentella, June 25, 1386) "because of the ignorance and incompetence of a general [Cortesia de Serego], who had nowhere seen battles except those he had seen in pictures or read about in books" (*nusquam nisi quae picta viderat aut scripta legerat*).

Through you Leonello was given precedence over his warlike brothers, and now sits on his lofty throne, from there admitting that he has profited from your advice; for he embraces you with all his heart, and hopes to entrust you with his late descendants; nor does he hide any domestic secrets from you, putting both his wife and children into your formative charge.

428: *picta palatia*: The Estensi palaces of Belriguardo (begun 1435) and Belfiore (begun at the end of the *Trecento*) are described in Gundersheimer, *Ferrara* 254-264. The Schifanoia Palace (or "Diamond" Palace, from the diamond shaped stones on its exterior), begun in 1391, was receiving much attention from Borso when Ianus was writing. It is the only palace (except Mesola) which has survived, probably because it was within the walls. All of these were heavily decorated by artists like Cosimo Tura, Francesco del Cossa, and Ercole de' Roberti, but most of the decoration was not done until the 1470's. Gundersheimer, *Ferrara* 231, notes, "But it may well be true that the Estensi owned more square meters of frescoed walls than any other family in history." See also n. on 443.

430. *tyrannus*: In its original Greek sense this word meant someone who had seized power by illegal means. Here it simply means a man ruling alone. Gundersheimer, however, well observes (*Ferrara* 69, n. 5) that Niccolò III could not have maintained his position without noble and perhaps even popular support, and that the willingness of the people to be dominated was a crucial condition to the success of the Estensi. Similarly, L. Simeoni, *Le Signorie* (Milan, 1950) 1. 248 makes the point that to the Ferrarese *libertà* (freedom) meant *signoria* (the rule of a lord).

432. *per te*: Guarino may have spoken well of Leonello to his father, but there is no doubt that Niccolò had made up his own mind. Six years older than Borso, and an experienced soldier who had served under Braccio da Montone, Leonello was the obvious choice to succeed as marquis. His humanist accomplishments were a very secondary consideration to Niccolò, and probably meant little or nothing to the nobles and people. It was not until Leonello became marquis that Guarino exercised any real power.

Per te, Mars alias lituis dum perstrepit oras,
Sola vacat citharis Ferraria, sola triumphat
Principibus fecunda piis, fecunda disertis   440
Civibus et pariter cunctis habitata Camenis.
Nec solas, quas ipse doces, hic cernimus artes:

433. *fatetur:* Cf. Pliny, *N.H.* Praefatio: *Est vero benignum et plenum ingenui pudoris fateri per quos profeceris,* a favorite quotation of Guarino, which Ianus perhaps had in mind.

443. *reliquae:* Architecture, the visual arts, and music all flourished under Leonello and Borso. Gundersheimer, *Ferrara* 252, n. 36, takes Kenneth Clark's *Civilization* (1969) to task for failing to discuss the architectural wonders of the Castello di San Michele, ducal palace, and Schifanoia within the city, and the various *delizie* (see n. on 428) beyond the walls. Justly, he claims that after Milan, Naples, and the Vatican, Ferrara had the grandest buildings in Italy. Leonello erected only two, the Palazzo Trotti and the Spedale di Santa Anna, the latter a medical facility still in use. According to Johannes Ferrariensis, *Excerpta ex Annalium Libris Illustris Familiae Marchionum Estensium 1409-1454* col. 456 (in Muratori, *R.I.S.* 20), he also decorated the chapel at Belfiore, and brought a choir from France to sing in it. He patronized the artists Oriolo and Pisanello, both of whom painted his portrait and other fine works, including a famous Madonna by Pisanello (1432). Oriolo's career extended into Borso's reign, but the best period of Ferrarese art did not come until later. The fine exhibit in the *Museo del Duomo* of paintings, statuary, and illustrated manuscripts is no more than a sampling of it. The best guide to the visual and decorative arts in Ferrara are the works of G. Campori listed in Gundersheimer, *Ferrara* 119, n. 52. Particularly noteworthy are the medals cast by Pisanello (who also designed Leonello's coinage) and Matteo Pasti (See n. on 822-24). Guarino was not wholly averse to the non-literary arts: he wrote a poem in praise of Pisanello (*Epistolario* 1. Ep. 386) and two (Epp. 389, 390) in praise of a musician, whom I have identified with Giocchino dei Cancellieri (Thomson, "Two Unpublished Items in Toledo MS 100.42," *Traditio* 25 (1969) 412-14).

Because of you, while Mars sounds the clarion in other places, Ferrara alone has time for the lyre, she alone glories in a wealth of conscientious leaders and eloquent citizens, and is the home of all the muses. Nor do we see here only the arts that you yourself teach:

There is no indication, however, of real appreciation. His references to art and artists almost always hark back to such ancient names as Zeuxis and Apelles (e.g. *Epistolario* 1. Ep. 346. 11; Ep. 386. 76-79), which he could have known only from such passages as Pliny, *N.H*. 34. 69-71. His view on the relative value of the two arts is expressed in *Epistolario* 2. Ep. 864. 27-35, where after thanking his son Battista for a pen-portrait of Chrysoloras, he claims that Battista's work is better than that of Zeuxis, Apelles, and Polyclitus among the ancients, and of Gentile Bellini, Pisanello, and Angelo da Siena among the moderns, "because they painted, or paint, in ephemeral pigments, and made their figures mute, such that the artist's glory dominates the subject's, but you give coloring and artistic expression to my teacher Manuel in such firm, lively, and enduring lines, that his life and the immortality of his name increase by the day."

445. *triplicem ... sophiam*: The traditional *trivium*; of grammar, rhetoric, and logic; or possibly the three traditional; disciplines of law, medicine, and theology (see n. on 53-56).

446. *Syrtis*: The Syrtes was a dangerous sandbank off the north coast of Africa.

448: *Sarmaticis*: The Sarmatians were a Slavic people living between the Rivers Vistula and Don.

449: *Getulis*: The Gaetuli (or Getuli) lived in what is today Morocco.

452-54: The ancient rite followed in marking out a city's boundaries.

462: *Amphion*: The son of Zeus and Antiope, he is said to have raised the walls of Thebes by music; see, e.g., Horace, *Od*. 3.11. 2.

Tyrios: So called because Cadmus, the legendary founder of Thebes, was son of Agenor, king of Tyre.

Adsunt et reliquae, sed tu dux omnibus illis.
Tot siquidem medici, gemino tot iure periti,
Tot triplicem amplexi sophiam te propter in istum 445
Confluxere locum. Tu, si vada Syrtis iniquae
Incoluisse velis Scythicove in vertice sidas,
Si vaga Sarmaticis figas tentoria campis
Aut in Getulis habites magalibus, illic
Gymnasium fiet, studia illuc cuncta meabunt.   450
Verius ergo potes dici tu conditor huius,
Quam qui cornigerum iungens cum matre iuvencum
Primus ei ducto sanxit pomeria sulco
Transtulit et curvum, portam dum signat, aratrum.

468: *Nivento*: Niventum was an ancient Roman settlement on or near the site of what was later Ferrara.

469: *Cynthia*: i.e., Diana (Gk., Artemis), goddess of the moon.

472: *illecebris*: Carbone paints the same gloomy picture of Ferrara before the arrival of Guarino, but we need not believe literally that the ancient authors lay neglected. Ugo Mazzolati, *referendarius* to Niccolò III, had corresponded with Guarino since 1415 (G., *Epistolario* Ep. 34), and Giacomo dei Zilioli, a later *referendarius*, was showing interest in humanism by 1417 (*Epistolario* 1. Ep. 80), and in 1426 sent his sons to be educated by Guarino at Verona. Flavio Biondo was welcomed to Ferrara in 1422, and Giovanni Aurispa came to tutor Niccolò's son, Meliaduse, in 1427. In earlier times, Azzo VI (1208-12) and his son, Azzo VII Novello, protected French troubadours such as Aimerac de Pelguilhan and Ralmenz Bistors, and under Obizzo II (1264-93) and Azzo VIII (d. 1308) a collection of Provencal poetry was made (see G. Bertoni, *La Biblioteca Estense e la Coltura Ferrarese ai tempi del Duca Ercole I* [Torino, 1903] 4, 81-84). The picture of pre-humanist culture in Ferrara painted in Bertoni, *Guarino da Verona fra letterati e cortigiani a Ferra* (Geneva, 1921) is far from dim.

the others are here, too, but you are the guiding spirit of them all. It is because of you that so many physicians, so many men skilled in both laws, and so many who have embraced the triple wisdom, have flocked to this place. If your fancy was to live in the shallows of the hostile Syrtes, or were you to settle on a Scythian peak, or set up your nomadic tents on the plains of Sarmatia, or dwell in Getulian huts, there a school would surely come to life, and all the disciplines would find their way to it. More truly, then, can you be called the founder of this city than he who, yoking together a horned steer and its mother, first drove a furrow and consecrated its boundary, and carried his plough over it, thus marking the gate.

474: *Oenotria*: Properly, the extreme south-eastern part of Italy; here simply "Italy."

477: *Dalmatia*: Ianus is referring to himself and other "Pannonians."

478: Filippo, Carlo, and Lodovico Podatero (and possibly also a Gian Podocatero) were students from Cyprus: see G., *Epistolario* 3. 508-12. No Rodian student is known to me. For the Cretan, see n. on 632-35.

480. Henri Jouffroy and Henri de Bruges: see G., *Epistolario* 3. 055-06, 512.

481: Peter Luder; Gaspar Schmidthauser; and the sons of Samuel Karoch: see G., *Epistolario* 3. 502, 443-44.

482: The brothers Valesius and Alfonso from Portugal: see G., *Epistolario* 3. 26-27, 77-78.

444–483: Mikolaj and Jan Losowski, and Zavissius Operowski: see G., *Epistolario* 3. 411, 414. From Hungary, Ianus might have mentioned Elia Czepez, Georgius Hando, Georgius Augustinus Zagabriensis, and two students called Simon and Paulus; see G., *Epistolario* 3. 411, 441, 442-43, 444.

Scilicet est maius fragiles attollere pinnas,   455
Aggeribus fossas praecingere, turribus arces,
Quam populo silvis excito ac vallibus imis
Ingenuas artes et vitae inducere cultum?
Quin et structorum celebravit honoribus illos
Fama prior, per quos vaga turba coivit in unum   460
Corpus et insulsum gentes posuere rigorem.
Nec secus Amphion Tyrios me iudice muros,
Cynthius erexit Phrygios, dum pectine dulci
Attractas cogunt in moenia crescere petras:

452 cornigeram iungens cum Marte iuvencam *A*
459 nomine tales *A*
463 Phrygias *A*

484: Cf. Vergil, *Ecl.* 1. 66. The English students were William Grey, John Free, John Gunthorpe, Robert Flemming, and John Tiptoft; see G., *Epistolario* 3. 500.

486-88: See *Introduction*, p. V-VI.

491: *Hiberum*: The River Ebro in Spain.

492: *Tanain ... Cydnus ... Albis*: The Rivers Don, Kara-Su (in Cilicia), and Elbe.

496: *abscondita*: Cf. 535.

508: *Pharon*: An island near Alexandria in Egypt, where Ptolemy Philadephus built a lighthouse, but here (as in Statius, *Silvae* 3. 2. 102) used poetically for Egypt itself.

Is it really a greater achievement to raise frail battlements, to gird moats with ramparts and citadels with towers, than to bring civilization and the liberal arts to a people called forth from the woods and depths of the valleys? Indeed, it is said that in ancient days those by whose efforts a mob of vagabonds joined together as one body, and tribes abandoned their unintelligent and uncouth ways, were honored as builders. Thus, as I see it, did Cynthius raise the Phrygian, and Amphion the Tyrian walls, drawing rocks together with their sweet quills and

511: *Timavus*: A river in Istria, between Aquileia and Trieste. Vergil, *Ecl.* 8. 6 refers to the rocks at its mouth; see also *Aen.* 1. 244.
513: *provectior aetas*: See n. on 370-77. Latin and Greek were studied simultaneously but Greek was started later.
519: Cf. Vergil, *Geo.* 1. 42, *alta petens*, of a fisherman seeking the catch at the bottom.
526: Guarino made a collection of homonyms, discussed by Sabbadini in *La Scuola e gli studi di Guarino Veronese* (Catania, 1896; repr. in *Guariniana* ed. M. Sancipriano, Torino, 1964) 56-57. Sabbadini prints (p. 57) a thirteen-line sample, the first two lines of which illustrate the type: *Dicitur esse nepos de nepa luxuriosus,/Ast natum gnati dic post natum esse nepotem*. Here the difference between *nepos* in its original sense "grandson" is made clear.

Vox chelys illa fuit, duri saxa illa coloni.   465
Hoc, Guarine, tibi nuper Ferraria pacto
Fundata est, talem tua quam praesentia fecit,
Ut iam nunc veteri tam sit diversa Nivento
Plena senescenti quam distat Cynthia Lunae:
Ante rudis rerum, nunc ipsis aemula Athenis,   470
Nulli nota prius, totum nunc clara per orbem,
Illecebris quondam, magni nunc hospita mundi.
   Nam te audituri terrarum ex omnibus oris
Huc coiere viri; tua nec te Oenotria tantum
Miratur, movere tuae praeconia famae   475
Hos etiam, Musas qui condemnare solebant:
Ad te permenso descendit Dalmatia ponto;
Ad te Creta Rhodos properavit et ultima Cypros,
Sole Rhodos, Iove Creta, Cypros Cythereide felix;
Pro te Sequanicos Galli sprevere magistros;   480
Germani argutam pro te liquere Viennam
Venit et Herculeis vicina Hispania metis;
Axe sub Arctoo positi venere Poloni;
Venerunt alio volitantes orbe Britanni.
Me simul hos inter fatis et sorte deorum   485
Pannoniae tellus tenero tibi misit in aevo,

468 iuventa A

530-34: The practice in narrative poetry of permuting the natu-
ral temporal sequence of events (*ordo naturalis*) goes back as far as
Homer, who plunges, as Horace tells us, "in medias res." The an-
cients were aware of the difference between *ordo naturalis* and *ordo
artificialis*, ("artistic" order), but detailed instruction on how to use
the artistic order was not elaborated before the Middle Ages, e.g., by

forcing them to become city walls. Your voice was that lyre, those rocks the rough farmers. Thus was Ferrara founded by you, Guarino, in modern times, and your presence has made her now as different from old Niventum as is Cynthia, fully grown, from Luna as she grows old: once boorish in every way, now the rival of Athens herself; unknown to any throughout the whole earth; once obscure, now the hostess of the mighty world.

For men have gathered here from all corners of the earth to hear you. Not only does your native Oenotria marvel at you, but stories of your fame have stirred even those who used to despise the muses: Dalmatia has crossed the length of the sea and come to you; to you have hastened Crete, happy in Jove, and Rhodes, happy in the Sun, and furthest Cyprus, happy in the Cytherean; for you the Gauls have spurned their Sequanic teachers; for you the Germans have left sharp-witted Vienna, and Spain, neighbor to the Pillars of Hercules, has come, and the Poles that live beneath the Arctic sky, and the Britons, flitting from another world. By divine fate, the land of Pannonia, where Dravus, soon to mingle his name and waters

Geoffrey of Vinsauf in his *Documentum de modo et arte dictandi et versificandi* and *Poetria nova*, both published by E. Faral in *Les Arts poétiques du xiie and du xiiie siècle* (Paris, 1924). The *Poetria nova* (publ. with English translation by Jane B. Kopp in *Three Medieval Rhetorical Arts* ed. J. J. Murphy [Berkeley, Los Angeles, and London, 1971] 32-108) opens, after his Introduction, with a detailed exposition of

Qua mox Danubio mixturus nomen et undas
Pinguia culta secat leni iam gurgite Dravus.
Urbs si quem tota una colit, satis esse beatus
Creditur et tumida resupinus laude superbit   490
Ludi turba tui est, quicquid latet inter Hiberum
Ac Tanain, quicquid discedunt Cydnus et Albis.
Qualiter in mediis reddens oracula Delphis
Gentibus a cunctis acceditur augur Apollo;
Hunc Notus et Boreas nec non Occasus et Ortus   495
Consulit in dubiis et rerum abscondita discit:
Quis bello morbisve modus, prudentia cuius
Prima viri, miseros quis felicissimus inter
Mortales, quae longarum fortuna viarum.
Ille licet caecis penitus demersus in antris,   500
Tempora cuncta tamen momento cernit in uno,
Volvere nec Parcae populive inquirere tantum
Sufficiunt, quantum solus valet edere Paean:
Sic ad te toto certatim ex orbe profecti
Agrestes animos et barbara corda reponunt.   505
Nec tuus assiduo fons unquam deficit haustu,
Purior et maior sed in omnia pectora manat,
Ut Pharon immenso fecundat flumine Nilus,
Magnus et Euphrates Chaldaeos irrigat agros.
Gurgite nec tantum collectus laberis uno,   510

492 quantum *A*

---

ordo artificialis (Murphy, 36-41). Geoffrey states (Kopp's translation, p. 36) "The line of nature's avenue governs when the action and the words follow the same course and the discourse does not deviate from

with the Danube, cuts through rich tillage with his now
gentle current, sent me also to you at a tender age.

If a whole city worships a man, he is considered blessed
enough, and walking erect, he glories in the clouds of praise.
But enrolled in your school is all that lies between the Hi-
berus and the Tanais, between the Cydnus and the Albis.
Thus do all races approach the augur Apollo, giving ora-
cles in the midst of Delphi; North, South, East, and West
consult him in matters of doubt, and learn what is hidden:
when diseases or a war will end, whose wisdom is greatest,
who is happiest among wretched mortals, what will hap-
pen on long journeys. Though sunk in the depths of a dark
cave, he sees all in a single moment, and the Fates cannot
unroll nor whole peoples ask as much as Paean alone can
give forth. Even so do men from all over the world set out
emulously to reach you, and when they have, they put away
their untutored minds and barbaric hearts.

Nor does your fountain ever fail from constant draughts,
but it flows purer and stronger into every heart, as the Nile
enriches Pharos with its immense flood, and the mighty
Euphrates waters the fields of Chaldea. Nor do you flow in
a single body of water, but

the natural order of events. The work proceeds along the footpath of
art, on the other hand, if, as being more suitable, the plan places ensuing
things first, or draws to the rear things intrinsically prior."

Sed velut innumero prorumpens ore Timavus
Multiplices aperis rivos: scatet ille Latinis
Artibus, hic Graiis; bibit hinc provectior aetas,
Inde minor, prima seu quis maduisse Minerva
Rhetorico potius cupiat seu nectare tingi   515
Seu velit annales seu dia poemata vatum,
Quos tu non trito vulgi de more retexis
Plana et aperta sequens, ceu qui vaga retia summis
Ducit aquis fundo nec praedam quaerit in imo,
Grandia sed parvis, sublimibus infima miscens   520
Nil indiscussum penitus dubiumve relinquis,
Syllaba uti nullum tenuis vel littera fallat,
Qui structurae ordo, quae sit sententia vocum,
Quae nota verborum servata fidelibus annis,
Quodlibet a quanam decurrat origine nomen,   525
Quid distent, unum quae significare videntur,
Qui stilus aut numeri species, quis carminis auctor,
Argumenta quibus veniant a sedibus et quos
Excuset ratio, commendet forma colores,
Narrandi quae lex potior, quod saepe per artem   530
In medio soleant prima et postrema locari
Nec se a principiis moveat tractatus et imos

522 Syllaba vel nullum ut *A*
527 author *A*
530 quae saepe *A*
532 se principiis *A*

535. *rerum abstrusa*: Allegorization of the classics, especially
Homer and Vergil, was fundamental to Guarino's defence of their use as
the basis for a liberal education. Nearly every important humanist, from

like Timavus erupting from countless mouths, you open up a vast network of streams: one gushes with the Latin arts, another with the Greek; older students drink from the latter, younger ones from the former, whether one's wish is to be steeped in the primary Minerva or touched with the nectar of rhetoric, whether one wishes history or the divine works of the poets. These last you interpret not in the usual trite way, following the plain and obvious, like one who casts his trailing net over the surface of the water, without going for the catch at the bottom; but rather, mingling great with small, the highest with the lowest, you leave nothing whatever in doubt or undiscussed, so that no one will make a mistake over a short syllable or an individual letter, about the construction, the meanings of words, what words have faithfully kept their meaning over the years, the etymology of any expression, the difference between words that seem to have only one meaning, the style or the metre, the author of a poem, the sources of subject matter, what figures of speech are permissible in argumentation, which ones best fit a particular literary form, and which rule is the more effective in narrative, because often first and last events are artfully set in the middle, nor does a tract always progress in chronological order,

Petrarch on, had something to say on the matter (See E. Garin, *Il pensiero pedagogica dello Umanesimo* 42-124). By Guarino's time, their general arguments had become stereotyped. They are summarized by

Desinat in fines, sed gratius ordine verso
Ultima praeveniat, longe prius acta reservet.
Tu tamen exuperas, cum rerum abstrusa recludis,535
Cum veterum sectas inter figmenta latentes
Producis. Nec te sollertior edere quisquam,
Mystica secreto quid celet fabula sensu,
Quod vastum sine lege Chaos, quae bella Gigantum,
Qui Pyrrhae lapides Phaethonteive calores,   540
Quas Progne plumas, quae cornua sumpserit Io,
Daedalus arma quibus Minoia fugerit alis,
Quae vis reppulerit solem, quo robore caelum
Fulciat altus Atlas, quod virus Gorgonos atrae,
Quid facies habitusve notent et sacra deorum.   545

Antonio Stäuble in "Francesco da Fiano in difesia della Poesia," *Bib-
liotheque d'Humanisme et Renaissance* 26 (Droz, Geneva 1964) 256-57:
1). Poetry has a divine origin; (2) The Scriptures themselves are alle-
gorical and sometimes introduce scenes of vice; (3) Poets were honored
in times past as educators; (4) Various Church Fathers studied the
pagan poets with understanding and found them useful. The more lib-
eral churchmen, such as Ambrogio Travesari and Guarino's students,
Bernardino da Siena and Alberto da Sazana, saw no contradiction be-
tween studying the classics and leading a Christian life; but others,
such as Giovanni da San Miniato and Giovanni Dominici in the four-
teenth and early fifteenth century saw humanism as corrosive of Chris-
tian life. Guarino himself came under attack on April 5, 1450, when
Giovanni da Prato, sent by the Pope to preach an Easter sermon at
Ferrara, criticized the reading of pagan authors, particularly Terence,
on whom Guarino happened to be lecturing about that time (see Gio-
vanni's remark in G., *Epistolario* 2. Ep. 824.47). Giovanni had warned
Guarino in advance that he would attack, as is clear from the opening

and end with the very last event, but more pleasingly, by switching the sequence, it puts the last action first, and postpones what happened earlier until much later. You excel, however, when you are unlocking secrets, when you parade the sects of the ancients that hide their doctrines in fantasy. No one is shrewder than you at revealing the hidden meaning of a mystical tale, the significance of vast and lawless Chaos, of the battles of the giants, the stones of Pyrrha or the fires of Phaethon, the plumage that Procne, and the horns that Io assumed, the wings that Daedalus used to escape the arms of Minos, the force that held back the sun, the strength by which tall Atlas supports the sky, the poison of the black Gorgon, and the aspects, natures, and rites of the gods.

of G., *Epistolario* 2. Ep. 823, which is Guarino's defence. It was a dangerous situation, since the preacher had demanded burning at the stake for all those who bought or possessed copies of Terence. Guarino opens by wondering why Vergil, too, was not condemned, and defends him as a potent force in educating children. Then he attacks philosophers who assert that the Universe is eternal, and agrees that certain books should be denied to students. The aim of education is the love of God, and Theology is admitted to be the chief branch of knowledge, but those who would study it must have minute knowledge of all the other arts and sciences. He quotes Basil, Augustine, and Jerome in support, in particular pointing out that in Gregory Nanzianzenus' funeral oration on Basil, the latter's conversion is attributed to his "all-round education" (i.e., the *enkyklios paideia* of later Greek times), and that Basil himself had said that one should first be steeped in the poets, orators, and historians before moving on to "sacred and abstruse matters." However, when passages about vice occur, we should close our ears. Guarino agrees, fulminates against actors, and

Nempe etiam quotiens divinam Aeneida versas,
Haud frustra Aeolio ventos in carcere ponis,
Ter quater et dictos ostendis iure beatos,
Quid supplex Erycina patri mutatave divae
Effigies vel nube cava contectus Achates,   550
Illa tot in primis stabulantia faucibus Orci
Quid sibi monstra velint, quae tres ex ordine Parcae,
Quae totidem Furiae, quod rami divitis aurum,
Quam pulchrum occulta condant sub imagine verum

542 arva *malit Sabbadinus*

concludes that certain pagan authors must be read as we pluck roses,
"with the thorns left out." He then shows that Jerome is full of echoes of
the classics, and would be incomprehensible to anyone but a classically-
trained scholar. He also states that Jerome explains the *Aeneid* as an
allegory of human life. Now follows a defence of Terence as a teacher
of rhetoric and good morals. He appeals to the doctrine of *proprietas*,
(found, e.g., in Catullus 16. 5-9) whereby, for example, when the evan-
gelist condemns Judas and describes his sin, we condemn Judas but not
the evangelist: the same principle applies to pagan writers who describe
vicious acts. Jerome's Epistle 21. 13. 5f. is cited, an interpretation of
Deuteronomy 21. 10, in which the "captive maiden" is equated with the
classics, and the paring of her nails, etc. with the process of bowdleriza-
tion. Guarino also quotes Augus- tine, *De Doctrina Christiana* 2. 61,
in which Lactantius and other converts are likened to Israelites leaving
Egypt, laden with precious trinkets (i.e., the pagan classics) which God
has arranged for them to use in a noble way. He stresses that authors
must not be rejected because dubious passages occur in them; without
the complete text, discrimination is impossible. But downright pornog-
raphy, magical spells, and dainty recipes must be forbidden. "There
are books, ancient and modern, that I would not even allow young men
to touch," he says, particularly condemning books "on the art of love-
making," meaning in particular Ovid's *Ars Amatoria*.

And when you take in hand the divine Aeneid, not with-
out purpose do you locate the winds in the prison of Aeolus,
and show how rightly named are those called thrice and four
times blessed, and explain the scenes where Erycina sup-
plicates her father, where the goddess's image changes, or
Achates is hidden in a hollow cloud, and the meaning of the
many monsters stabled in the front jaws of Orcus, the three
Fates in order, and the like number of Furies, the gold of
the rich bough, and the beautiful truth

538: Implicit in the allegorical method used by Guarino (see n. on
535) was the assumption that ancient writers, particularly the epic po-
ets, concealed scientific and philosophic truths under their fictitious nar-
rative (narratio fabulosa) by means of a wrapping (involucrum) or pro-
tective covering (integumentum); for a good discussion of these terms,
and the difference between involucrum and integumentum, see Brian
Stock, Myth and Science in the Twelfth Century (Princeton, 1972) 45-
55. The habit of allegorizing goes back at least as far as Xenophanes
in the sixth century B.C., who regarded parts of Homer as repositories
of philosophic truth: for a history of the method, see F. Buffière, Les
mythes d' Homère et la pensée grecque (1956), and for specific examples
of the method in operation, the best modern discussion is Michael Mur-
rin, The Allegorical Epic (Chicago and London, 1980) 3-25. It is implicit
in Servius' commentaries on Vergil, Macrobius' commentary on Cicero's
Somnium Scipionis (esp. 1. 2. 14 and 1. 2. 17-18), Fulgentius' De Con-
tinentia Virgiliana, various passages of John of Salisbury, and the com-
mentary on the first six books of Vergil's Aeneid ascribed to Bernardus
Silvestris, to name but a few medieval authors (for whom, see the Intro-
duction, pp. xi-xxxiii, in Commentary on the First Six Books of Vergil's
Aeneid by Bernardus Silvestris, trans. with introduction and notes by
E. G. Schreiber and T. E. Maresca [Lincoln and London, 1979]). It

Trux avis unda fugax volucris rota pendula moles   555
Ac reditura silex et futilis urna sororum,
Quae rabidi tria colla canis, quae cruda senectus
Remigis, Elysiae quae pigra oblivio Lethes,
Cur novies fusam metuant Styga fallere divi,
Cocytus lacrimis, Phlegethon cur igne redundet,   560
Per geminas diversa volent cur somnia portas.
Nec Smyrnaea minus belle penetralia pandis,
Qua tenuit Siren, qua vi Titania vertit,
Qui Veneris cestos, triplicis quae flamma Chimaerae,

continued in the Renaissance, e.g., in Cristoforo Landino's allegoriza-
tion of the *Aeneid*, contained in Bk. 4 of his *Camaldulensian Dialogues*
(1480). Guarino's interpretations were not therefore out of line with
mainstream humanist thinking, which looked back to the medieval tra-
ditions rather than to the rationalist tendencies of the sixteenth and
seventeenth centuries.

539: *Chaos*: Literally, "gaping void," the beginning of the universe,
according to Hesiod, *Theogony* 116 ff. Here, as elsewhere, we cannot
tell what interpretation Guarino gave such terms. *bella Gigantum*: The
myth in Hesiod, *Theogony*, 453 ff, that when Zeus grew to maturity he
raised a rebellion against his father, Kronos (Lat., Cronus, identified
with Saturn), and defeated him with the help of Cronus' elder children
and certain of this brethren who had been imprisoned in Tartarus: the
Cyclopes (makers of thunder and lightning) and the Hecatonchires (gi-
ants with a hundred hands each). The Titans fought with Cronus in the
war, which came to be known as the *Titanomachia*. Later, Zeus battled
with the Giants, whom the Earth stirred up against him. The war had
three stages: the *Gigantomachia*, the first account of which is in Pindar,
Nemeans 1. 67 ff. and *Isthmians* 6. 32 ff, the fullest in Apollodorus
1. 34 ff.; the assault by Typhoeus, recounted in Hesiod, *Theogony* 820
ff.; and the attempt of Otus and Ephialtes to scale Olympus (in, e.g.,
Odyssey 11. 305 ff.)

hidden under secret imagery by the grim bird, the receding water, the revolving wheel, the hanging mass, the stone fated to roll back, and the leaky urn of the sisters; the meaning of the three necks of the rabid dog, the harsh old age of the rover, the oblivion of Elysian Lethe; why the gods are afraid of swearing falsely by Styx with its nine coils, why Cocytus overflows with tears and Phlegethon with fire, and why dreans fly in different directions through the twin portals.

Just as handsomely, you open up the inner chambers of the Smyrnean, explaining by what force the Siren laid hold on men, and Titania changed their shape, the nature of the girdle of Venus, and the flame of the tri-form Chimaera,

540: *Pyrrhae lapides*: The myth, told in Ovid, *Metamorphoses* 1. 211-421, was that in the time of Deucalion, son of Prometheus, Zeus was angry at the wickedness of mankind and destroyed them with a flood. Only Deucalion and his wife Pyrrha were saved by building an ark. When the waters went down, they emerged on Mt. Parnassus, and were advised by an oracle to throw the "bones of their mother" (stones) over their shoulders. The stones thrown by Deucalion became men, those thrown by Pyrrha became women.

Phaethonteive calores: See n. on 409.

541: *Progne*: The legend was that Tereus, husband of Procne (or Progne), the daughter of king Pandion of Athens, imprisoned her, pretending she was dead, and married her sister, Philomela. Philomela discovered Procne, and for revenge on Tereus, killed their son, Itys, served his flesh to Tereus in a meal, presented him with Itys' head, and then fled to Procne. Tereus pursued, and to escape, Procne prayed to be changed into a bird. She became a nightingale, Philomela a swallow, and Tereus a hoopoo. See, e.g., Vergil, *Ecl.* 6. 78-81.

Io: The story, told in Ovid, *Metamorphoses* 1. 588-747, was that Hera discovered Zeus making love to Io. In a vain attempt at concealment, Zeus turned her into a heifer, which Hera pursued with relentless torments.

Quid Iovis adiutor Briareus, deiectus ab alto   565
Mulciber, inclusus cavea Gradivus aena,
Aethiopum mensae, cum coniuge Tethyos irae,
Aurea quid signet pendens ex aethere funis.

542: *Daedalus*: The Athenian master craftsman of legend, who took refuge in Crete after murdering his nephew Perdix. Tiring of his life there (some say he was shut up in the labyrinth for assisting Minos' wife, Pasiphaë, to fulfill her passion for a bull sent by Poseidon for sacrifice, but kept by Minos), he invented wings, by which he and his son escaped. The story is told in Ovid, *Metamorphoses* 8. 200-30.

arma: In quoting this passage in G., *Epistolario* 3. 420, Sabbadini suggests the emendation *arva* (fields), presumably because Ovid's account (see n. above) says nothing about Minos pursuing Daedalus with arms, while he was in Crete.

543: *vis*: It is not clear whether this is a general statement (in which case *reppulerit* must be taken as a gnomic perfect), or simply refers to Daedalus' advice to Icarus, which he himself followed but Icarus did not, to avoid flying too close to the sun, so that the wax holding their wings would not melt.

544: *Atlas*: A Titan who was punished by Zeus by having to support the sky on his shoulders.

Gorgonos: i.e., Medusa, the mortal one of a triad of female monsters with snakes for hair and the power to change anyone who gazed upon them to stone. Perseus slew Medusa and put her head into a *kibisis* or sack. A late addition to the myth has it that as Perseus passed over Libya, blood dripped from the sack, each drop creating a poisonous serpent. The poison, however, might also refer to the snakes on Medusa's head.

546: *Aeneida*: See. n. on 535. Note that the citations from the *Aeneid* are all from Books 1 and 6. For the adjective *divinam*, cf. Statius, *Thebais* 12., *nec tu divinam Aeneida tenta*.

and the meaning of Briareus, the ally of Jupiter, of Mul-
ciber's ejection from on high, of Gradivus' capture in the
bronze cage, of the feasts of the Ethiopians, of Tethys' anger
with her husband, and of the golden chain hung from the
upper air.

547: *Aelio*: One of Ianus' earliest compositions at Ferrara was a
long poem on a contest of the winds, *Eranemos, seu carmen de cer-
tamine ventorum* (*Poemata* 1. 6). Published at Debrecen in 1594, it
was the last of Ianus' poems to be published in Hungary until 1754
(Birnbaum, 36, n. 44; see also her discussion of the poem, pp. 29-31).
Drawing mainly on Vergil, Ovid, Seneca, and Lucan (see Huszti, *Ianus
Pannonius* 70-76 and Dezsö Pais "Janus Pannonius Eranemosa és a latin
klasszikusok," *Egyetemes Philológiai* Közlöny [1910] 760-76), Ianus rep-
resents the winds arguing over who is the strongest. Their king Aeolus
judges the rhetorical talents of each, and awards the palm to Boreas,
the north wind, who is the most garrulous. The winds probably repre-
sent various students, Aeolus Guarino, and Boreas Ianus himself (in his
Epigr. 1. 185 [Kombol, 190] he speaks of himself as coming from the
chill axis of the northern sky).
    carcere: Cf. Vergil, *Aen.* 1. 54 and 141. The storm scene in
Aen. 1. 82-142 probably suggested the idea for Ianus' *Eranemos*, but
in Vergil it is Neptune who calms the waters (*Aen.* 1. 125). We know
from *Epistolario* 1. Ep. 25. 127 that Guarino interpreted Neptune
here as reason. Ianus, however, seems to take Aeolus to mean reason
embodied in Guarino.
    549. *Erycina*: i.e. Venus, who in Vergil, *Aen.* 1. 223-53 points
out to Jupiter the plight of the Trojans, and contrasts it with the high
destiny he had promised them. Her speech begins at line 239.
    549-50 *mutata ... effigies*: Venus' disguise as a mortal huntress is
described in Vergil, *Aen.* 1. 314-20.
    550: *Achates*: The faithful companion of Aeneas. In Vergil, *Aen.*
1. 411-12 Venus wraps them both in a cloud, to prevent them being
seen as they approach Carthage.

Talia dictantem pronis te aurita iuventus
Sensibus attendit. Sic, cum Lesbous Arion   570
Dorsa recurva premens mediis tinniret in undis
Dulce melos (toto cantu commota profundo
Monstra maris saevos damnarunt mitia nautas),
Sternuntur fluctus, rupto caput excita somno
Phoca levat nec tarda ducem balaena moratur,   575
Raucum Nereides rident Tritona protervae,

563 Tytanida A
566 grandaevus ahena A

551: *monstra*: In Vergil, *Aen.* 6. 273-289 the jaws of Orcus contain
Cares and Woes, Diseases, Old Age, Fear, Hunger, Poverty, Death,
Hardship, Sleep (brother of Death), Evil Joys, War, the Furies, Discord,
Empty Dreams, and (285,89) Centaurs, Scylla, Briareus, the Hydra of
Lerna, Chiamaera, Gorgons, Harpies, and Geryon (giant with three
bodies).
    552: *Parcae*: Roman birth-goddesses identified with the Greek
Moirai ("Alloters" or "Fates"). Vergil does not place them in Tartarus
(see n. on 1012).
    553: *totidem Furiae*: See Vergil, *Aen.* 6. 552-53, where Allecto,
chief of these spirits of vengeance, calls on "throngs" of her sisters. The
usual number in most writers is three.
    rami ... aurum: The Golden Bough is referred to in Vergil, *Aen.*
6. 136-48, 204-11, 406-07, 629-36. It gains Aeneas entrance to the
Underworld, whereupon he leaves it fixed to the gate-posts.

As you lecture on such matters, the attentive young
men listen, all ears. As when Arion of Lesbos, stradling
the dolphin's arching back, played his sweet melody in the
midst of the waves (the monsters of the sea, roused from all
its depths by the song, with their gentleness condemned the
savage sailors), the billows are stilled, the seal, wakened from
its broken nap, raises its head, nor does the slow whale delay
its conductor, or the forward daughters of Nereus laugh at
hoarse Triton, Galatea does not

555-56: Refer to some of the torments of sinners described in Vergil,
Aen. 6. 580–627: the vulture (*avis*) which fed on the regenerating liver
of Tityus (6. 595-600); the impending mass (*moles*) that threatens
the Lapiths, Ixion, and Pirithous (6. 601-03),and the rock (*silex*) that
Sisyphus rolls vainly to the top of a hill (6. 616); the wheel (*rota*)
on which people like Ixion are tied (6. 616-17). Vergil does not place
in Tartarus the daughters of Danaus, who killed their husbands, the
fifty sons of Aegyptus, and were condemned to keep putting water in
jars (*urna*) with holes in them, but Guarino (if Ianus is reflecting his
teachings) seems to have taken 6. 608, *quibus invisi fratres*, to refer to
them. Likewise, the punishment of Tantalus (not mentioned by name)
in *Aen.* 6. 603-05 is to have an unreachable feast placed before him. The
receding water is a detail from Homer, *Odyssey* 11. 581. Ianus, however,
may have been confused by a reminiscence of Ovid, *Metamorphoses* 10.
1-85, in which Ixion, Tityus, Sisyphus, Tantalus, and the Danaids all
figure.

Non Acin Galatea gemit, non mater Achillem
Nec plus Inoae meminit Melicerta ruinae,
Non centum saltare vetant Aegaeona nodi,
Fatidicus Proteus stat vultu immobilis uno,   580
Nec vitasse velit mutantia gramina Glaucus,
Iam silet, Isthmiacis siccat iam solibus udos
Ille sinus et adhuc fervent freta lata choreis.

557: *canis*: i.e., *Cerberus*, the three-headed dog that guarded the
entrance to Tartarus; Vergil, *Aen.* 6, 417-23.

558: *remigis*; i.e., *Charon*, who rowed souls across the Styx. His
squalor and strength are described in Vergil, *Aen.* 298-304.

558: *Lethes*: i.e., the River of Forgetfulness.

559: According to Hesiod, *Theogony* 337 ff, when Zeus fought the
Titans, he was helped by Styx, goddess of one of the rivers that flow in
the Underworld. As a reward, he decreed that any god swearing falsely
by her name would be banished for a fixed term from Olympus.

560. *Coctyus ...Phlegethon*: Rivers flowing in the Underworld.

561: Guarino's interpretation of the twin gates is likely to have
been of the sort given by Macrobius, *In somnium Scipionis* 1. 3. 17-20,
where the authority cited is Porphyry, commenting on Homer, *Odyssey*
19. 562. Drawing on this passage of Macrobius, Bernardus Silvestris
interprets the twin gates as follows: "By sleep is meant the soul, which
has two parts, one of horn, the other of ivory. Of horn, because just
as horn is translucent when it is shaved thin, so the soul, when it is
not too much weighed down by the body, sometimes sees the truth
without hindrance, though not with total clarity ...Of ivory, because
just as ivory, when pared to the limit, can never be made thin enough
to see through, so also the soul is sometimes ...so depressed by the
weight of the body and its dullness, that it is completely blocked from
recognizing and distinguishing the truth." (*Commentum qui dicitur
Bernardi Silvestris super sex libros Eneidos Virgilii* ed. J.W. Jones and
E.F. Jones [Lincoln and London, 1977] 128).

mourn for Acis, nor his mother for Achilles, Melicerta no
longer remembers Ino's fall, the hundred knots do not stop
Aegaeon from dancing, the seer Proteus stands motionless,
without changing shape, and Glaucus no longer wishes he
had escaped the herbs that transformed him: Arion falls
silent, and is already drying his wet clothes in the sunshine
of the Isthmus, while the broad straits are still seething with
dances.

562. *Smyrnaea*: i.e. Homeric, because there was a tradition that
Homer came from the city of Smyrna in Asia Minor: see Lucan *Pharsalia*
9. 24, and Statius *Silvae* 8. 595.
    563: *Titania*: i.e., Circe, the witch.
    564: *Chimaerae*: The chimaera, offspring of Typhon and Echidna,
was a fire-breathing lion in front, a dragon behind, and a goat in the
middle. It was slain by the hero Bellerophon (Homer, *Iliad* 6, 179-93).
    565: *Briareus*: See n. on 579.
    566: i.e. Vulcanus, identified with Hephaistos, the Greek god of
metal-workers. There are two accounts in the *Iliad* of his ejection from
Heaven. The first is that his mother Hera did it, because she was
ashamed of his lameness: the other is that Zeus cast him out when he
intervened in a quarrel between him and Hera.
    Gradivus: A cult title of the Roman deity, Mars, identified with
the god of war. In Homer, *Odysses* 8. 266-366 it is recounted how Ares
was cuckolding Hephaestus, who constructed a net to catch him and
Aphrodite in the act.
    567: *Aethiopum*: In the story above (on 566, Gradivus), Hephaes-
tus pretends to be going to visit the Aethiopians, a people who lived in
Central Africa, proverbial for their hospitality to the gods.
    Tethyos: Tethys was wife of Oceanus; both were Titans, and said
in Homer, *Iliad* 8. 479 ff. to be the parents of the gods.
    568. *aurea ...funis*: A reference to Homer, *Iliad* 8. 19, where Zeus
offers to hang a cord from heaven and pull against all the other gods

Ipse dies pulchro distinguitur orbe laborum.
Mane salutatis petitur schola publica divis   585
Socratis antiquo nil concessura Lyceo,
Tot iuvenum clara fulget stipata caterva.
Vergilius primum legitur vel proximus illi
Quilibet. Hunc sequitur, qui contudit arma togatus,
Aut implere vicem Ciceronis idoneus alter.   590
Exin vicinam conscendis principis aulam.

at the lower end of it. This image caught the fancy of many commen-
tators ready to read mystical meanings into Homer, e.g. Macrobius, *In
Somnium Scipionis* 1. 14. 15: "Accordingly, since Mind emanates from
the Supreme God and Soul from Mind, and Mind, indeed, forms and
suffuses all below with life, and since this is the one splendor lighting
up everything and visible in all, like a countenance reflected in many
mirrors arranged in a row, and since all follow on in continuous suc-
cession, degenerating step by step in their downward course, the close
observer will find that from the Supreme God even to the bottommost
dregs of the universe there is one tie, binding at every link and never
broken. This is the golden chain of Homer which, he tells us, God or-
dered to hang down from the sky to earth." (version from *Macrobius'
Commentary on the Dream of Scipio*. Translated with an Introduction
and Notes by William Harris Stahl [New York and London, 1952] 145).
This was probably Guarino's interpretation.

   571. *Arion*: a legendary musician from Methymna in Lesbos, who
was rescued from drowning by dolphins charmed by his final song: see,
e.g., Ovid, *Fasti* 2. 79ff.
   Tritona: The sea deity, Triton, often depicted as blowing on a
conch.
   577. *Galatea ...mater*: The Nereid Galatea was beloved by the
uncomely Cyclops, Polyphemus, but she rejected him in favor of Acis,
a handsome youth. Finding them embracing, Polyphemus killed Acis,
whose blood became the river of that name (Ovid, *Metamorphoses* 13.

The day itself is divided up in an impressive round of tasks. After prayers in the morning, you go to the public school, no whit inferior to Socrates' ancient Lyceum, so packed is it with brilliant young men. First, Vergil is read, or some similar author. He is followed by the man who, though a civilian, crushed an armed conspiracy, or by some other author suitable as an alternative to Cicero. Then you go up to the court of the prince nearby.

750-897). Galatea's sister, Thetis, was the mother of Achilles, who died young in the Trojan war.

578. *Melicerta*: Melicerta (or Melicertes) was the son of Ino, who to escpae her insane husband, Athamas, plunged with Melicerta in her arms into the sea, she becoming the marine goddess Leucothea, he the sea-god Palaemon (Ovid, *Metamorphoses* 4. 416ff.).

579. *Aegaeona*: Cf. Statius, *Achilleis* 1. 209-10; Claudina, *De raptu Prosperpinae* 1. 46-47. According to Homer, *Iliad* 1. 396-404, Aegaeon was the name given by mortals to the hundred-handed son of Ouranos and Ge, called Briareus by the gods (see also Hesiod, *Theogony* 502, 714, 817). Cronos put him in chains, but Zeus released him; hence he was a type of release from tyranny and ally of the values represented by Zeus. His name is confused with that of the Aegean Sea by Euripides, *Alcestis* 595, which may be why Ianus makes him representative of it here.

581. *Glaucus*: A fisherman of Anthedon in Boeotia, who became immortal after swallowing a magic herb. He leaped into the sea and became a marine deity (Ovid, *Metamorphoses* 13. 920ff. and 2. 8-10, where he is depicted with Triton and Proteus, with his arm cradling two whales).

583: Cf. Vergil, *Geo*. 1. 327.

584: Cf. Juvenal, 1. 127, which has *ordine rerum* for Ianus' more expressive *orbe laborum*.

585. *salutatis ... deis*: See n. on 810 for Guarino's religious views.

Hic te Nicoleos audit Leonellia proles
Ac morum simul et studiorum insignia sumit.
Talis Aristoteles rerum secreta docebat
Pellaeum iuvenem, quibus ille accensus in omnes   595
Extendit terras animos nec digna magistrum
Destituit merces, nam compensante Philippo
Instaurata manet pretium Stagira laboris.

592 hinc *A*
598 manent *A*

schola publica: In the fifteenth century the University of Ferrara
had no permanent home. Classes seem to have met in Franciscan and
Dominican churches (Gundersheimer, *Ferrara* 101). The ruins of such
a church, said to have been "the earliest university" are still stand-
ing behind the Palazzo Bentivoglio, only a few minutes' walk from the
Castello. The public school was distinct from Guarino's *contubernium*
(see n. on 591).
    586. *Lyceo*: The Lyceum, together with the Academy and the
Cynosarges, was one of the three gymnasia outside the walls of ancient
Athens. Dedicated to Apollo Lykeios, it lay in the eastern suburb, not
far from the River Ilissos. It was here, rather than in the market place,
that Socrates conducted most of his discussions: see Plato, *Symposium*
223D 8; *Euthyphron* 2A 1, etc.
    589: As consul in 63 B.C., Cicero crushed the Catilinarian conspir-
acy. Technically, he was still a civilian, since he was not in command of
an army in the field.
    591. *vicinam*: From the bill of sale for Guarino's house, published
in extracts by Sabbadini in G., *Epistolario* 3. 382, we know that the
purchase took place on October 5, 1437, and that the property was
bounded by the Via San Michele (now Vie del Turco, running south
and north from the old church of San Michele to the Via Cortevecchia),
the Via Cortevecchia (the same street that still runs east and west
past the Corte Vecchia or Palazzo Municipale on its south side), the

Here Niccolò the son of Leonello, hears you, and takes on the distinctions of morality and scholarship together. So too did Aristotle teach the young man of Pella the secrets of nature that inspired him, and caused him to spread his ideas world-wide. And the teacher did not fail to be well paid, for the restored city of Stagira stands to this day as Phillip's reward for his work. After you return,

Vico Podestà (now Vicolo del Podestà, running almost on a southern parallel to the Via Cortevecchia), and the house of the Podestà (now the Torre del Podestà, just to the right as one enters the Contrada di San Paolo, or Corso Reno, from the Piazza. The street known as Via Bocca-leone or Tombesi could not have existed in 1437, since it would have cut through the property described in the deed. The house must have had frontages of about 100 metres east and west, and about 70 metres north and south. It is described in a verse epistle from Girolamo Castello to Guarino (G., *Epistolario* 2. Ep. 778A): "In the middle of the city there is a house that can be seen from far off; they call it the Council of Pheobus and the daughters of Pieria. As it grows, it looks up on the one side to the august palaces of the ruler, and on the other the urban prae-tor touches its atrium." The main entrance was therefore from the west, and it was one of the grander dwellings in the city. Originally the town house of the aristocratic Boiardi, it cost Guarino 3,500 lire marchesane, as we know from a document (Archivio di Stato di Modena. Registro dei mandati 1436-1438) dated April 8, 1437, which conferred citizenship on Guarino and granted him the privilege of paying only 200 lire march-esane in taxes: "Et pertanto sapiando nui che luy ha comprato in quest nostra citade de Ferrara, per usare la civilita sua quesita, la casa di nobili di Boiardi per libre IIIm Vc ..." The same document authorizes a grant of 500 lire from Niccolò III towards the purchase price. This suggests that Guarino was in favor with the marquis, and that Niccolò realized the importance of his presence in the city. It is impossible to say how many *contubernales* the house could accommodate, but it was

Post reditum prandere datur, gula dicere possit
Quod modicum, natura satis. Post prandia rursus   600
Lectio codicibus miscetur Graia Latinis
Ac variae sub te certantur iudice lites,
Donec in occiduum declinet Cynthius axem.
Haec inter cunctis late tua ianua tota
Luce patet, notae deservit vespera turbae   605
Quam tecum domus una tenet. Non temporis illic
Incassum momenta volant: saepe exule somno
Ad pingues longa vigilamus nocte lucernas
Aetheriis nostros astris mirantibus ignes.
Agmine tu medio sublimis vel nova dictas   610
Vel dictata iteras non intellecta paratus
Quaesiti decies aenigmata solvere nodi.

perhaps more than the twelve at any given time that was the usual allowance for public professors who took private students.

592. *Nicoleos*: Leonello's son, Niccolò, was born in 1438. We do not know when Guarino took charge of his education, but he was his teacher in 1450 (*Epistolario* 2. Ep. 380. 4), and Niccolò had a "repedidore" in 1452, i.e. a *repetitor* or assistant tutor who drilled students and helped them with their assignments. This man's name was Alberto Maiolino (See G. Pardi, *Borso d'Este* 47, in *Studi Storici* 15 [1906]), but there is no indication that he had taken over from Guarino, however much the latter was in disfavor with Borso (see n. on 390-92). On the other hand, Borso was shrewd enough to realize that Guarino, who had exercized such power over Leonello and loved him like a father, would almost certainly have favored Niccolò over himself for the marquisate, if the lad had been old enough to contend for it. Despite his promise to the dying Leonello to secure power eventually for Niccolò, Borso had no intention of relinquishing it. He spoiled Niccolò only to neutralize his threat, and part of his

a midday meal is served, which a hearty appetite might term light, but nature sufficient. When the meal is over, different Latin and Greek texts are again read, and various cases are argued, with you acting as judge, until Cynthius sinks on his western axis. Meanwhile, during the hours of daylight your door is wide open to all; the evening is given over to the familiar group of students who live with you in your home. There not a fleeting moment is lost: often we banish sleep and stay awake by the oily lamps until well into the night, as the stars in heaven marvel at our fires. You sit high up in the middle of the group, and either lecture on new material or go over old lessons that have not been understood, prepared to unravel the mysteries of a puzzle that has been tackled ten times over.

precautions may have been to keep Guarino from having too much to do with him. Borso's apprehensions proved sound, because even as he lay dying, Niccolò and his *Veleschi* (supporters who rallied to his emblem, a sail) were disputing the succession with Ercole (see Gardner, *Dukes and Poets in Ferrara* 118-19) and in 1476 Niccolò tried again, this time bloodily, to wrest power from Ercole (see Gundersheimer, *Ferrara* 80-83).

595. *Pellaeum iuvenem*: Alexander the Great, whose Macedonian capital was Pella. The implied comparison of Niccolò di Leonello to Alexander might not have pleased Borso, if he ever saw these lines (see n. on 592).

598. *Stagira*: Birthplace of Alexander's tutor, Aristotle. Plutarch, *Alexander* 7 and Diogenes Laertius, 5. 4 both agree that it was Alexander himself who restored the city.

599-60: Cf. Vergil, *Geo.* 3. 527, where moderation in eating is praised.

Sed minus est, cultas abs te quod discimus artes,
Plus, quod virtutes. Procul hinc malesuada libido,
Improba rixa procul. Sic te sub praeside cuncti   615
Degimus aeditumos templis ut degere fas est:
Tanta quies animis, ea casti cura pudoris!
Vidi ego non unum, quem perditus ante ferebat
Transversum luxus, postquam tua limina dextris
Contigit auspiciis, mores posuisse sinistros.   620

603. *Cynthius*: i.e. Apollo, as the sun (by a late confusion of
his functions with those of Helios), and, by extension, Guarino, who is
identified in this poem with the sun (see n. on 920-40). Like the sun,
even Guarino must eventually sink to his well-earned rest.

606-09: Cf. *Elegia ad Galeottum Narniensem* (Eleg. 2. 4; Kom-
bol, 112-18) 57-62: "We shared the same room, and one table always
provided the food we shared. Quite often the two of us were up until
midnight, although our weary eyes longed for the gift of sleep. Often,
when we were enjoying lying in our warm beds, we rose before dawn at
three in the morning."

614. *libido*: See the discussion of Ianus' sexuality in my Introduc-
tion, 39-42.

615. *rixa*: For Ianus' dislike of Lodovico Carbone and Basino da
Parma, see my Introduction, 34-37.

621: Polemon of Athens (d. 270 B.C.) was head of the Academy
from the death of Xenocrates (c. 313 B.C.), who had converted Polemon
from a life of dissolution (Diogenes Laertius, 4. 17).

623-34: These sententious lines are more medieval than humanis-
tic in tone and style. Each is a close hexameter, embodying a striking
single thought of a general nature. The first, an echo of Matthew 7. 20,
balances and says much the same as the second, which may be based on
John 15. 1-5 or Vergil, *Geo.* 1. 47-49. This doubling, and other devices
with *sententiae* (properly, general moralizings introducing or cinching
a number of illustrative *exempla*) are discussed in, e.g., Geoffrey of

But it is less important that we learn the graceful arts from you than that we learn virtue. Far from this place is the lust that leads us to no good, far away is mischievous squabbling. With you in charge, we all live the proper lives of church sacristans: so deep is our peace of mind, so much so we value chastity. I myself have seen more than one fellow, once led astray by profligacy and self-indulgence, lay aside his bad habits, after having had the good luck to reach your door, even as they say

Vinsauf's *Poetria Nova*: see *Three Medieval Rhetorical Arts* ed. J. J. Murphy, 37-38.

626-27. *Daunia ... Terra*: i.e. Apulia, said to have been once ruled by Daunus, father (or ancestor) of Turnus, and father-in-law of Diomedes (Vergil, *Aen.* 10. 616 and 688).

628. *Cyrene*: The chief town of a province in Libya by that name, famous as the birthplace of Callimachus, Eratosthenes, and Aristippus (Pliny, *N.H.* 5. 5. 5; Pomponius Mela 1. 8. 2.)

630-31: Possibly the punctuation should be a comma after *Bar-barus*, thus making *duplex gloria* refer to Francesco and Ermolao Barbaro, uncle and nephew. Ermolao, a student of Guarino's 1421-24, and later Bishop of Treviso and Verona, was just as important as Francesco.

631. *Barbarus*: Francesco Barbaro (1390-1454), the life-long friend of Guarino, and a student of his for Greek at Venice 1414-1416. He translated Plutarch's *Aristides* and *Cimon*, wrote a funeral oration on Giannino Corradini and a laudation of Perugio Guidaloti on the latter's graduation at the University of Padua, and (in 1416) his most famous work, *De re uxoria*, a treatise on marriage, the second book of which is about the education of children. The standard edition of *De re uxoria* is by Attilio Gnesotto in *Atti e Memorie della Reale Accademia di Scienze e Lettere di Padova* 32 (1915). Barbaro's prime interest in life, however, was politics. He had a long career in the service of Venice, finally becoming Procurator of San Marco, the most prestigious position after that of Doge.

Ut quondam audito Polemona Xenocrate dicunt
Corruptum subito vitae mutasse tenorem.
Scilicet a fructu felix agnoscitur arbos:
Laeta probat messis, quam pingui creverit arvo.
Haud aliter qualis tua sit doctrina patescit   625
Discipulis, Guarine, tuis. Non Daunia tantos
Olim terra viros nec dives Ionia fudit
Siccave Cyrene vel Nilo interflua tellus,
Quantos ut latum sparsisti solus in orbem.
Inde duplex Venetae processit gloria gentis,   630
Barbarus et plectro celeber Leonardus eburno.
Inde Iovis genitus de stirpe Georgius alti
Cretaea, simili pavit quem lacte sub Ida
Digna polo nutrix et apes non rauca secutae
Cymbala purpureis mel congessere labellis.   635
Hinc veterum nulli cedens Castellus avorum
Martius et, Latiae nunc iam lux altera linguae,
Martius, undisono quem Narnia monte creavit,
Martius, aeternum Iani sub pectore nomen.
Hinc Aganippeo Tobias fonte rigatus: 640
Sed Titus hac ipsa longe perfusior unda,
Seu lituo pugnas cithara seu cantet amores

Leonardus: Leonardo Giustinian (1388-1446), scion of an old and wealthy Venetian family, was a statesman, poet, musician, and scholar. A student of Guarino's with Barbaro, he translated Plutarch's *Cimon* (as did Barbaro), *Lucullus*, and *Phocion* into Latin, but his fame today rests on his popular songs in the Venetian dialect, for which he also wrote music. His public career was long and varied. In 1428 he became

Polemon once suddenly changed the evil course of his life
after listening to Xenocrates. The healthy tree, of course, is known by its fruits: the
fertile crop is proof of the rich soil from which it grew. In like
manner, Guarino, the quality of your teaching is apparent
in your students. Not the land of Daunus, not rich Ionia or
parched Cyrene or the land through which the Nile flows,
ever produced such great men as you have scattered through
the wide world. From your teaching sprang the twin pride of
the Venetian race, Barbaro and Leonardo, the latter famous
for his ivory plectrum. From it comes George, a scion of
lofty Jupiter's Cretan stock, whom a nurse worthy of heaven
fed under Mount Ida with the same divine milk, and on
whose rosy lips bees that chased no raucous cymbals have
piled honey. From your teaching rose Castello, the equal of
any of his ancient forebears, and Marzio, already the second
light of the Latin language, Marzio, whom Narni created by
the mountain where the waves resound, Marzio, whose name
will live forever in Ianus' heart. From it rose Tobia, washed
in the fount of Aganippe: but Tito is much deeper laved
in this very same water, whether he sings of war with his
clarion or of love on his lute, interweaving

one of the Council of Ten, and he ended his career as Procurator of San
Marco.
    632-35: Almost certainly a reference to George of Trebizond (1396-
1484), who was born in Crete, but adopted the style Trapezuntius,
because his family emigrated from Trebizond as one of the earliest set
of refugees from Turkish aggression (for the attraction and importance
of Crete for refugees, see D.J. Geanakoplos, *Byzantine East and Latin*

Intexens Paphiae laurum Parnasida myrto.
Clarus et historia Facius nec dignus iniquis
Iam Petrus podagris et acerbo Lamola leto.   645
Multi praeterea, quorum si nomina quaeram,
Promptius enumerem veris tibi gramina fetus
Autumni brumae nimbos aestatis aristas,
Astra quot in caelo, pelagi quot in aequore conchae.
Quos inter nec me venientia saecla tacebunt: 650

West [Oxford, 1966, repr. Archon Books, 1976] 140-42). The myth
Ianus uses is that of the Cretan Zeus. Cronos swallowed all his children
one by one, but Rhea saved the youngest by feeding Cronos a stone
wrapped in a blanket, and spiriting Zeus away to a cave on Mt. Ida
(or Dicte) in Crete. There he was suckled by the goat Amalthea, and
protected by the Curetes, who covered the infant's cries by clashing
cymbals. Bees, attracted by the noise, provided honey (see Vergil, *Aen.*
12. 412 and *Geo.* 4. 64; Ovid, *Metamorphoses* 4. 293 and *Fasti* 4.
207). Ianus obviously respected George, but Guarino, who was George's
teacher for only short periods in 1416 and 1417, nursed a feud with him
for over thirty years (G., *Epistolario* I. Esp. 197. 36-40 and Ep. 245.
54-55; 2. Epp. 707 and 840).
    636. *Castellus*: Girolamo di Lodovico Castello (d. before 1485)
is named by Carbone as one of Guarino's best students, "equally dis-
tinguished in eloquence, philosophy, and medicine." His skill in Greek
is mentioned in a letter of 1450 from Girolamo Guarini to Bartolomeo
Fazio (G., *Epistolario* 3. 449; for other notices, *Id.* 3. 381-82). He took
his doctorate in medicine at Ferrara in 1445, and taught there from
1446. He was particulary friendly with Basinio da Parma in the years
1447-1450. Two books of Basinio's *Meleagris* are dedicated to him.
    637. *Martius*: Galeotto Marzio da Narni (1426-?1497), Guarino's
student 1447-1449, and Ianus; closest friend at school. In lines 63-
66 of an elegy to him (see n. on 606-09), written when they were
both at Padua in 1454, Ianus recalls: "I had no one to trust, no one

the laurel of Parnassus with the myrtle of Paphos. Another is Fazio the famous historian and Pietro, undeserving of the iniquitous gout, and Lamola, undeserving of a bitter death. And many others, whose names would be less easy for me to list, if I searched them out, than the grasses of spring, the fruits of autumn, the clouds of winter, the ears of corn in summer, and all the stars in the sky and the shells in the sea. And among them, ages to come will not fail to mention me:

who was willing to look after me, but you. You took the place of uncle and brother, and were like a father and mother to me." Galeotto started his career as a soldier, and was already widely traveled and not unversed in Latin poetry when he met the Pannonian in his first year at Ferrara. He had a fine physique (which the later-consumptive Ianus probably did not), but Ianus professed to admire his mind even more (30-42); he helped Ianus to handle metre (69-70) and dazzled him with his poetic talents (71-90) and sturdy morality (92-108). Ianus never quite lost his hero-worship, even when in later years Galeotto turned out to be more of a self-seeker than a true friend. After teaching humanities at Padua for several years after 1449, he studied medicine there, eventually marrying the daughter of his professor, Bartolomeo da Montegnana. In 1461 he spent a few months in Hungary, and came again 1465-1472, seeking Ianus' help and gifts. Birnbaum (p. 62) says the friendship gradually cooled, Ianus becoming a little patronizing as Galeotto looked upon him more and more as a useful resource. When Ianus was disgraced in 1472, Galeotto did nothing to help him, and withdrew to Bologna. In 1477, Matthias invited him back to Buda, where Galeotto had a successful career as a courtier until 1480. He left briefly, but was back again in late 1481 or early 1482. When the king died in 1490, Galeotto is thought to have taken service with Charles VIII of France. The place and date of his death are uncertain.

Primus ego Eridani patrium de gurgite ad Histrum
Mnemonidas Phoebo ducam comitante sorores;
Primus Nysaeos referam tibi, Drave, corymbos
Ac viridi in ripa centum sublime columnis
Constituam templum: media, Guarine, sedebis   655
Aureus in camera picto super Iridis arcu
Insistens lunam radiis et solis amictus,
Ut nec Phidiacum miretur Pisa Tonantem
Nec Rhodos immani surgentem mole colosson.
Stabunt et vivis spirantia signa figuris: 66o
Idaeam assimilans coniunx Thaddaea parentem,
Bis senae iuxta facies, tua sancta propago
Caelicolum totidem vultus imitata serenos.
Omnis ibi Europae sacris operata iuventus

Galeotto wrote a number of polemical letters, but his main literary
work was a collection of Matthias deeds and witticisms, *De egregie sapi-
enter iocose dictis ac factis regis Mathiae* (1458), which he presented
at court in 1485. His scientific work, *De incognitis vulgo* (1477) stirred
the wrath of the Inquisition at Venice, a sure sign that it contained
heterodox and therefore stimulating views.

640. *Tobias*: The Veronese Tobia dal Borgo, whose birth date
is unknown and who seems to have died about 1448 before finishing
work on the Rimini chronicle, is recorded to have been at Ferrara in
1432 and again in 1437, in which year he was a law student. In 1446
Guarino addressed to him an important letter (*Epistolario* 2, Ep. 796)
on the way history should be written (translated and discussed by I.
Thomson in *Explorations in the Renaissance* 3 [1976]). After being
at the University of Pavia 1438-41, he returned to Verona, where he
probably set up as a private master. In 1445 or 1446 he was hired as
a historiographer by Sigismondo Malatesta to revise and up-date the
Rimini chronicle, but he completed very little of it, perhaps because of
ill health. He was dead by May 29, 1451. Carbone describes him as a
very charming poet, who wrote the deeds of Sigismondo; which leads
one to speculate that an epic poem was in the making. If so, it has not
survived.

I shall be the first to take the daughters of Mnemosyne and their companion, Phoebus, from the waters of Eridanus to my native Hister; I shall be the first to bring back to you, Dravus, the ivy berries of Nysa, and to build on your green banks a lofty temple with a hundred columns: you, Guarino, will sit in gold in the middle of a room, with Iris' rainbow painted overhead, and you with your feet on the moon and clothed with the rays of the sun, such that Pisa will cease to marvel at Phidias' Thunderer, and Rhodes at its colossus rising in gigantic bulk. There will be standing statues of life-like realism: your wife, Tadea, looking like the Idaean mother, and nearby, twelve figures representing your sacred family, with serene expressions like the twelve inhabitants of heaven. All the youth of Europe will be there making sacrifice,

641. *Titus*: Tito Vespasiano Strozzi (1424-1505), the scion of a powerful Ferrarese family, he served as a court official under Borso, Ercole, and Alfonso I, earning great unpopularity from the stiff financial and other burdens his duties compelled him to lay on the people. Posterity, however, remembers him for his exquisite Latin eclogues and elegies.

643. *larum ... myrto*: The laurel was sacred to Apollo, the myrtle to Venus. For the intertwining image, see Vergil, *Ecl.* 8. 13.

644. *Facius*: Bartolomeo Fazio (1400-1457) studied under Guarino at Verona 1420-1426, after which he became tutor until 1429 of the children of Doge Francesco Foscari. Later, after a spell in Florence, he taught the children of Raffaele Adorno, later Doge of Genoa. From 1443 onwards he was Genoese ambassador to Naples. His history *De*

Suspendet tibi dona tholo, certabit et omnis   665
Non caestu crudo pubes nitidave palaestra,
Sed fidibus tentis et suave crepantibus hymnis;
Victores apio crinem cingentur amaro.
Ipse coronatus vittis et fulgidus ostro
Inter psallentes candenti in veste ministros   670
Pontificis ritu fumos adolebo Sabaeos.
Interea has tenerae tibi me sacrare iuventae
Primitias triplici iubet haerens Gratia nexu,
Gratia Lethaeos nunquam potura liquores.

viris illustribus, covering the last years of the fourteenth century to the middle of his own, and an account of the reign of Alfonso I of Naples, are his best known works.

645. *Petrus*: Perhaps Pietro del Monte, a student of Guarino's at Venice and Verona.

Lamola: Giovanni Lamola (1410-1449) studied under Guarino at Verona 1422-24 and again for a few months in 1425, before transferring to Vittorino's school at Mantua, where he stayed until the end of the school year in 1426. He also studied with Barzizza at Milan 1427-1429, and with Filelfo at Florence 1429-1430, after which he became Guarino's collaborator at Ferrara until May, 1433. In 1432 he and Guarino completed an edition of all the works attributed to Julius Caesar. Though greatly loved and much respected as a scholar by his contemporaries, he seems to have had a critical rather than a creative mind, and left no enduring original writing.

647: Cf. Vergil, *Geo.* 2. 105.

650-55: Modelled on Vergil, *Geo.* 3. 10-16.

653. *Nysaeos*: i.e. pertaining to Dionysus (Bacchus), whose nurse was said to have been the nymph Nysa, so called from the mysterious Mt. Nysa on which she raised him (Servius, *ad Ecl.* 6. 15). Nysa was also the name of a city in Caria on the slopes of Mt. Messogis (Pliny, *N.H.* 5. 29. 29), or of a city in Palestine (Pliny, *N.H.* 5. 18. 16), or of a city in India on Mt. Meros, said to have been

and hanging up offerings to you in the round shrine. All the young men will contend, not with the crude cestus or on the glistening wrestling-ground, but with taut strings and sweet-sounding hymns; the winners will be crowned with bitter ivy. I myself, garlanded with fillets and blazing in purple, amid acolytes robed in white and playing stringed instruments, shall burn Sheban incense, like a priest. Meanwhile, the Grace that clings to me with triple bond, the Grace that will never drink the waters of Lethe, bids me consecrate to you these first fruits of tender youth.

the birthplace of Bacchus (alluded to in Vergil, *Aen.* 6. 805-06: see the note *ad loc.* in the Heyne-Wagner ed.) Just as Bacchus brought foreign, new ecstasies to Greece, so Ianus will take similar ones to his native parts.

657. *radiis ...amictus*: The iconography is adapted from *Revelation of St. John the Divine* 12. 1: "and there appeared a great wonder in Heaven: a woman clothed with the sun, and the moon under her feet, and upon her head a crown of twelve stars." The twelve stars became statues of Guarino's children (662-63). The image of the rainbow in 656 is borrowed from *Revelation* 10. 1. Ianus identifies Guarino with the sun (and Apollo), and sees him as the agent and distributor of light, i.e. knowledge and civilization. See also n. 920-40.

658: The statue of Zeus at Olympia by the fifth-century B.C. sculptor, Phidias, was coutned one of the Seven Wonders of the ancient world (Pliny, *N.H.* 34. 8. 19; Cicero, *Tusculans* 1. 15. 34).

659. *colosson*: The gigantic statue of Helios (the Sun) that straddled the harbor entrance at Rhodes (Pliny, *N.H.* 34. 7. 18) was also one of the seven ancient wonders. The implication is obvious: Ianus considers Guarino, his Sun, a wonder, perhaps *the* wonder, of his modern world.

660: Cf. Vergil, *Geo.* 3. 34.

661: *Idaeam ...parentem*: Cybele, worshiped on Mt. Ida in Phrygia, said to be the mother of the gods in Vergil, *Aen.* 10. 252 and Ovid,

Tempus erit, cum iam maturis viribus audax   675
Sanguineas acies et Martia bella tonabo
Ioannis magni, quantis modo caedibus acres
Turcorum obruerit populos, quibus ille profundas
Aequarit valles cumulis; scit saepe cruentus
Hebrus et albentes etiam nunc ossibus agri   680
Paeoniae ac mediis Rhodope calcata pruinis:
Nunc te, qua possum, tenui modulabor avena.

Fasti 4. 182. As "house mother" to the students in Guarino's boarding school, she would in that sense be mother of gods (cf. n. on Prologue 30). She is, of course, also the mother of Guarino's god-like children.

Thaddea: Guarino married Tadea Zendrata, daughter of a prosperous Veronese family, on December 27, 1418 (marriage document published in L. N. Cittadella, *I Guarini* [Bologna, 1870] 25-27). Already forty-four, he went on to sire thirteen children (see n. on 662). The money and property at Val Policella he acquired with her dowry, and the help she gave in running Guarino's *contubernium* were, I believe, the turning points in his career. He rarely mentions her, but always with affection and respect. Her last child was born in 1438, and the last mention of her is in *Epistolario* 2. Ep. 778 of 1446. Carbone says she predeceased her husband, as does Ianus in the epitaph he wrote for her (Epigr. 1. 135; Kombol, 184): "Here buried lies Tadea, wife of the great Guarino; she went gladly before her husband, who will be late to follow her. No marble will pride itself on such a great name. She out-did Pallas in her arts, and Rhea in her offspring." By "arts" he means the domestic ones; Tadea was not an educated woman.

662: In *Epistolario* 2. Ep. 831. 25, Guarino stated in 1450 that he had twelve children. In the funeral speech, however, Carbone says there were seven males and six females, but this includes a child who dies in 1441. Guarino's figure twelve refers only to those still alive in 1450. Sabbadini's claim (G., *Epistolario* 3. 435) that there had been

The time will come when, emboldened by mature strength, I shall speak in ringing tones of the bloody battle lines and warlike exploits of the great John, of the immense slaughter with which he lately crushed the Turks, and filled deep valleys with the piles of their dead; the oft-bloodied Hebrus knows of it, as do the fields of Paeonia, still white with bones, and Rhodope, trampled amid the frosts: for now, with what powers I possess, I shall sing of you on the slender reed.

fourteen children in all is, I think, incorrect: the baby Esopo mentioned in *Epistolario* 1. Ep. 231. 48 is surely the same as Agostino. He had two names, but was always referred to as Agostino, just as Manuel had another name, Ambrogio (*Epistolario* 1. Ep. 288. 53-54), but was always called Manuel.

666: Cf. Vergil, *Geo.* 1. 343 and 3. 20. In the second of these passages the youth contend *with* the cestus.

668: *apio*: Parsley was used for chaplets of all kinds in antiquity (Vergil, *Ecl.* 6. 68; Horace, *Od.* 4. 11. 3 etc.), but especially for victors at the Nemean and Isthmian Games.

673. *triplici*: The Graces were usually given as three in number.

675: Cf. Vergil, *Geo.* 3. 46-47. Ianus seems to have projected the development of his own poetical genius as roughly corresponding to that of Vergil: shorter poems in his youth (his epigrams corresponding to Vergil's *Eclogues*), a more ambitious and sustained poem as his strength increased (the *Panegyricus* corresponding to Vergil's *Georgics*), and the promised epic on Hunyadi (for whom see n. on 677) corresponding to the *Aeneid*. Unfortunately, the epic was never written, either because Ianus did not live long enough or he lost interest in the idea. He could hardly have had a better subject than Hunyadi, whose wars against the Turks had made him the hero not only of Hungary but of the Slavic world, where he was celebrated in many folk-poems: see Tvrtko Čubelić, *Epske Naradne Pjesme* (6th. ed. Zagreb, 1970) 71, where the most famous of

Otia forte tibi si quando parva legendi
Festave lux annive quies consueta remisit,
Cetera dum solos discurrit turba per agros   685
Messe perusta genas pressive immunda racemis,

679 stet *A*

these poems is listed as *Zenidba Sibinjanin Janka* (about his wedding).
One may speculate on several reasons why the Latin epic was never
written: the gradual divergence about 1452 of Vitéz, who favored a cen-
tralized administration, from Hunyadi, who supported the prerogatives
of the feudal nobility; the possibility of offending Matthias Corvinus,
whose military skills became established in the 1460's, by writing about
Hunyadi rather than his son; or even a loss of interest in Hunyadi be-
cause of a gradual disenchantment with his son. But the real reason
may have been Ianus' aversion to war (see n. on 912), and a feeling
that he could not sustain the inspiration necessary for an epic.

677. *Iohannis*: János Hunyadi (c. 1387-1456), the son of a Vlach
magnate, began his spectacular rise to fame in the service of Sigismund
I of Luxemburg, king of Hungary from 1387, who became Holy Ro-
man Emperor 1411-1437. His successor, Albert of Hapsburg, entrusted
Hunyadi with a frontier defence against the Turks (1437-1438), which
established his military reputation. When Albert died in 1439, Hun-
yadi and the lesser nobility supported Wladislas III of Poland in his
claim to the throne of Hungary against the prince who later (1444)
was recognized as Ladislas V. Wladislas of Poland became king of Hun-
gary in 1440 as Wladislas I Jagiello, thus freeing Hunyadi to prosecute
the resistance to the Turks, who had been pressing again on North-
ern Serbia and by 1439 possessed all of it except the town of Novo
Brdo, forcing the Despot Djuradj Branković to take refuge in Hun-
gary. Hunyadi defeated a Turkish general at Hermannstadt in 1442,
and followed this up with a major victory over Sultan Murad II at
Nish on November 3, 1443. He then took Sofia (near the Rhodope
mountain range), won another battle in the valley of the River Maritza
(Hebrus), and threatened Constantinople, whose emperor was a vassal

If perchance a feast day or the year's traditional season
of rest ever allow you a short spell of leisure to read, while
the rest of the crowd goes scurrying off through the lonely
fields, with cheeks bronzed by the harvest sun and stained
from the wine press,

of the Sultan. Branković was restored to his domain, and Turkish power
was broken, temporarily, in the Balkans. Undoubtedly, this was the
"recent" campaign Ianus is referring to.

A ten-year truce was concluded with the Turks, but against Hun-
yadi's advice, Wladislas broke it, and was defeated and killed at Varna
on November 10, 1444. Before the battle, Hunyadi had withdrawn his
forces to Hungary. The Diet recognized Ladislas V, at that time a pris-
oner of the emperor Frederick III, and meantime, in 1446, named Hun-
yadi regent, a duty he discharged with the help of Vitéz, for whom he
had secured the lucrative bishopric of Várad in 1445. In 1448 Hunyadi
resumed the struggle against the Turks, but was defeated at Kosovo
on October 17 and imprisoned for a time by Branković, who forced
him to acquiesce in the restoration of Ladislas. Hunyadi resigned when
Ladislas returned in 1452, but was made commander-in-chief in 1453,
when Sultan Mohammed II (the Conquerer) took Constantinople, thus
establishing a secure European base for further aggression. In 1454 Mo-
hammed invaded Serbia, and had control of most of it by 1455. In 1456
Hunyadi had his greatest military success when he raised the siege of
Belgrade and drove the Turks back to Constantinople, thus securing
the safety of Hungary for the next seventy years. Three weeks later,
he died, probably of plague, on August 11. In 1458 his son Matthias
Corvinus became king, largely through the efforts of Vitéz.

679: Cf. Statius, *Achilleis* 1. 12, *scit Dircaeus ager.*

681: Paeonia was the region roughly corresponding to modern
Macedonia; Rhodope is the mountain range between modern Greece
and Bulgaria.

682: Note the sudden quietening as Ianus reverts to a more modest,
pastoral tone. Vergil makes similar transitions at *Geo.* 3. 48-49 and 4.
562-63.

Tu condis transfersve aliquid, quod prosit in usus
Communes et te nemori procul inserat aevo,
Aut, vernum ad solem cum garrit aprica senectus
Vel mediis brumae tenebris Caprive diebus   690
Cum stertunt reliqui, cella tu clausus in alta
Adrodis digitos pluteum vel caedis et atro
Paulatim niveam signas humore papyrum,
Unde licet tanto curarum pondere pressus
Plura secuturis animi monumenta dedisti   695
Quam qui secreta vacui spatiantur in umbra.
Illa docent structis adnectere nomina verbis,
Haec vocum explanant proprias ex ordine vires;
Iungis ad haec, magni fuerit quae vita Platonis,
Blandus adulator rigido quid distet amico.   700
Missa nec in levibus iuvenatur epistola nugis,
Sed semper studiis aliquid vel moribus affert.
    Haec etiam possim multorum aequare libellis,
Ouae seris in cathedra vel si qua ex tempore profers.
Sin meditata sonas, funduntur pectore ab uno   705
Isocratis numeri Xenophontis gratia torrens
Isaei cultus Lysiae Demosthenis ardor,
Qualem te ingenuas laudantem audivimus artes,

702 amoribus A

686. *immunda*: Cf. Vergil, *Geo.* 2. 8, where Bacchus' legs are stained with the new must. Contrast the frenzied self-indulgence of the holiday-makers with the calm dedication of Guarino to scholarship.

you compose or translate something that will be of use and benefit to all, and make you remembered for long ages to come; or when old men gossip as they bask in the spring sunshine, or others are snoring in the middle of a deep winter's night or in the dog days of summer, you shut yourself up in a lofty room, and bite your nails or strike the bookshelf, and gradually mark the snowy paper with black ink. So despite your many worries, you have given more memorable works to posterity than those who stroll in the cloistered shade with nothing to do. One teaches the rules of grammatical writing, another explains the meanings of words in order; and to these you add an account of great Plato's life, and of the difference between a glib flatterer and a staunch friend. When you send a letter, it does not prattle on about trifles, but always brings something conducive to study or morality.

The seeds you sow when teaching, or your chance remarks, I could also say are worth the books of many men. But if you intone some practiced piece, there pours forth from you alone all the rhythm of Isocrates; the charm of Xenophon, the torrential flow of Isaeus, the polished art of Lysias, and the fire of Demosthenes, as when we heard you praising the liberal arts, when the new

687: Cf. G., *Epistolario* 2. Ep. 796. 241-43 (of his letter to Tobia dal Borgo on the writing of history): " ...the work will please me just as much, because I have devoted as much time through the better part of this holiday season to refreshing my mind as others have given to their games, masquerades, and lusts."

Cum pridem Octobres studiorum exordia nobis
Restituere Idus et misso in dolia musto   710
Garrula solliciti rediere ad scamna comati
(Quis tunc Musarum sacris non ignibus arsit?
Quem tuus Aonio non impulit Euchius oestro?)
Aut qualem rapti nuper te in funere diro
Principis orantem tristis Ferraria sensit.   715

692. Cf. Persius, 1. 106. The actions described are the conse-
quences of frustration, the desperate effort of the creative artist to find
the right word, the perfect expression.
693: A beautiful line. Ianus had learned from Vergil (and Guarino)
the value of simple, clear-cut imagery.
695. *monumenta*: By 1454 Guarino had written, apart from an
enormous number of letters (only some of which have survived, and only
because the best of them were preserved by the recipients and passed
around as models of style), a treatise on the diphthongs (*Epistolario*
1. Ep. 29; 3. 38); a didactic poem on homonymns (see n. on 526);
an abridgement of Chrysoloras' *Erotemata* (*Epistolario* 1. Ep. 95.
41; 3. 76); a Latin grammar (see n. on 371); a lexicon to Servius
(see n. on 698); the first Greek-Latin dictionary by a humanist (see
n. 698); an original life of Plato (see n. on 699); editions of Pliny
the Younger's *Epistles* (*Epistolario* 1. Ep. 141. 25; 3. 100), Pliny
the Elder's *Naturalis Historia* (*Epistolario* 3. 307-308), Aulus Gellius
(*Epistolario* 2. Ep. 631. 3; 3. 307), Julius Caesar (see n. on 645,
Lamola), and possibly, Cornelius Celsus (*Epistolario* 3. 199-200); and
translations of Lucian's *Musca* and *Calumnia* (*Epistolario* 3. 7 and 47),
Herodotus 1. 1-71 (*Epistolario* 3. 45-46), Isocrates' *Ad Nicoclem* and
Ad Demonicum (*Epistolario* 3. 6-7 and 47), parts of Basil's *Exemeron*
(*Epistolario* 3. 356, 420, 423, 433), and many Lives of Plutarch (see n.
on 729-30). In 1454 he was translating Strabo (see n. on 732).
697. *Illa*: The *Regulae* and Chrysoloras' *Erotemata*.
698. *Haec*: The Servius lexicon and the Greek-Latin dictionary.
The former dates from 1420 or earlier (*Epistolario* 1. Ep. 29, which is
its dedicatory letter). Its entries are alphabetically arranged, following

wine had been bottled, and the Ides of October had brought us back to our studies, and the long-haired, nervous students returned to the noisy benches. (Who then did not burn with the sacred fires of the muses? Whom did your Euchius not inspire with Aonian frenzy?) Such, too, was your eloquence when stricken Ferrara heard your oration at the tragic funeral of the prince she had just lost.

the typical scheme Sa Se Si So Su, Sca Sce Sci ..., Spa Spe ..., Sta Ste ...etc. Servius' glosses are given, occasionally varied by Guarino, who also gives the Vergilian reference. (Sabbadini, *La scuola e gli studi di Guarino* 54). Sabbadini (id., 57) deplores the loss of the Greek-Latin lexicon, but I believe it to be extant in "Österreichische Nationalbibliothex Cod. suppl. gr. 45, recently item 37, "Griechisch-lateinisches Wörterbuch des Janus," in *Matthias Corvinus und die Renaissance in Ungarn* (Catalogue of the Schallaburg Exhibition, May 8-November 1, 1982) 157-58.

699. *vita Platonis*: Based on the life of Plato in Diogenes Laertius 3, this biography was written in 1430 and dedicated to the Milanese physician and humanist, Filippo di Giovanni Pellizone. For the list of Platonica it contains, see my article, "Some Notes on the Contents of Guarino's Library," *Renaissance Quarterly* 29. No. 2 (1976) 169-77.

700: Guarino's compendium of Plutarch, *De blanditiis*. The dedication is *Epistolario* 2. Ep. 676, probably of 1437. The compendium was circulating by 1439 (*Epistolario* 3. 331). Garin, *L'Umanesimo* 482, n. 4, incorrectly dates it 1444, this being merely the year in which Francesco Barbaro requested a copy of it (G., *Epistolario* 2. Ep. 790. 8).

708-10: The school year began on October 18, just after the grape harvest, but students would start returning about the 15th (Ides). Customarily, some distinguished professor would deliver a *prolusio* (inaugural address), such as the one Guarino gave in 1442 to mark the reorganization of the university by Leonello (for which see Gundersheimer, *Ferrara* 101). Extracts of the 1442 *prolusio* are published in Garin, *L'Umanesimo* 488-90. Guarino gave another address in 1447, which

Tempore non homines tantummodo luximus illo,
Mite genus: planxere ferae, planxere volucres,
Maesta comas nullis excussit flatibus arbor,
Maesta cavis gemuit plorabile rupibus Echo.
Ipsa dolor tetigit caelestia. Fletibus auctum   720
Vix ripae tenuere Padum nec largius unquam
Gemmea populei lacrimarunt succina trunci.
Orphea ab Elysiis remeasse elementa putabant
Vallibus et nuptae mortem deflere secundam.
    Inachiae vero tibi tanta peritia linguae,   725
Ut sacer haud alio traduci interprete malit
Plutarchus chartis nec plus se agnoscit in ullis
Ambiguus, patrione magis sermone nitescat,
Sive rudimentis pueriles instruit annos,
Sive altera ducum committit facta priorum.

is published by Sabbadini in *Biblioteca delle scuole italiane* 7 (1897)
33-37. This was the first formal lecture by Guarino that Ianus heard.
    713. *Euchius*: A title of Bacchus, from the ritual cry *eu-hai* or
eu-hoi.
    714. *funere diro*: This phrase is often used in Latin poetry to
signify a premature death (cf. Vergil, *Ecl.* 5. 20; *Aen.* 6. 429; *Geo.* 3.
263). Leonello died, probably of a stroke, on October 1, 1450. Guarino
gave the funeral oration, which is extant in many codices (*Epistolario*
3. 424).
    716-24: Cf. Ovid, *Metamorphoses* 10. 1-85 and 11. 1-66 (Orpheus
and Eurydice).
    717. *mite genus*: The colon Juhasz places after *genus*, making this
phrase refer to *humans*, creates an effective contrast between the mourn-
ing of men and that of wild nature, and points Ianus' neat reversal of
durum genus, used of humans at Vergil, *Geo.* 1. 63 and Ovid, *Meta-
morphoses* 1. 414. For the ritual lament of nature after a premature
death, see Vergil, *Ecl.* 5. 20-33.

We, the gentle race of humans, were not the only mourn-
ers on that occasion: the wild beasts lamented, the birds
lamented, the trees in sorrow shook off their leaves, though
no breezes blew, and sad Echo heaved a piteous sigh from
her caves in the rocks. Grief reached the very heavens.
Flooded with tears, the Po almost overflowed its banks,
and never did the poplars more copiously weep their am-
ber gems. Nature thought that Orpheus had returned from
the vales of Elysium, and was bewailing the second death
of his wife.
    In truth, your skill in the language of Inachus is so great
that sacred Plutarch prefers no other translator, nor does he
recognize himself more in any other writings. Whether he
is teaching young children their first lessons, or comparing
and contrasting the deeds of ancient leaders, he wonders
whether he shines to better effect in his own language or in
your translation.

722: Cf. Vergil, *Ecl.* 8. 55 (tamarisks sweating amber) and 6.
62-63 (Phaethon's sisters turned to alder trees).
    723. *Orphea*: For the mourning of Eurydice a second time by
Orpheus, see Vergil, *Geo.* 3. 504-26.
    725. *Inachiae*: i.e., Greek, cf. Vergil, *Geo.* 3. 153. Inachus was
the legendary first king of Argos. His name evokes the ancient language
rather than the demotic which Guarino also knew.
    peritia: Guarino's translations from Greek are generally accurate,
although sometimes over-literal, but he must have been able to speak it
rapidly and well, since he was chosen as an interpreter at the Council of
Ferrara in 1438. We have only three samples of his original composition.
The first (*Epistolario* 1. Ep. 1), an exercise written at Constantino-
ple to Marcello, another Italian also learning Greek, is over-elaborated
and contains a few minor errors. The second (published by E. Lobel,
"A Greek Letter of Guarino and Other Things," *Bodleian Quarterly*

Iste tamen iuveni dederat praeludia quondam;
Maiorem natu magnus nunc Strabo fatigat
Pontificis summi iussu. Quae gaudia pubis
Pieriae, cum iam supremum rasus ad unguem
Cedron olens minio rutilans et pumice levis   735
Servantis tandem loculos evaserit arcae!
Felices annos, felicia nostra profecto
Tempora, quis tantum duce te cognoscere primis
Auctorem licuit, quo non diffusius alter
Explicat, inclusum Neptunus ut ambiat orbem,   740

Record 5 1926-29, 134-35), was written in 1416 to Leonardo Giustinian
to keep its contents private. Its style is freer, but it is clearly a hasty
composition, with few particles. The third (*Epistolario* 2. Ep. 829),
written in 1450, contains two grammatical blunders and is stylistically
more Latin than Greek.

    729-30: Guarino translated *De liberis educandis* (see n. on 370-77),
and the following Lives of Plutarch: *Flamininus* (see n. on 325-29),
Marcellus, Alexander, Caesar, Coriolanus, Brutus and Dion, all by
1416 (*Epistolario* 1. Ep. 47. 90-05); *Themistocles, Phocion, Eumenes,
Pelopidas, Philopoemen, Breves clarorum hominum inter se contentio-
nes*, and part of *Homer* (for which see Sabbadini, *La scuola e gli studi
di Guarino* 130-31), all by 1419.

    732-33: The translation of Strabo was the last great labor of Guar-
ino's life. After writing a letter (*Epistolario* 2. Ep. 803) congratulating
Nicholas V on his election in 1447, he was taken into the pope's plan to
sponsor translations of all major Greek works into Latin. Sabbadini (*La
scuola e gli studi di Guarino* 126) claims that this did not happen until
1453. Certainly, it was only in March of that year that Guarino sent
the first samples of his work to Rome, but in the covering letter (*Epis-
tolario* 2. Ep. 871) he refers to two letters, the latest dated (as he tells
us) January 13, 1453, in which the Pope's librarian, Giovanni Tortelli,
had discussed the Strabo project. Guarino complains about the Strabo
text from which he had produced his first installments of the transla-
tion, and indicates that he is waiting for a better exemplar from the
Pope, which Tortelli had evidently promised. The Pope's interest must
therefore have begun in 1452 at the latest. We know from a letter of

But he merely gave you practice as a young man; now, by command of the supreme pontiff, great Strabo taxes your mature powers. How the young Pierians will rejoice when, polished to the last detail, fragrant with cedar, glowing with red minium, and smooth from the pumice, he will finally emerge from the desk drawers where he is being kept safe! Happy our years, happy indeed our times, when for the first time it has been possible, with you to guide us, to make the acquaintance of an author, who more fully than any other, tells how Neptune goes round his globe,

Filelfo dated August 3, 1448 (*Philelphi Epistulae* Venetiis, 1502 f. 41) that Guarino was already searching for manuscripts of Strabo; Filelfo admitted that he had once had one, but said that he no longer had it. In another letter of Filelfo (*Epistulae* f. 63v), dated February 26, 1451, he tells Flavio Biondo that Giovanni Aurispa (then Abbot of Pomposa in Ferrarese territory) had a good Strabo, and rumor had it that Guarino had one also. It is not clear whether he means that each had a Strabo, or that they were sharing the use of one. At any rate, Biondo, who was in Ferrara during parts of 1449 and 1450, cites passages from Book 5 of Strabo in Book 3 of his own *Italia Illustrata*, which came out in 1453. B. Nogara, in *Studi e Testi* 48 (1927) 137, raised the question of how Biondo could have used Strabo before Guarino's translation of Books 1-10 came out in 1455. The answer could be because Guarino had given him the information in 1449 or 1450.

Aubrey Diller, first in "The Greek Codices of Palla Strozzi and Guarino Veronese," *Journal of the Warburg and Courtauld Institutes* 24. Nos 304 (1961) 31, and later at more length in *The Textual Tradition of Strabo's Geography* (Hakkert Amsterdam, 1975) 101-103 and 126-129, established that for translating Strabo 1-10 Guarino used a Strabo now in the library of Eton College, which was the first volume of a two-volume set written at Constantinople in 1446 for Ciriaco d'Ancona and brought by him to Italy in 1448. Diller believes that when Ciriaco visited Ferrara in July, 1449, he gave or sold the set to Theodore Gaza, who was teaching Greek there at that time, and that when Gaza went to Rome in late 1449, he left the first volume with Guarino and took the other to Rome, where it was made available to Gregorio Tifernate

Quo de fonte ruant medias dirimentia terras
Aequora, vicinis quaenam discrimina regnis,
Qui passim populi silvae iuga flumina portus
Oppida, quo quaevis fluitet circumsona ponto
Insula, distantum quae sit mensura locorum!   745
O, qui nosse cupis, quicquid de Tethyos undis
Eminet, Alcides quantum vel Liber obivit,
Hoc lege creber opus! Brumales haec tibi somnos
Contrahat et multum membrana absumat olivum!
Quod, si Cecropiis non summus in artibus esses,   750
Primus eras. Reliqui vel te didicere magistro
Aut in discendo tua sunt exempla secuti.

735 laenis *A*
738 queis *A*

(for whom, see Diller, *The Textual Tradition* 130-131), who went on to
translate Books 11-17. It may be that the Pope had ordered a division
of labor between Guarino and Tifernate, in which case Ianus' words
Pontificis summi iussu (in 733) could just as easily apply to any date
between 1449 and 1453. It seems likely that each set about translating
the parts of Strabo they had in the hope of eventually being able to
translate the whole seventeen books, which could then be dedicated to
the Pope.

Guarino was working on the Pope's manuscript by September 12,
1453, because in a letter of that date (*Epistolario* 2. Ep. 878. 1-7)
he refers to it being "more cock-eyed" (*strabonior*) than the defective
manuscript (the Eton Strabo) he had been using. Diller has securely
identified the Pope's manuscript with Vaticanus graecus 174, once the
property of the Russian cardinal, Isidorus Ruthenus, and shown that
its role in Guarino's translation was secondary. Both it and the Eton
Strabo have very corrupt texts. Little wonder that as late as February,
1455, he was begging Tortelli to find him a better exemplar (*Epistolario*
2. Ep. 888. 29-32). The process had been very laborious, as Ianus says
(732-49), and extremely frustrating, as is reflected by Guarino's letters

from what source rush the seas that separate the various lands, what the boundaries are of adjacent countries, what forests, mountains, rivers, ports, towns, and peoples there are in different places, in what sea a given island floats, girt with the sounding waves, and the distances from one place to another. Ah, read this work often, you who desire to know whatever juts out from Tethys' waves, and all the lands visited by Alcides or Liber! Let these pages shorten your hours of sleep in winter, and use up much oil. But you are not only supreme in the arts of Cecrops: you were also the first to get them. The others either learned from your teaching, or in learning them followed your example.

relating to it. Evidently to keep the Pope's interest alive, Guarino kept sending quaternions of the work as it was done over the period 1453-1455 to Tortelli in Rome. Diller believes, correctly I think, that Burney MS 107 in the British Library, which bears the arms of Pius II, is a binding of these collected installments.

Guarino sent the completed version of Books 1-10 to Rome in March, 1455, together with the dedicatory letter, but Nicholas died in the night between March 24 and 25, and probably never even saw the finished product. The often-quoted statement of Vespasiano da Bisticci (*Vite di uomini illustri del secolo* XV ed. P. D'Ancona and E. Aeschlimann Milan, 1951 39 and 313) that Guarino received 1,500 florins for the work savors of romantic fiction: Vespasiano says that 500 florins were paid for each of the parts dealing with Europe, Africa, and Asia; but this cannot be true, because by the time Nicholas died, Guarino had translated only the part dealing with Europe. Certainly by June 22, 1454, he had been bold enough to remind Tortelli that he was not a wealthy man and might not be able to continue his work beyond Book 6 (*Epistolario* 2. Ep. 880. 9-12). It is unlikely that Guarino received any compensation from Nicholas. If he had, he could not easily have rededicated the work to another patron, as we shall see was the case.

Having completed Books 1-10, Guarino went on to translate Books 11-17, ignoring the fact that Tifernate had already translated this part.

Praecepta et multis tribuisti, exordia cunctis
Nec quisquam norat Cadmea elementa Latinus
Ante tuum in Thracas felix iter: At modo nemo   755
Iam Sicyona petat fabicatricemve Corinthon,
En habet in mediis illud, quod quaerit, Etruscis
Italia, ut per te maior sit Graecia rursus
Ac redocere rudes sua dogmata possit Achivos.

Tifernate seems to have had the same idea about translating Books
1-10, to this end enlisting the aid of Francesco Sforza of Milan, who
on September 27, 1456, wrote the Gonzaga family in Mantua, asking
for a loan of a Strabo that was said to be in their library (E. Motta,
in *Bibliofilo* 7. 129). Whatever the outcome of this request, Tifernate
never did a translation of Books 1-10.

For Books 11-17 Guarino used, as Diller has shown, Codex Mos-
quensis graecus 204 (Vladimir 506), now in the State Historical Mus-
esum in Moscow. Once the property of Maximus Margunius, Bishop
of Cythera residing in Venice, it passed form him to a monastery on
Mt. Athos, from which it was brought in 1655 to Moscow by the Rus-
sian monk Arsenius Suchanov for the library of the Holy Synod. The
Moscow Strabo may have been one of two Strabo manuscripts brought
from Constantinople in 1423 by Giovanni Aurispa (*Ambrogii Traversari
Epistulae* ed. L. Mehus and P. Canneto [Florentiae, 1759] 24. 53).

Guarino dedicated all seventeen books of his translation in 1458 to
the wealthy Venetian, Giacomo Antonio Marcello (*Epistolario* 2. Ep.
890), with a large portrait of himself at the beginning (see n. on 822-
24). If anyone paid him for his work, it is more likely to have been
Marcello than the Pope. Marcello had a calligraphic manuscript made
from Guarino's original, and presented it to King René of Naples. In
the first edition of Strabo, by Giovanni Andrea Bussi in 1469, Guarino's
translation is printed for Books 1-10, Tifernate's for Books 11-17.

732. *nunc*: Sabbadini (*La scuola e gli studi di Guarino* 2, n. 3)
argues that since Guarino began to translate Strabo in early 1453, and
Pope Nicholas died in March, 1455, the *Panegyricus* must have been
written sometime between these dates. Since Ianus speaks of the trans-
lation as well advanced, Sabbadini favors the dating 1454.

You gave lessons to many, and their start to all; no Latin knew the first thing about the language of Cadmus before your productive journey to Thrace. Let no one now go to Sicyon or Corinth, famous for its wares. Lo, amid the Etruscans Italy has what she is looking for, to become through you a second and greater Greece, able to reteach the untutored Argives their own lessons.

746. *Tethyos*: Tethys was the consort of the sea deity Oceanus.
751. *Primus*: Strictly, Guarino was not the first humanist to learn Greek; the honor belongs to the pupils of Chrysoloras at Florence, especially Leonardo Bruni. But he was the first to do so in Constantinople.
754. *Cadmea*: Cadmus, the legendary founder of Thebes, was said to have introduced alphabetic writing into Greece (Pliny, *N.H.* 7. 56. 57).
756. *Sicyona ...Corinthon*: Corinth and Sicyon slightly to the N.W. of it were noted centres of art, but neither is evocative of literary learning. Ianus probably chose these names to avoid detracting from the associations of *mediis ...Etruscis* in 757.
759. *rudes*: As D. J. Geanakoplos has shown in *Greek Scholars in Venice* (Cambridge, Mass., 1962) and *Byzantine East and Latin West* (Oxford, 1966) the Greeks who came to Italy before 1453 were anything but untutored.
769. *obscuras ...mentes*: See n. on 535.
775–76: The basic heroic metre was a dactyl (– ◡◡), for which a spondee (– –) could be substituted in any but the fifth foot of the hexameter (consisting of six feet). The iambus was a short syllable followed by a long (◡–). Elegiac metre is exemplified by the hexameter-and-pentameter combination of the *Praefatio* to the *Panegyricus*. Anapaests were scanned ◡◡– (two shorts followed by a long). The favored quantitative metres in the Middle Ages were hexameters and elegiacs, usually without elisions, and sometimes with end or internal rhymes. The humanists also favored hexameters and elegiacs, but also extended the number of other metres used. Guarino's own poetry, a selection of which is published in Sabbadini, *La scuola e gli studi di Guarino* 225–30, is technically sound, but uninspired, with the possible exception of his poem on Lake Garda. It is hard to see why Biondo (*Italia Illustrata* f. K VIv) called Guarino's poem on Pisanello (*Epistolario* 1. Ep. 386) "easily the most famous poem of the century."

Ergo, quae reliquis contingunt singula, solus   760
Iuncta tenes et plena datur tibi summa bonorum.
Sunt, qui scripta animo penetrant aliena sagaci,
Ipsi nulla queunt inopi deducere vena;
In latebris aliqui non sane vilia cudunt,
Sed coram densis nil hiscere coetibus audent;   765
His Latia claris lingua deest Graia facultas
Vel, si forsan adest, non sic, ut vertere possint:
In te concurrunt simul omnia nec prior ullus
Auctorum arcanas penitus deprendere mentes,
Reddere Romana Danaum gravitate leporem   770
Dicere vel nexa pedibus vel voce soluta,
Quae duo vix unquam tribuit caducifer ulli.
Vatibus et cum sit vel simplicis ardua metri
Gloria, tu pariter quaevis in carmina promptus

---

pater (of Jupiter; Ennius, *Annales* 5. 179), *Bacche pater* (of Bac-chus; Horace, *Od.* 3. 3. 13), *pater patriae* (of a great benefactor to one's country; Cicero, *in Pisonem* 3. 6), *pater Aether* (of ether as a creative power in nature; Lucretius, 1. 250), *Zeno pater Stoicorum* (of the founder of a school of philosophy; Cicero, *De nature deorum* 3. 9. 23), and *Isocrates pater eloquentiae* (of a teacher, as a source of inspi-ration and paradigm of excellence; Cicero, *De oratore* 2. 3. 10), its application to a teacher taking a parent's place in the upbringing of a child was made explicit by Juvenal, 7. 208–11, a passage quoted by Carbone in the funeral oration on Guarino: "May the gods grant that the earth lie soft and light upon the shades of our forefathers, may the sweet–scented crocus and eternal spring bloom over their ashes, who desired that their teacher should hold the place of a revered parent." Guarino uses the word *pater* of his own teacher, Marzagaia, in *Epis-tolario* 1. Ep. 133. 43–44: "Me vocitet gnatum per tempora quaeque Guarinum/Quem voco corde meo natus et ore patrem" ("May he whom I, his son, call father with my lips and in my heart, call me, Guarino, his son for all time.") Isotta Nogarola, who was not Guarino's pupil, calls him *Guarine pater* in G., *Epistolario* 2. Ep. 704. 22.

IANUS PANNONIUS ON GUARINUS VERONENSIS

The single qualities, then, that fall to others are yours all together, their total belongs to you. Some there are, who have shrewd and penetrating insights into the writings of others, but cannot produce anything original themselves; others hide themselves away and pound out quite good work, but dare not so much as open their mouths in large meetings; others, who are brilliant Latinists, do not know Greek, or if they do, do not know enough to translate it: all things come together in you, and no one is better at understanding the deepest secrets of authors' minds, at turning a Greecian grace with Roman gravity, or at writing in prose or verse, twin skills that the Staff-bearer hardly ever grants anyone. And although even simple metre is hard to do, and a source of pride to poets, you have equal facility in any kind of verse; now you march in stately

792. *tres Arretini*: Leonard Bruni (1370–1444), Carlo Marsuppini (1398–1453), and Giovanni Tortelli (c. 1400–1466). Bruni began his career as a protégé of Coluccio Salutati at Florence, where he learned Greek from Chrysoloras. He was an apostolic secretary 1405–1415, except for brief service as chancellor of Florence, a post he later held from 1427 until his death. A superb Latinist, he wrote many works, including orations, dialogues, a history of the Florentine people, translations from various works of Plato, Aristotle, Plutarch, and Demosthenes, and a large number of letters (*Epistolarum Libri VIII*. 2 vols. ed. L. Mehus, Florentiae, 1741), as well as Lives of Dante and Petrarch in Italian. Bruni gave Guarino his first career opportunity as a humanist (see n. 325–29).
  Marsuppini was born in Genoa, but his family was from Arezzo. He studied Greek under Guarino at Florence, and Latin under Giovanni Malpaghini, the one-time amanuensis of Petrarch. He was tutor to Lorenzo, brother of Cosimo de' Medici, and lectured at the University of Florence 1441–1444, but most of his life was spent in the service of the republic, finally as chancellor after the death of Bruni. He

Nunc gravis heroo graderis, modo curris iambo,   775
Nunc tristes elegos, modo laeta anapaestica ludis.
Quidam nil aliis tradunt, cum plurima norint,
Seu livore aliquo seu, quae sit norma docendi,
Ignorant fugiunt seu taedia dura laborum.
Haec tua praecipue laus est: Quippe haud tibi credis   780
Te soli genitum, sed toti protinus orbi.
Viventes hinc ore mones, per scripta futuros,
Ut iam uni triplex aeque tibi debeat aetas:

translated parts of Homer into Latin, but most of his writings were official state letters and orations.

Tortelli began his career in medicine, but became a doctor of theology in 1435, in which year he went to Constantinople to perfect his Greek. He entered the service of Pope Nicholas V in 1449, and is usually considered to be the first librarian of the Vatican. He wrote a history of medicine, and an important *Orthographia*, extracts of which are published by Garin, *L'Umanesimo* 425–27. For his contact with Guarino, see n. on 732–33.

Lusci duo: Antonio Loschi (c. 1365–1441), a native of Vicenza, served in the chanceries of Naples, Verona, and Milan, and as an apostolic secretary under Martin V and Eugenius IV. His fame comes mainly from his work at Milan 1388–1420, during which he produced much pro–Visconti literature, commentaries on several orations of Cicero, a translation of Quintilian (from the imperfect medieval text) into Italian, two tragedies (*Achilles* and *Ulixes*). He had two sons, Francesco and Antonio, the latter of whom was Guarino's student in 1433 (*Epistolario* 3. 295). Ianus is probably referring to Antonio and Niccolò, but possibly to Niccolò and Francesco, the second of whom was a famous lawyer (*Epistolario* 3. 416). The Latin *luscus* means "one–eyed," so the phrase *Lusci duo* may be a verbal sally.

Poggius: Gian Francesco Poggio Bracciolini (1380–1459) early became a protégé of Salutati and an intimate of Niccolò Niccoli at Florence. He served as an apostolic secretary 1403–1418 under Boniface IX, John XXIII, and Martin V. During the Council of Constance 1414–1418 he journeyed to various monasteries and brought to light a number of manuscripts of works thought lost or available only in imperfect texts: Cicero's *Pro Caecina*, *Pro Roscio Amerino*, *In Pisonem*, the heroic time, now race in iambics, now move in mournful elegiacs or light-hearted anapaests. Some men know a great deal, but fail to pass it on to others, perhaps because they are somehow jealous, or do not know how to teach, or because they shun its hard, boring work. Your signal glory is your belief that you were not born for yourself alone, but for the whole world. So you teach the living with your voice, and posterity with your writings. Thus three ages are now equally in your debt:

two *Pro Rabirio* and the three *Pro lege agraria*; Columella's *De re rustica*; Lucretius' *De rerum natura*; and a complete Quintilian at St. Gall in 1417, and another one in 1418, a copy of which Guarino requested (*Epistolario* 1. Ep. 83. 20–21). The next year he went to England, but returned in 1423 to Rome, where he resumed work as an apostolic secretary until in 1453 he became chancellor of Florence. His many works include a collection of ancient inscriptions; *De varietate fortunae* in four books, describing the ruins of ancient Rome (1431–1438); *De avaritia* (1428–1429); *De vera nobilitate*, propounding the idea that ability, not birth, is the mark of a person's worth (1440); *De infelicitate principum* (1440); *Contra hypocrita* (1447– 1448); a *Liber facetiarum*, containing a series of witty, sometimes spicy, anecdotes collected in the "Bugiale" (Liars' room), a retiring room for apostolic secretaries (1438–1452); a history of Florence from 1350 down to the Peace of Lodi; and a translation of Xenophon's *Cyropaedia*, which is little more than a turgid paraphrase. He also wrote many orations and letters, often of a polemical nature. On the whole, however, he was popular with his fellow humanists, including Guarino, who taught his son (G., *Epistolario* 2. Ep. 900. 9–13, and Ep. 903. 1–8).

794. *Scipio ... Caesareis*: Refers to the controversy between Poggio and Guarino over the relative merits of Scipio Africanus (symbolic of republicanism) and Julius Caesar (symbolic of monarchy). Guarino, whose prejudices in favor of Caesar and monarchical government were sincere (see n. on 418), entered the lists in March, 1435, with a letter to Leonello d'Este (*Epistolario* 2. Ep. 668), congratulating him on his "recent defence" of Caesar when word had reached Ferrara of a debate at

Praeterita, extinctos veterum quod reddis honores,
Postera, quod calamo, praesens, quod voce laboras,   785
Pro quibus officiis doctorum iure virorum
Te chorus omnis amat, reveretur, laudibus ornat,
Tu pater et princeps, tu censor et arbiter illis,
Si quando dubiis discors sententia pugnat
Iudiciis; fastu nec sic tumet ullus inani,   790
Ut non esse tibi se praedicet ipse secundum.
Tres te Arretini, Lusci duo, Poggius unus
Suspiciunt pariter, quamvis laudatus ab illo
Scipio Caesareis te vindice cesserit actis.
Te Victorinus veneratur et ipse Philelphus,   795
Sfortia qui laxis cecinit modo proelia nervis,

777 norunt A

Florence over "great men and their deeds," and offering to supply schol-
arly ammunition against "anyone who wants a fight." Leonello visited
Rome in April, and heard more about the debate, which was begin-
ning to assume political overtones. In a letter of April 10, 1435, Poggio
had written to Scipione Mainente, impugning Caesar's moral charac-
ter and insisting that Scipio had been at least his equal as a gen-
eral and his superior as a person. When a copy of this letter was
brought to Ferrara, Guarino wrote to Leonello (*Epistolario* 2. Ep.
669), promising to combat the "scourge of Caesar" (*Caesaromastix*),
and insisting that one prince must protect another. The result was
a long attack on Poggio's position (*Epistolario* 2. Ep. 670, contain-
ing 1,142 lines in Sabbadini's text). Based on 113 passages from 17
ancient sources (Vergil, Servius, Pliny the Elder. Horace, Cicero, Ju-
venal, Livy, Plutarch, Plato, Augustine, Macrobius, lsidore, Homer,
Valerius Maximus, Ovid, Lucan, and above all, Suetonius), the let-
ter concentrates on Caesar's military and personal virtues, saying lit-
tle about Scipio. The sources are not always acknowleged, nor cited
in their precise wording: most were probably done from memory,
with slight changes in wording and with the grammar and syntax of

the past, because you are restoring the vanished glories of the ancients; the future, because you work with your pen; the present, because you work with your voice. For these services the whole chorus of scholars rightly loves and respects you, and lavishes praise on you. You are their father and guide, their critic and their arbiter in any difference of opinion or moot point; no one is so puffed up with conceit that he will not admit to being your inferior. The triad from Arezzo, the pair of Loschi, and the unique Poggio, all equally respect you, even if the deeds of Scipio, whom Poggio praised, did lose out to those of Caesar, whose champion you were. Vittorino reveres you, as does Filelfo himself, who recently sang on trembling strings of the battles

the original quotations adapted to Guarino's own. Sometimes the argument descends to special pleading: if Caesar was guilty of a few moral lapses, then we must remember that not every pope has been as virtuous as Peter; if he used bribery, so does the Vatican; if he was prone to sins of the flesh, he was only human after all, and at least he loved a queen (Cleopatra), not a serving wench, like Scipio. There is also a sixty–four line digression aimed at Poggio's "holy Cato," which fits into the argument because Cato, like Scipio, was a stereotype of republican virtue. Guarino, besides, had a particular ill–will against Cato, whom he regarded as a sanctimonious hypocrite (cf. a similar attack on him in 1425, *Epistolario* 1. Ep. 300. 5–11). Though far from watertight, and relying on selected authorities, flat denials of Poggio's points and hardy assertions of his own, Guarino's defence of Caesar is really a spirited, even passionate, defence of Leonello himself. Poggio responded with restraint, answering Guarino's points one by one, and expressing surprise that such a fuss should have been made over so little. As was usual when a reconciliation was being sought, Poggio addressed his letter not to Guarino directly, but to Francesco Barbaro, a common friend, who was asked to adjudicate. A copy of the letter was sent to Leonello. Barbaro tactfully intervened, giving the palm to neither party, and the matter was dropped between them. The general controversy continued, however, in 1436, when Ciriaco d'Ancona again defended Caesar against

Rupibus et sparsos decorans Vergerius Histros.
Te placidi vates Clarium ceu numen adorant.
Te colit et tantis e milibus approbat unum
Nec tua dicta unquam stellis verubusve notavit   800
Corrector veterum, contemptor Valla novorum.
Me tamen haudquaquam tua tam facundia praestans
Quam perfecta movet virtus; et desino linguam
Mirari nimium, quotiens considero vitam,
Eximium quamvis adeo sanctissima vincit   805
Eloquium probitas et cedunt moribus artes.

Poggio, as did Pietro del Monte yet again in 1440 (E. Walser, *Poggius Florentinus: Leben und Werke* Leipzig, 1914 168–73 and 437–38). Birnbaum (188–89) makes the statement: "In terms of humanist thought, Janus's ideology was anyhow closer to the tenets of Poggio, who postulated …that brilliant minds disappeared after power had been concentrated in one hand and Roman letters have [*sic*] suffered by the loss of liberty …Janus's political credo was not participatory democracy, but a broad basis of popular representation within the framework of Matthias's kingdom."

795. *Victorinus*: Vittorino dei Rambaldoni da Feltre (1378–1446), Guarino's only peer as a humanist teacher. In 1396 he entered the University of Padua, then the centre of the incipient humanist movement, and studied with such luminaries as Giovanni da Conversino da Ravenna, Paolo Veneto, and Pier Paolo Vergerio. After taking his doctorate in Arts, he studied mathematics under Biagio Pelicani (d. 1416). Vittorino maintained himself as a private teacher at Padua until 1415 (or 1416), then learned Greek from Guarino at Venice and Padua in the period 1416–1417. He seems to have been short of money, because Guarino in a letter of 1416 (*Epistolario* 1. Ep. 55. 30–33) mentions a debt he wants Vittorino to pay. From about 1420 Vittorino taught at the University of Padua, and perhaps took student boarders also. In 1423, however, his fortunes rose: on Guarino's recommendation, he became tutor to the children of Gian Francesco Gonzaga I, marquis of Mantua. There in the famous *Casa Giocosa* he founded a school in which Vergerio's idea of

of Sforza, and Vergerio, a credit to the Histrians, scattered by their rocky terrain. The peaceful poets adore you as they adore the god of Claros. Valla, corrector of the ancients and despiser of the moderns, is your devotee, approves of you alone among so nany thousands, and has never marked your words with asterisks or spits.

But your flawless virtue impresses me for more than your outstanding eloquence; and my exceeding wonder at your speech breaks off, whenever I think about your life, so far above eloquence, however remarkable, is honor and sanctity, so much less important are the arts than good character.

education as a harmonious blend of mental and physical training was realized for the first and perhaps only time in the Renaissance. His students are responsible for the hagiography of Vittorino (see the various documents in Garin, *L'Umanesimo* 504–718), and this adoration is echoed in Woodward's influential study, *Vittorino da Feltre and Other Humanist Educators* (1897), still a standard text.

Philelphus: Francesco Filelfo (1398–1481) received his early education at Padua, Venice, and Vicenza. He became Professor of Rhetoric at Padua at the age of eighteen, displaying a linguistic brilliance that never deserted him. In 1420 he went on a diplomatic mission to Constantinople, where he stayed for seven years, among other things studying Greek under John Chrysoloras and marrying John's daughter, Theodora, who eventually bore him many children. Economic necessities weighed heavily upon him, causing tensions which sometimes made him run foul of others, for example, Carlo Marsuppini and Cosimo de' Medici, the latter of whom secured his dismissal in 1434 from the University of Florence, where he had lectured with great success since 1429. He moved to Siena, but soon found employment at Milan, where he was favored by Duke Filippo Maria Visconti and his successor, Francesco Sforza. In 1474 he went to Rome, but soon became restless. Lorenzo de Medici, setting aside Filelfo's earlier hatred of Cosimo and the Medici in general, helped in restoring him to Florence, but Filelfo died within a few weeks of returning. He was a prolific writer of letters (many of them invectives), orations,

At bona pars vitiis animi decus oris opimi
Inquinat et, quantum doctrinae luce refulget,
Tantum criminibus sordet polluta nefandis.
Prima tibi est semper magnorum cura deorum,   810
Quos te prae cunctis mortalibus unice amantes
Aequali pietate colis mox ipse colendus
Proxime post superos hominum, quos rite ferino
Aevum agitare vetas, quos ore et corde politos
Ac vere facis esse homines, quin morte subacta   815
Vincere fata doces et iter super aethera monstras.
Nec te unquam trepidae rapuit ruber impetus irae,
Quin etiam dentes passus livoris iniqui

817 rubor A

poems in Latin, Greek, and Italian, and an incomplete epic, the *Sforzias*,
on the deeds of Francesco Sforza (see n. on 796). He appears to have
offended many of his fellow scholars, and his reputation as a vicious
and acerbic character has lingered, perhaps unfairly: see Diana Robin,
"A Reassessment of the Character of Francesco Filelfo," *Renaissance
Quarterly* 36. No. 2 (1983) 202–24.

796: In June, 1451, Filelfo wrote Pietro Tommaso that he had
begun work on the *Sforzias*, an epic on Francesco Sforza, who had
become Duke of Milan the previous year (*Filelfi Epistulae* Venetiis, 1502
f. 65). In October, 1452, he wrote his son, Xenophon, who was then
at Rome, that he was sending him part of the *Sforzias*, which some of
Xenophon's friends had expressed an interest in seeing (*Filelfi Epistulae*
f. 73v). In March, 1453, Filelfo wrote Alberto Zancari that he was
sending him an excerpt from the second book of the *Sforzia* (*Filelfi
Epistulae* f. 75v). In June, 1455, he wrote Lodovico Casella, asking him
to pass a copy of the *Sforzias* he had given him on to Pietro Tommaso,
who was waiting for it (*Filelfi Epistulae* f. 89). Copies of the unfinished
poem were therefore in circulation from at least 1452.

797. *Vergerius*: Pier Paolo Vergerio (1370–1444) was born at
Capodistria, where, as Ianus well knew, the coastline is rocky, and vil-
lages nestle in folds of the hills. As was common for young scholars from
that area, Vergerio went to Padua for his education, and stayed in Italy,

Yet a good many people tarnish the glory of a rich tongue with vices of the mind, and are as much defiled by unspeakable crimes as they glitter with the light of learning. Your first concern is always for the mighty gods, who love you above all other mortals, and whom you worship with equal devotion. O next among mankind to the gods, soon to be worshiped yourself, you forbid men to disturb the times with their bestial ways, you polish their minds and tongues, and make real men of them; you even teach them how to conquer fate by trampling death underfoot, and point the way to the highest heavens.

The crimson tide of trembling rage has never taken you; indeed, even when you suffered the sting of unfair envy,

where there were more openings for talent. In 1386 he became a friend of Coluccio Salutati and Francesco Zabarella both enthusiasts for the new *studia humanitatis*. Himself a teacher of logic, Vergerio nevertheless embraced humanism, resigning his post at Padua to learn Greek from Chrysoloras at Florence 1397–1400. For the next five years, he studied medicine, law, and the humanities at Padua, taking his doctorate in 1405. He then worked in the papal curia, immersing himself in its affairs but maintaining his interest in humanism. At the Council of Constance he met the Emperor Sigismund, who crowned him poet laureate, gave him a pension, and invited him to his court, Vergerio accepted, and remained in Hungary from 1417 until his death, save for a few brief absences. Vergerio's works include a treatise on metrics, an invective against Carlo Malatesta, many letters and orations, the treatise *De ingenuis moribus et liberalibus studiis adulescentiae* (1404), and a Latin comedy, *Paulus*, written at Bologna in 1389 or 1390. The *Paulus* is in five acts. It represents a young student (perhaps Vergerio himself) torn between a life of study and virtue (promoted by a good servant, Stichus)

Carpentum nunquam potuisti carpere mores
Nec tua in alterius valuit facundia famam,   820
Ausoniis hodie vitium commune disertis,
Sed semper facies hilaris tibi, mixta lepori
Semper inest gravitas ac mitis ruga severae
Frontis et in laeto non dura modestia vultu.

and one of dissipation (abetted by a bad slave, Hermotes). It is a surprisingly lively piece, with some excellent dialogue, all the more remarkable because it was the first of its kind by a humanist. The text, with facing translation in Italian, is in *Teatro goliardico dell' Umanesimo* ed. Vito Pandolfi and Erminia Artese (Milan, 1965) 52–119. Like *Paulus*, the *De ingenuis moribus* was written for a moral purpose. Bolgari (*The Classical Heritage and its Beneficiaries* 258) states that in it "we may reasonably assume that he was putting on paper the principles which had guided him throughout his career." Though somewhat piecemeal in its presentation, it contains most of the ideas that dominated humanist education for at least the next hundred years: those born in humble circumstances can achieve status through learning; reason is the best spur to merit, but praise is most effective with the young; the nature of a child's abilities and character is early recognizable; parents and teachers must set a good example, and not permit extremes in behavior; boasting, lying, and foul language should be curbed; the state is ultimately responsible for education; youths must be shielded from sexual temptations; teachers and text books should be very carefully selected; too much sleep, food, and drink is harmful; religious values should be implanted early, but without undue coercion; parents, elders, and guests deserve respect; upper-class children are best educated away from home; students should be worked hard and exposed to wisdom at an early age; some students require, and should receive, more attention than others; it is never too late to learn new things; encouragement and rewards and the natural spirit of emulation, all in moderation, stimulate learning; books must not be banned or destroyed; the pace of instruction should match the pupil's capacities; students should develop the skills that really interest them; everything learned during the day should be reviewed in the evening; one should study with a friend; it is best to set aside regular hours for study; hunting, hawking, fishing, walking, riding, and ball-games are good leisure-time activities; training in weaponry should precede intellectual training; wit, humor, and music all have their place in life; good grooming is essential; a prince must be a good

you never could criticize your critics, and your speaking
ability has never been used to defame another, a failing
common today among Ausonian wits, but your face is al-
ways cheerful, its everpresent seriousness is softened with
charm, there are kind wrinkles on your stern brow, and a
winning humility in your pleasant expression.

general; at times it is permissible to do nothing. Practical teachers
followed these general recommendations as their own inclinations led
them. Vittorino paid great attention, for example, to physical educa-
tion, whereas Guarino was more permissive about it. They also stressed
what was congenial to themselves out of Vergerio's list of "subjects" to
be studied: grammar, syntax, rhetoric, poetry, history, logic, arithmetic,
astronomy, geometry, medicine, ethics, music, natural history, theology,
the weights of bodies, and perspective. Vittorino taught the sciences
(really the medieval *quadrivium*), more fully than Guarino. Guarino
gave a series of lectures on the *De ingenuis moribus* in 1429 (*Episto-
lario* 2. Ep. 570. 22–25), the *prolusio* to which is extant (see *Epistolario*
3. 268). The treatise ran through at least twenty printed editions be-
fore 1500 (Woodward, *Vittorino* 95), and as many or more came out in
the sixteenth century. According to Paolo Giovio, *Elogia veris clarorum
virorum imaginibus apposita* (Venetiis, 1546) 68, it was a common text
book in schools of his time.

798. *Clarium ...numen*: Claros, a small town near Colophon in
Ionia, was famous for its temple and oracle of Apollo.

801. *Valla*: Lorenzo Valla (1407–1457) was born at Rome, where
he received his first education and wrote a work *De comparatione Ci-
ceronis Quintilianique* (now lost) in which he argued that Quintilian
was a better stylist than Cicero, thus early acquiring a reputation
for exact scholarship and bold, original thinking. In 1429 he became
Professor of Rhetoric at Pavia, but was dismissed as a result of two
controversial works: *Epistula de insigniis et armis*, in which he crit-
icized the style and methods of the almost sacrosanct jurist, Bartolo
da Sassoferrato (1314–1357); and *De voluptate* (later renamed *De vero
bono*), actually a dispassionate examination of Stoicism and Epicure-
anism, concluding that a blend of Stoicism and Christianity was the
ideal philosophy, but a work often misunderstood as a defence of he-
donism. Valla was never an enemy of Christianity or anti–clerical,
but he was impatient with fools, even if they were clerics. After a

Inter discipulos et caros inter amicos   825
Iucundi sine felle sales et melle faceto
Conditi nec rus sapiunt tua dicta, sed urbem,
Qualia Cecropiis olim sonuere theatris,
Quae doctus magni praeferret Tiro patroni
Lusibus et prompti mallent strinxisse Lacones.   830

stay in Milan and Florence, he went in 1437 to Naples as secretary to
Alfonso I. There he wrote his most brilliant work, a study (1440) of the
Donation of Constantine, a document purportedly of 324 in which tem-
poral and spiritual authority in the West was conferred on the Bishop
of Rome. Valla proved from its style, vocabulary, and syntax, that it
could not have been written before the eighth century. The more in-
telligent clergy realized that Valla was not attacking the Church or the
primacy of the Pope, but many did not. Valla's reputation as the best
philologist of his time was confirmed by his *Elegantiae linguae latinae*
(1435–1444), a collection of pure Latin usages drawn from Cicero and
Quintilian, intended as guides to good style not a prescriptive classi-
cism. In 1448 he became one of Nicholas V's apostolic secretaries, and
was given the task of translating Herodotus and Thucydides. When
Nicholas died he continued to work under Calixtus III until his own
death in 1457. Among his other works were *Disputationes dialecticae,*
an attack on scholasticism; *De libero arbitrio,* arguing that free will is
maintained by faith, not reason; and a history of the reign of Ferdinand
of Aragon, the mediocre quality of which shows that he was at his best
in close argumentation and Latin philology. His translations from Greek
are likewise disappointing, tending to introduce florid additions hardly
justified by the originals.

810: No humanist (or medieval) teacher gave formal instruction in
religion, this being left to the students' spiritual confessors, but most,
like Guarino, were careful to encourage ordinary devotions. This was
particularly necessary when traditional churchmen mounted periodic
attacks on the classics as a basis of education (see n. on 535 and 614).

812. *mox ipse colendus*: Cf. *Praefatio* 31 and note; also Vergil,
Geo. 1. 24, where Augustus is invoked as a future god.

817–20: The Anonymous Veronese provides the best conment:
"Though Guarino has been too often attacked by the malicious and
envious words of certain reprobates whose vices he particularly loathes
and abominates, he has never lost his temper and ...never shown any-
thing but impartiality. What is more, when he had in his power certain

With students and close friends your wit is agreeable and harmless, and spiced with the honey of good hunor; your words smack of the city, not the country, and have the quality once heard in Cecropian theatres, which the learned Tiro thought more of than the jokes of his great patron, and which the quick-witted Lacedaemonians preferred to unleash.

individuals who had harmed him, the only penalty he assigned was to say that he was satisfied to have had the power to pay them back; apart from that, he left them unharmed ... Quite often he has been called upon by certain people to help them against those who envied and disliked them (and with some justice), but he loftily refused, and did not hesitate to chide those who had sought his aid for trying so brazenly to turn him from the path of honor, further cautioning them that if their rivals ...wanted his help, he would give it ...and energetically plead their case, the moment they had put aside their grievance and taken up a love of justice."

822–24: The most famous likeness of Guarino is the medal (c. 1440–1446) by the Veronese artist, Matteo Pasti, now in the British Museum. He appears in left profile as a thick-set, vigorous man with an aquiline nose, large eyes, receding forehead and hair-line, thick at the back and sides. This medal or a copy of it may be the one sent by Ianus to Janos Vitéz about 1449: "I am not sending any books at the moment, especially since the messenger found me unprepared, but ...I have given him a likeness in bronze of our Guarino to take to you ...so that your Excellency may now know by his form and features the man you have for long known by his fame and writings. He himself gave this likeness to me a long time ago, with the specific purpose of getting it to you eventually" (G., *Epistolario* 3. 440–41). Sabbadini suggests (*ibid.* 441) that the medal Vitéz received was actually one by Pisanello, referred to in a poem of Basinio da Parma (F. Ferri, *La giovinezza di un poeta: Basinii Parmensis carmina* Rimini, 1914 26).Neither it nor the Pasti medal is likely to be the portrait referred to in an inscription by Cristoforo Lafranchino, published by A. Segarizzi in *Nuovo Archivio Veneto* 20 (1910) 110: "Et latiae et graiae linguae laus ampla Guarinus/Ille Veronensis pictus hic emicuit./Qui lauro illustris cinctus sua tempora vates/Clarus et orator notus in orbe fuit." Laurels can be metaphorical, but not surely in a poem describing a likeness of someone shown bare-

Haud tamen idcirco tibi disciplina tuorum
Laxior; horrescit rigidos domus intima frenos
Ac famuli dominum nati novere parentem,
Quos tu temperie tali moderaris, ut illos
Non premat asperitas, non indulgentia solvat.   835
Hinc animis vigor et probitas, hinc pectora sacris
Culta deo studiis et, ne morer, omnia patris.
Sed longe ante alios minimus de stirpe virili
Eminet et fratres tantum Baptista verendos
Antevenit, quantum reliquis intermicat astris   840

830 struxisse *A*

headed, and the participle *pictus* (painted) seems to exclude likenesses
in bronze. Neither can Lafranchino's poem refer to the only known
painting of Guarino, now in the library of the University of Minnesota,
which acquired it in 1950 with the purchase of what was formerly MS.
6645 in the Phillipps of Cheltenham collection in the Bodleian Library at
Oxford. This portrait, according to Henri Omont ("Portrait de Guarino
de Verone," Bulletin de la Societé Nationale des Antiquaires de France
[1905] 323–26), was a copy of an original in Canonic. lat. 301, Guarino's
holograph of his translation of the whole of Strabo (see n. on 732–33),
which went missing in 1817, when the Bodleian acquired the manuscript.
The Minneapolis portrait shows Guarino as a very old man wearing a
hat, but the features are recognizably the same as those on the Pasti
medal. Since it is unsigned and undated, the artist remains unidentified.
I suspect, however, that the original may be the "monument" referred to
in *Epistolario* 2. Ep. 874. 34–39, as a gift which the Veronese Damiano
dal Borgo had given or intended to give Guarino to "immortalize" him.
The letter is dated June 18, 1453, which I believe was Guarino's birthday
(see n. on 879). If, as the letter suggests, the gift was a portrait, it would
have been an appropriate addition to the finished Strabo manuscript,
the crowning achievement of Guarino's scholarship.
      828. *Cecropiis*: i.e. Athenian, from Cecrops, legendary first king
of Attica.
      828. *Cecropiis*: i.e. Athenian, from Cecrops, legendary first king
of Attica.

Nevertheless, the discipline you exercise over your charges is far from lax; your intimate household shudders at the tight reins, and the servants know the master, the children their father. You control them in such a way that they are not crushed by tyranny nor made careless by indulgence; so their hearts are strong and honest, their minds filled with religious devotion and, in short, all their parent's qualities. But standing far out before the rest is Battista, the youngest of a virile line, who surpasses his admirable brothers as Sirius or Bootes, who turns the icy Oxcart, outshine the other

829. *Tiro*: Marcus Tullius Tiro, the learned slave and secretary of Cicero, and his freedman after 53 B.C. He survived Cicero, edited some of his letters and orations, and wrote his biography. Tiro wrote a work on grammar (*De usu atque ratione linguae latinae*) and one on miscellaneous questions (Aulus Gellius 13.9.1). A system of Latin shorthand known as *notae Tironianae* is associated with him. Plutarch (*Cato Minor* 23) says Cicero introduced shorthand into Rome; but almost certainly this was a Greek system, adapted by Tiro for the purposes of Latin.

830. *Lacones*: The Spartans had a reputation for brief, droll sayings: see, e.g., Cicero, *Tusculans* 5.14.40.

831. *disciplina tuorum*: Contrast this with *Epigr.* 1. 63 (Kombol, p. 186), which Birnbaum (p. 31) says is a reprimand "in the style of Renaissance comedies": "Why, Guarino, most indulgent of fathers, don't you keep your sons away from shameful vices? Maybe you don't know what one of them has just done. He made you the father–in–law of your own maid, and the grandfather of a homemade female slave. You are the talk of the town. Do you still not know about your shame? Guarino, softest of papas, why don't you, I say, keep your sons from shameful vices? If they often get by with this sort of thing with the servants, others will take liberties with your daughters, believe me." This poem, which Sabbadini dates about 1450 (G., *Epistolario* 2. p. 555), seems to have been based on a real incident. The serving girl who bore Guarino's illegitimate "granddaughter" is almost certainly the Maria Linnata on whom Guarino settled a dowery of 128 lire marchesane in a legal act of January 12, 1457 (Cittadella, *I Guai* 34). Obviously, he bore

Sirius aut versans Plaustrum glaciale Bootes.
Iam cathedram doctor, iam scandere pulpita rhetor
Audet et intentas fando suspendere mentes.
Plausibus exultant aedes aut templa deorum,
Dum favet et iuvenem laudatrix contio flammat,   845
At tibi praedulces rumpunt pia gaudia fletus;
Non secus, ad patrium carmen gentile Caystrum
Cum tener edidicit defuncti pullus oloris,
Tentat et ipse modos nec iam genitore canoro
Deteriora crepat; tum protinus agmine denso   850
Mirantum saeptus volucrum candentibus alis
Tollitur et dominum quaerit super aethera Phoebum;
Ille volat, pulsae resonant modulamine nubes.

her no ill will, but it is difficult to imagine that he found Ianus' "repri-
mand" anything but the impudence it was.

839. *Battista*: Battista Guarini (1438–1503) was Guarino's
youngest son and his successor in the chair of Rhetoric at Ferrara (1460).
Four years younger than Ianus, he nevertheless became his friend at
Ferrara, and remained loyal to him all his life (see Birnbaun, 56–57).
Indeed, a letter written by Battista 1467 to Giovanni Bertuccio (in
Abel, *Analecta* 203–11) provides most of the essential biographical ma-
terial for Ianus. Birnbaum believes that Battista wrote it as a favor,
to re-establish Ianus' name in humanist circles in Italy. After teach-
ing at the University of Bologna 1456–1457 (G., *Epistolario* 2. Ep. 8,
4. 24, and 3. 478), Battista returned to Ferrara, where he translated
Xenophonis *Agesilaus* in 1458 (G., *Epistolario* 3. 504) and wrote his
De modo et ordine docendi ac scribendi (see n. on 370) the following
year. Both were probably done at his father's suggestion, to make sure
that Battista would succeed him. That this was by no means automatic
emerges from Carbone's threat in the funeral oration on Guarino that
he would take employment with John Tiptoft in England if the Fer-
rarese proved ungrateful and the tasteless peroration in which he makes
the ghost of Guarino designate Carbone as his successor. Borso, nev-
ertheless, appointed Battista and continued to favor him. Battista, very

stars. Already he ventures to ascend the chair as teacher and the pulpit as speaker, and to hold attentive minds in suspense with his words. The palace or the temples of the gods ring with joyful applause, as the approving audience shows its favor and inspires the youngster, while for you, Guarino, a father's joy breaks out in tears too sweet for words. So is it when the tender cygnet of a dead swan has learned well the song of his breed beside their ancestral Caystrus, tries it out himself, and is already sounding as sweet as his tuneful sire: at that moment, surrounded by a dense throng of his admiring fellows, he rises on shining wings and looks for Phoebus his lord beyond the upper air, and as he flies away the clouds quiver and ring with his song.

much the courtier, was even more favored by Duke Ercole, for whom he translated Plautus, *Menaechmi* and other comedies into Italian. His other works include many letters, orations, and poems. His poems were published in *Baptistae Guarini Poemata* (Mutinae, 1496). The fact that Battista was the only one of Guarino's sons mentioned in *Panegyricus* so upset him that in a manuscript of the poem on which he later worked in Venice (Abel, *Analecta* 212) Battista added twelve lines extolling those Ianus had passed over (Huszti, *Janus Pannonius* 109; Birnbaum, 65, n. 22).

842. rhetor: Battista Guarini at the age of fifteen delivered the *prolusio* at the opening of the academic year in 1453. This speech (published by K. Müllner in *Wiener Studien* 19 [1897] 126–43) ends with a tribute to Duke Borso: "He has undertaken the support of the university at his own expense. With good salaries he has attracted and invited to this most flourishing city of his, to be your teachers, those distinguished scholars whom you see in this praiseworthy assembly. And lest any burden fall upon us, lest warfare hinder our devotion to literature, he has brought peace to his dominions, although on all sides we see Italy ablaze with war, and in his wisdom he is ruling in person over this gracious city and his other subjects, who abound in the good arts and the things necessary to life."

Sed nec munificum quisquam neget esse, quod amplas
Haud dispergis opes contentus et ipse pusillo,   855
Quod non ulla tuo fremitant spectacula sumptu
Nec Paron imminuunt tacturae sidera moles,
Quod tua plaudentem non pascunt horrea vulgum
Nec populare pluit rapiendos missile nummos.
Non ideo non tu longe diffusior illis,   860
Quos tam vana iuvant. Donis meliora caducis
Te tribuente tui capiunt, Guarine, clientes,

859 placet rapiendos mittere A

847. *Caystrum*: The River Caystrus, rising on Mt. Tmolus in
Lydia and flow in into the sea at Ephesus, was famous for the many
swans on its banks.
848. *defuncti pullus oloris*: Swans were famous for their death-
song, consecrated to Apollo (Cicero, Tusculans 1. 30. 73; Pliny, *N.H.*
10. 23. 32; Vergil, *Ecl.* 7. 38) Carbone twice uses the same image of a
dying swan to describe Guarino in the funeral oration.
855. *pusillo*: Though personally frugal, Guarino was not the poor
man "avendo più figliuoli e non molte sustanze" that Vespasiano da
Bisticci says he was (*Vite di uomini illustri* ed. D'Ancona and Aeschli-
mann, 313). This is clear from his will, published by Cittadella, *I Guar-
ini* 33–34. To his married daughters, Libera and Fiordimiglia he left
dowries "already stipulated" (the sums are not specified); to his two
surviving unmarried daughters, and to his son Girolamo's orphan, 800
lire each; to Agostino (majordomo to the duke) the family house in
Verona and some land; to Manuel (a canon in the Church of San Giorgio
Maggiore) part ownership in the large house in Ferrara (see n. on 591);

None would say you were lacking in generosity, because
you do not spread great wealth around, being content your-
self with very little, or because no noisy shows are put on at
your expense, or vast piles that reach for the stars diminish
Paros, or because your barns do not feed a clapping rabble,
nor does a popular largesse rain down coins to be scrambled
for. Even so, you are far more generous than those who de-
light in such vanities. Your dependants get better things
from you, Guarino, than perishable

to Gregorio (a leading physician) a villa in Montorio, some land, and
a mill; to Leonello (a notary) the villa and land at Val Policella (see
n. on 661); and to Battista, the controlling interest in the house in
Ferrara plus some minor property and income. He also ordered 136
masses said for various intentions (7 for remission of the Seven Deadly
Sins, 9 for the 9 orders of angels, 30 for expiation of sins against the
Ten Commandments and the Trinity, 40 in restitution for incorrectly
performed masses, and 50 for the Pope's intention in the Jubilee of
1450). He could hardly have been worth less than 18,000 lire, which
was sixty times his annual salary from the duke.

857. *Paron*: The Aegean island of Paros was noted for its white
marble (cf. Vergil, *Aen.* 3. 126). In Ianus' time most of the fine marble
in northern Italy came from the quarries at Carrara, but characteristi-
cally he chooses the ancient, more evocative image. He likewise ignores
the fact that in his time all the important buildings at Ferrara were of
brick, as they are today.

870–71: Carbone also says that Guarino helped students out of
his own pocket, but this may be a borrowing from the 1443 biography
of Vittorino by his pupil, Sassolo da Prato (in Garin, *L'Umanesimo*
504–33). Comparing Vittorino to Socrates (as Carbone and Ianus com-
pare Guarino to Socrates), Sassolo states (p. 516): "Socrates only
taught the young for nothing, but Vittorino not only does that, but
in every other respect does the duty of an excellent and most indul-
gent father." Vittorino is said to have applied constantly for subsidies

Quae saturent avidas indeficientia mentes
Nec senio valeant aboleri aut fulmine frangi
Ad furum secura dolos et tela latronum.   865
Haec tu dispensas, haec tu partiris in omnes
Tam iusta trutina, nulli ut sua portio desit,
Sed referat quivis, quantum cupit arca cerebri,
Tam tenui pretio, nemo ut non solvere possit.
Multi quippe tibi nulla mercede docentur,   870
Omnes exigua, quanquam quae digna Camenis
Pensio, quis totum virtuti aequaverit aurum,
Quod Scytha quod Bessus/
quod Arabs quod congerit Astur.
Quid memorem parcae frugalia fercula mensae,
Ingenium simul et nervos laedentia puris   875
Vina domas lymphis ac sola more vetusto
Contentus cena vix unquam prandia nosti?

from the Gonzaga family, but there is no documentation of such dis-
bursements from Borso. As for Guarino, his *contubernium* was a busi-
ness as well as a "house of the muses," and with his large family to
provide for, he did not displace his generosity. There were times, how-
ever, when he lent students money until such time as their funds could
be transferred to Ferrara. He was not hesitant to sue. For example,
in 1420 he sued Francesco and Niccolò Brenzon, who had failed to re-
pay 100 ducats loaned by Guarino to Bartolomeo Brenzon for "food,
clothing, and books (Archivio notarile di Verona. Ufficio del registro
1420. f. 197, 38.) He could also be unpleasantly insistent, as appears
from a letter of Zavissius Operowski to Bishop Mikolaj Lasowski: "
...I am so worried about this lack of funds that I don't know what to
do. Daily, nay hourly, my teacher Guarino keeps demanding what I
owe him and dinning it into my ears ...I beg you to help me." (G.,
Epistolario 3. 416–17). For a series of dunning letters to Lasowski
during the year 1448–1449, see *Epistolario* 2. Epp. 818, 819, 820, 821.
Ianus himself had similar difficulties in 1451, when Guarino would not

gifts things that never fail, that satisfy their eager minds, that cannot be destroyed by time or shattered by lightning, and are safe from the guile of thieves and the weapons of bandits. These you dispense and share with others in such just measure that no one goes without, and everyone gets as much as his brain cares to store, at such little cost that no one is unable to pay. You teach everyone for a modest fee, and many for no fee at all. But what payment is worthy of the muses? Who shall say that virtue is worth all the gold amassed by Scythians, Bessi, and the peoples of Araby and Asturia?

Why mention the frugal fare of your thrifty table? With pure water you dilute the wine that damages the nerves and brain, and like the ancients, content yourself with dinner alone, and have almost never known a midday meal.

permit him to travel to Buda for a brief visit until the Bishop of Mutina had provided surety for sums Ianus was owing (Iohannes Vitéz de Zredna, *Opera quae supersunt: Pars 1, Epistolarium* ed. I. Boronkai [Budapest, 1980] 159–60)

873. *Bessus ... Astur*: The Bessi were a savage people in north-eastern Thrace noted for piracy (Pliny, *N.H.* 4. 11. 18). The Astures lived between the Callaeci and the Cantabri Suae along the northern coast of Spain, extending across the mountains to the south. After their conquest by Augustus (26–19 B.C.), they supplied Rome with gold, chrysocolla, minium, horses, and auxiliary troops. The area was almost proverbial for its mineral wealth.

874–77: Cf. 614–16. The evils of over-indulgence in food and drink are often pointed to by ancient authors, e.g., Vergil, *Geo.* 3. 526–27; Juvenal, 1. 135–45.

879: This line provides the best internal evidence for dating the *Panegyricus*. Everything depends on knowing when Guarino was born, and on the assumption that Ianus was here reporting his age exactly.

Quae tibi sobrietas hos plane contulit annos,
Ut iam bis decimi tangens confinia lustri
Non pede, non oculo, non sensu debilis uno   88o
Purpureum clara serves cum voce colorem.
Vive, precor, quantum non ipse Gerenius heros,
Quantum non Phoebi volucris rediviva nec hausto
Pulvere mensa suam virgo Cumaea senectam,

868 capit A

The birth year 1370 given by Huszti and, following him, Birnbaum (p.
24) is traceable to Guarino's first major biographer, Carlo Rosmini, who
in his *Vita e disciplina di Guarino* 1.1 linked the certain date of Guar-
ino's death (see n. on 290) with two other pieces of evidence. The first
is Carbone's statement in the funeral oration that Guarino died "ad
nonagesimum usque annum perductus" ("when he had been brought
right up to his ninetieth year"). The second is an epitaph written on
his father by Battista Guarini: "Quam superis tua casta fides moresque
placerent/Lustra tibi vitae nona bis acta probant" ("The twice nine lus-
tra of life lived by you prove how your pure faith and character pleased
the gods"). Taking a *lustrum* here to mean five years (a sense it some-
times bears see article in Lewis and Short, *Latin Dictionary*), Rosmini
saw that Battista and Carbone both say Guarino lived until he was
ninety. He therefore concluded that since he died on December 4, 1460,
he must have been born in 1370. In n. 1 at the end of his first vol-
ume Rosmini attempts further precision by claiming in a brief dictum
that the year and month of Guarino's birth are revealed by those of
his death: hence, according to Rosmini, his birthday was sometime in
December. Sabbadini, however, disposed of the 1370 date by pointing
(*La scuola e gli studi di Guarino* 2) to the precision of Manuel Guar-
ini's notice of his father's death (see n. on 290) as occurring in his
eighty–seventh year i.e., before his eighty–seventh birthday. The round
figure given by Carbone and Battista Guarini may be dismissed as no
more than pleasing rhetoric. Moreover, the one may simply have been
following the other and they may not be independent witnesses. Accept-
ing Manuel's testimony, Sabbadini arrived at 1374 as the correct birth
year and found confirmation by taking a *lustrum* to mean four years
(its usual sense) in Ianus' *Panegyricus* 879. He concluded that Guar-
ino was 79 in 1453, and for this reason dated the *Panegyricus* to that

Such moderation has clearly brought you to these years, so that, though now getting close to your twentieth lustrum, you have no defect in the feet, the eyes, or any of the senses, and you still retain your fresh complexion and clear voice. Live, I pray, longer than the Gerenian hero himself, longer than the bird of Phoebus that comes to life again, and the virgin of Cumae, who measured her old age in countless grains of dust;

year or the next. It seems likely that Ianus would present his poem to Guarino at or just before the completion of his studies, i.e., about May or June of his last year. Moreover, we know from Battista Guarini's letter to Giovanni Bertuccio (see n. on 839) that Ianus completed his legal studies at Padua in only four years. Since he took his doctorate and went back to Hungary in 1458, he must therefore have left Guarino's school after the close of the academic year 1453–54. The *Panegyricus* was probably presented to Guarino in May or June, 1454.

882. *Gerenius heros*: The epithet regularly used by Homer of Nestor, king of Pylos, famous for his long life. See also Martial, 2. 64. 3, and Juvenal, 10. 249, where he is said to have lived through three generations, i.e., for 100 years.

883. *volueris*: The phoenix, a fabulous bird said to live for 500 years, then incinerate itself with fire taken from the sun, and come to life again as a young bird (Pliny N.H. 10. 2. 2; Ovid, *Metamorphoses* 15. 393; Statius, *Silvae* 2. 4. 6).

884. *virgo Cumaea*: The Sibyl of Cumae (a Greek settlement near Naples), who promised her virginity to Apollo in exchange for a life of as many years as there were grains in a handful of dust). But she forgot to ask for lasting youth also. When she reneged on her promise, Apollo allowed her to become progressively older and more decrepit (Ovid, *Metamorphoses* 14. 132–53).

887. *Hebe*: Goddess of youth.

889. *Elysium*: Ianus is here using a pagan term for the abode of blessed spirits to express the Christian concept of Heaven, for which the usual word was *caelum*.

889–90: The *Cyllenes alumnus* is the god Mercury, and also the planet named after him. It is *rarus visu* (rarely seen) because of its

Vel potius gravior, quotiens acceserit aetas,   885
Vernantem primo reddat tibi flore iuventam
Diva ministratrix aeterni nectaris Hebe
Nec te prae nostro capiat, pater inclyte, mundo
Elysiumve nemus vel caeli tertius orbis,
Qua rarus visu Cyllenes errat alumnus,   890
Sed sis perpetuus studiorum praesul et istis
Mersarum in tenebris animarum publica lampas.
Dum servant elementa fidem, dum sidera currunt,
Haec studia, hic omnes vitae tibi cursus in annos,
Haec clara humanum merita in genus, inde per orbem 895
Victurum, mundi dum stabit machina, nomen.

proximity to the sun. The *tertius orbis* of the sky is the sphere of
Mercury (alluded to by Paul in *Corinthians* 2. 12. 2), i.e., the three-
dimensional space between the spheres of the planets on either side of
it, the outer sphere having a diameter equal the maximum distance
from the earth the planet ever reaches as it travels through the sky,
the inner sphere having its diameter equal to the minimum distance
from the earth the planet achieves (see V.E. Thoren, "The Comet of
1577 and Tycho Brahe's System of the World," *Archives Internationales
d'Histoire des Sciences* 29. No. 104 1979 59). This sphere is mentioned
as another possible location of souls after death. The belief perhaps
arose because Mercury in myth is the god who brings death by touching
the eyes of mortals with his magic wand (*caduceus* and conducts the
souls to the next world. Note that Ianus was thinking in terms of a
geocentric universe, and following the order of the planets given by
Cicero, *Somnium Scipionis* 4. 2, and Macrobius, *In Somnium Scipionis*
1. 19. 1 and 1. 19. 14, which is Earth, Moon, Mercury, Venus, Sun,
Mars, Jupiter, Saturn (the correct order is Earth, Moon, Venus, Mars,
Mercury, Sun, Jupiter, Saturn).

890 891: Cf. Lucretius 3. 1–4, in which Epicurus is praised as a bringer
of light out of darkness.

896. *mundi ...machina*: An echo of Lucretius, 5. 96. Poggio had
uncovered a manuscript of Lucretius in 1417, but the work had little

or rather, as old age comes and weighs heavier, may Hebe, the divine dispenser of eternal nectar, restore you to a youth in the first bloom of its springtime, and may the Elysian grove, o illustrious father, or the third circle of heaven, where wanders the rarely-seen nursling of Cyllene, not take you from our world first. May you be a perpetual high priest of scholarship, and a public light for those sunk in the darkness of the soul. As long as the elements stay true to themselves, as long as the stars run their course, these studies, this way of life you follow, these splendid services to the human race, will last through the years, and from them your name will live on earth as long as the planned fabric of the world stands.

appeal to the humanists of Guarino's generation. There are only three seeming echoes of passages from it in the whole of Guarino's letters: *Epistolario* 1. Ep. 386. 16, *induperator*, which could have come from Aulus Gellius, 18. 9. 2, or Cicero *De divinatione* 1. 107; *Epistolario* 2. Ep. 586. 33, *creteae imagines*, an echo of Lucretius, 4. 298; and *Epistolario* 2. Ep. 702. 7, *sentiscerem*, an inceptive verb peculiar to Lucretius.

899. *instaurator*: There was no single "restorer" of classical learning. Vespasiano da Bisticci (*Vite di uomini illustri* ed. D'Ancona and Aeschlimann, 312-13) gives the palm to Bruni and Guarino jointly, and other authors of the time name other candidates for the honor. Guarino himself saw the revival of Latin as beginning with the spread of Greek (*Epistolario* 1. Ep. 43. 43-49), and regarded Latinists of the fourteenth century as inferior: e.g., in *Epistolario* 1. Ep. 34. 57-59 he puns on the name of Salutati's teacher, Pietro da Moglio, as representative of his whole generation: "...his style is so obscure and unusual that he seems not so much to speak eloquently (*loqui*) as to moo (*mugire*)." In the whole of Guarino's letters Petrarch is given only one brief mention (*Epistolario* 2. Ep. 826. 19). Most interesting is Epistolario 2. Ep. 862 of 1452, in which Guarino explains to his son, Niccolò, that when he himself was a boy he studied "barbaric" text books in school; he singles out Prosper of Aquitaine's *Epigrammata* a versification of key-passages from the writings of St. Augustine),

Salve, magne parens, cunctis decus addite saeclis,
Optime doctorum, doctissime, salve, bonorum!
Salve, instaurator Latiae, revocator Achivae
Pallados! Ipsa tuis titulis Euandria mater   900
Cesserit, Arcadio vates afflata Lyceo;
Illa bis octonas Latio intulit hospita formas,
Quas quondam Tyrius Graiis monstraverat exul:
Tu, quicquid veterum dederat sollertia patrum,
Reddis et in lucem longa e caligine promis,   905
Qui nisi prostratas relevasses funditus artes,

906 funditas *J*

Prudentius' *Dittochaeon* and Bernard of Morlay's *Chartula* as the worst
texts, and quotes this sample of what was considered good Latin style in
his boyhood, *Vobis regratiorde concernentibus capitaniatui vestri vestra me advisavit sapientitudo.* The reform began, he explains, "out of
nature's own goodness with no one leading the way, until Chrysoloras
came with the gift of Greek which made progress in Latin possible.
    900. *Evandria mater*: i.e. Carmentis (less correctly, Carmenta), a
native Italian goddess of prophecy, whom the Romans identified with
the Arcadian nymph Themis, mother of Evander, who according to
legend left Arcadia and founded the first community on what was later
the Palatine Hill in Rome (Vergil, *Aen.* 8. 54) is credited by Isidore,
Etymologiae 1. 4. 1 and 5. 39. 11, with teaching the latin aborigines
to write, but most authorities (e.g. Tacitus, *Annales* 11. 14. 4) say this
was done by Evander. In *Epistolario* 2. Ep. 813. 72-76 Guarino says
Evander's mother was Nicostrata, and repeats Isidore's statement that
the indigenous people called her Carmentis, since as a mere mouthpiece
of the gods, she was, "without mind" (*carens mentis*). He credits her
with initiating the second of the periods in the development of the Latin
language (see n. on 1035).

Hail, great father, a glory given to all the ages! Hail, best of the learned and most learned of the good! Hail, founder of the Latian, and restorer of the Greek Pallas! The Evandrian mother herself will yield to your titles, she a prophetess inspired by the Arcadian Lyceus. She brought to Latium as a guest sixteen shapes, which the Tyrian exile had once shown to the Greeks: you restore and from long darkness bring into the light all the gifts of wisdom of the ancient fathers. If you had not raised up

901. *Lyceo*: The Arcadian wolf-god, Pan Lykeios, identified by the Romans with their native deity, Faunus. According to Ovid, *Fasti* 2. 279 ff., Evander established his cult on the Palatine, and the fertility festival known as the Lupercalia.

903. *Tyrius ... exul*: See n. on 102. For the expression, cf. 96, *Samius exul*

907. *Quirinus*: The name given to Romulus, legendary founder of Rome, after his deification.

908. *Camillus*: Marcus Furius Camillus, the great Roman general and statesman of the early republic. For his capture of Veii from the Etruscans (c. 396 B.C. and his military and civil reforms after the Gallic invasions (387-86 B.C.) Livy (5.49.7) calls him "the father of his country and the second founder of Rome" ("pater patriae conditorque alter Urbis").

910: Cicero, *De officiis* 1. 22. 77, quotes this line from his own poem *De suis temporibus*. Most manuscripts, however, have *laudi* instead of *linguae*, but the line is quoted with *linguae* in Quintilian, 11. 1. 24, which may have been Ianus' source.

912. *Tirynthius heros*: Hercules. See n. on 4. Ianus does not undervalue Hercules as a type of warlike valor, but he implies that those who spread civilization through learning are the real heroes. Guarino says much the same of Chrysoloras in *Epistolario* 1. Ep. 27.

Priscorum vanus staret labor. Alta Quirinus
Fundavit Romae, reparavit regna Camillus,
Sed tantum ambobus maior tua gloria, quantum
Cedunt arma togae, concedit laurea linguae.   910
Nec quenquam proferre potest spatiosa vetustas,
Qui plus praestiterit populis. Tirynthius heros
Pestiferis terras purgabat et aequora monstris;
Ille et nigrantis custidem Cerberon Orci
Tergemina totidem religatum colla catena   915
Ostendit vivis et sidera ferre coegit.
Per te barbaries, qua nullum Tartara monstrum
Taetrius ima ferunt, supera de sede fugatur
Eminus et Stygias iterum gemit acta sub umbras.

910 caedunt A

37-46: "What generosity there was in him, what constancy, faith, in-
tegrity, what religiousness, modesty, and holiness what greatness of soul,
what a knowledge of all the arts and everything really important! If
some outstanding writer is found to record them, what a volume they
will fill! You see what an immense number of excellent verses Homer, the
supreme poet, puts out before he can be quit of that mythical demi-god
whom he had taken it upon himself to praise, a bad-tempered, lustful,
bloody savage, a fellow born to ravage and destroy cities. What do we
think a poet of the highest wisdom would do with a true story and a
case of sterling virtue?" Ianus could have seen this passage, since Ep.
27 was one of those included in the *Chrysolorina* (see n. on 155).
    914. *nigrantis ... Orci*: Hercules' last Labor was to fetch out into
the light Cerberus, the three-headed hound that guarded the infernal
regions. In Homer's *Odyssey* he himself says it was his hardest task, and
he could not have done it without the help of Hermes and Athena. The
myth, as Ianus seems to have realized, is really a "conquest of death."
The parallel with Guarino is therefore appropriate, since he is depicted
throughout the poem as bringing life out of death, light out of darkness.
The dark imagery of 914-19 prepares the way for the blaze of light in
920ff.

the fallen arts from their foundations, the work of the an-
cients would stand for nothing. Quirinus laid the founda-
tions of Rome's greatness, and Camillus re-established her
rule, but your glory is greater than both of theirs by as
much as arms yield to the toga and the laurel crown to the
tongue.

Nor can long antiquity produce anyone who has done
more for people. The Tirynthian hero cleared the lands and
seas of pestilential monsters; he tethered the three necks of
Cerberus, guardian of black Orcus, with as many chains,
showed him to the living, and forced him to endure the
stars. Through you, barbarism, than which lowest Tartarus
brings forth no fouler monster, is routed from its place on
earth, and now groans again, driven beneath the Stygian
shades.

920-40: This magnificent hymn to the sun brings to a climax the
many parallels of Guarino throughout the poem with the sun itself, and
with Apollo as the god of light and the arts (see 26, 87, 221, 255, 283–94,
328, 493–505, 603, 657, 798, 883, 892, 905). The ideas in it go back to
Cleanthes (331-232 B.C.), under whose leadership (263-232 B.C.) Sto-
icism (see n. on 174 and 214) became infused with a quasi-religious fer-
vor. Considerable fragments of his writings remain (*Stoicorum Veterum
Fragmenta* ed. Von Arnim, 1. 103-39). He taught that the universe is
a living being, with the sun at its heart, and this in part contributed
to the very gradual emergence of sun-worship throughout the Roman
empire. Elagabulus (218-222) was the first to promote it officially, but
it was not until the reign of Aurelian (270-275) that it became domi-
nant. The older gods continued to be worshiped, and Christianity was
making headway, but Sol Invictus (the Unconquerable Sun) was the
chief deity of the empire until the final triumph of Christianity at the
Council of Nicea (325). Macrobius in the early fifth century is merely
reflecting earlier doctrine when he says (*Saturnalia* 1. 17.4) that all
gods except the transcendental powers beyond the physical universe
are "powers" (*virtutes*) of the sun. Ianus could have been drawing on

Immensus nil sole gerit praestantius orbis: 920
Sol Iovis est oculus mens mundi lucis origo
Rerum temperies cor caeli spiritus aethrae
Astrorum dominus mensor revolubilis aevi
Sensilium sensus viventum vita propago
Nascentum largitor opum largitor honorum,   925
Telluris pariter coniunx fecundus et undae,
Fatorum rector, deus idem summus et omnes;
Phryx licet Attinem, Phoenix hunc dicat Adonin,

923 mensorque volubilis *A*
927 omnis *A*

Saturnalia 1.17.2-4, as Kardos claims in *Janus Pannonius bukása* (Pécs, 1935) 58 (quoted in Birnbaum, 172), but I believe a more immediate source was Martianus Capella, *De nuptiis Philologiae et Mercurii* 2. 185-86:

> Ignoti vis celsa patris vel prima propago,
> fomes sensificus, mentis fons, lucis origo,
> regnum naturae, decus atque assertio divum,
> mundanusque oculus, fulgor splendentis Olympi,
> ultramundanum fas est cui cernere patrem
> et magnum spectare deum, cui circulus aethrae
> paret, et immensis moderaris raptibus orbis:
> nam medium tu curris iter, dans solus amicam
> temperiem superis, compellens atque coercens
> sidera sacra, deum cum legem cursibus addis.

Following Kardos, Birnbaum (p. 172) says that "based on Macrobius's *Saturnalia*, Janus's Orphic sun hymn represents a new perspective, the sensing of a heliocentric system." But surely the sources are more identifiably Stoic than "Orphic," and there is nothing scientifically novel here. By calling the sun the *cor caeli* Ianus is reflecting either Cleanthes' view that it is the heart of a living universe, or the mistaken belief that the sun occupies the median point among the other planets (see n. on 889), or both. This is a far cry from the heliocentric doctrine of Copernicus.

The boundless world bears nothing more glorious than
the sun: the sun is the eye of Jove, the intelligence of the
universe, the source of light, the controller of nature, the
heart of heaven, the spirit of the ether, the lord of the stars,
the measurer of revolving time, the intelligence of the in-
telligible, the life of living things, the propagator of things
that come to birth, the dispenser of wealth and honors, the
fruitful consort of earth and sea alike, the ruler of fate, the
supreme god and all gods in one. The Phrygian may call
him Attis, the Phoenician, Adonis;

922. *aethrae*: In the Middle Ages and the Renaissance the most
commonly accepted division of the universe was that given in the
pseudo-Platonic *Epinomis*, into regions of fire, ether, air, water, and
earth. Ether was usually thought to be a lower form of the celestial fire,
but there was much controversy about its exact nature and location (see
Den Boeft,*Calcidius on Demons* 18-21).
927. *fatorum rector*: See n. on 68.
deus ...omnes: Cf. Martianus Capella, *De nuptiis Philologiae et
Mercurii* 191-92, where Egyptian, Libyan, Persian, and Phoenician gods
are syncretized in Apollo, who was frequently identified with Helios,
the sun god. For a discussion of the tendency to convert the Olympian
gods into deities of other religions, see J. Bayet, *Histoire politique et
psychologique de la religion romaine* (Paris, 1957) 244-54. As Stahl
points out (*Martianus Capella and the Seven Liberal Arts* 87-88), the
blending of Olympian religion with Neoplatonic, Neopythagorean, and
Stoic elements in Martianus gives rise to a fairly consistent theology
and an intellectually defensible philosophic system: all deities of all
religions can be fitted into a hierarchy of power; their numbers can be
reduced by syncretization; and a place in the universe can be assigned
to each. The Supreme Unknown and Unknowable God of Neoplatonic
thought (Plotinus, *Enneads* 6. 9. 4-7) glimpsed in Martianus 185 and
202, could, with a little goodwill, become the Christian God, the lesser
powers being converted into good or evil *daemones* (cf. n. on 71, 72,
568).

Hinc Persis Mithram, Pharos inde Serapin adoret,
Pana colat Tegee, Memphis deploret Osirin,   930
Verum Paeonia quamvis levet arte dolores,
Quamvis ille suis illuminet omnia flammis,
Saepe tamen tristi feralia tela sinistra
Iactat et obtenta radios abscondit in umbra,
Saepius hiberno declivis frigore torpet   935
Semper et obscurae iussus decedere nocti
Invidet alternam superis fulgere sororem,
At tua lux aninos, non segnia corpora lustrat,
Nec scit defectum nec tempore languet in ullo,
Noctibus et roseis simul irresticta diebus   940
Curat et assidue, quos fert inscitia, morbos.

928. *Attinem*: In Roman versions of the myth of Attis (e.g. Ovid,
Fasti 4. 221-44), he is the consort of Cybele, the Phrygian Great
Mother, and castrates himself, but the details of why he does so vary.
In the late empire his cult became associated with that of the sun.
    Adonin: The most familiar version of the Adonis myth is in Ovid,
Metamorphoses 10. 298-559, 708-39: the son of Cinyras, king of Cyprus,
by an incestuous union with his daughter, Myrrha, Adonis was beloved
of Aphrodite; he was killed while out hunting by a boar (in some other
versions by Ares, disguised as a boar); his blood became an anemone,
and Aphrodite decreed that her grief for his death should be re-enacted
annually. In Phoenicia he was worshiped under the title of *Adon* (Lord)
as a god of vegetation and the regeneration of nature. At Byblos there
was an annual mourning festival, to which a resurrection ritual, bor-
rowed from the religion of Osiris, became appended.
    929. *Persis*: i.e. Fars (or Farsistan) in S.W. Iran.
    Mithram: Originally an ancient Indo-European god of light,
Mithras in Persian Zoroastrianism was the ally of the good power,
Ahuramazda, and the enemy of Ahriman, the power of darkness and
evil. His cult became popular, especially among soldiers all over the

Persis may on the one hand adore him as Mithras, and
Pharos as Serapis on the other; Tegea may worship him as
Pan, and Memphis weep for him as Osiris. But although
he relieves pain with Paeonian art, and lights the universe
with his flames, he often hurls deadly shafts from his dire left
hand, and hides his rays under a drawn shade; more often
than not, he is sluggish as he sets in the cold of winter, and
when bidden to yield to dark night, he always begrudges
those overhead the succeeding gleam of his sister . But
your light, Guarino, shines on minds, not sluggish bodies;
it knows no setting, and it never fades; it is unquenched
by night or during rosy days, and it constantly cures the
diseases that ignorance brings.

Roman empire, from about the second half of the second century A.D.
Sometimes he was identified with Sol Invictus.
    Serapin: Serapis was an Egyptian god associated with the sun,
whose cult spread to Greece and Rome in the early empire.
    930. *Tegee ...Pana*: Tegee (or Tegea), an ancient town in Arcadia,
about 28 miles north of Sparta, figures in the most famous story about
Pan, recounted in Herodotus 6.105: when the runner Philippides was
sent on the eve of the Battle of Marathon 490 B.C.) to ask help from
the Spartans, he met Pan near Mt. Parthenion above Tegee, who called
him by name and ordered him to ask the Athenians why they paid him
no honor, since he had helped them before and would do so again; after
the victory the Athenians instituted a cult of Pan under the Acropolis.
Pan, whose name is probably to be connected with an Indo-European
root signifying nurture, was originally an obscure god of shepherds, but
when his cult spread from Athens throughout the Hellenistic world, it
gradually became that of a universal deity by false derivation of Pan
from the Greek word for "all" and the expression *to pan*, meaning "the
universe." His identification with the sun comes from the common idea
that the sun sees and knows all.

Haud igitur sine mente quidem, sine numine divum
Crediderim talem te nostra in saecula natum.
Nam tua Lucinae cum iam pia vota potenti
Conciperet genitrix et plenis mensibus infans   945
Viscera maturo premeres genitalia partu,
Orbe procul medio, qua Pegasis ungula sacras
Fodit aquas geminis et cornibus aethera rumpit
Deucalioneis Parnasus inobrutus undis,
Maestior ad maestas Clio sic orsa sorores: 950

Osirin: In Egypt Osiris represented the dead pharaoh, who was
thought to go to a new life as a ruler of the Underworld. The most
widespread myth about him was that he had originally been a divine
king, who was dismembered by his jealous brother Set, who scattered
the parts throughout Egypt. Isis, the faithful wife of Osiris, collected
the parts, which retained enough virility to beget Horus, who eventually
avenged his father on Set. The centre of his cult was Upper Egypt,
where annually his "death" was mourned, and his resurrection hailed
with rejoicing. Osiris was therefore periodically resurrected, like the
sun, and was regularly called the Sun of the Underworld. His cult
spread through the Hellenistic and Roman world as part of the ritual
enactment of his resurrection by Isis.

931. *Paeonia ... arte*; i.e., with medicine.

934. *obtenta ... umbra*: Cf. Vergil *Geo.* 1.248, *obtenta nocte.*

940. *roseis*: Cf. Lucretius 5. 610, where this adjective is used of
sunlight.

944. *Lucinae*: A title of Juno in her capacity of goddess of women
in childbirth.

945. *genitrix*: Libera di Zanino (Giannino), wife of Bartolomeo
Guarini, a worker in metals. Her own and her husband's names are
known from Libera's will, extracts of which are published in G., *Epistolario* 3. 195-96. Guarino himself records (*Epistolario* 2. Ep. 904. 15-2)
that he had only a dim memory of his father, who died as a prisoner

I cannot therefore believe you were born the man you are in our times without the divine intent of the gods. For when your mother was already forming her pious prayers to potent Lucina, and in the fullness of months you, her child, were pressing out of her womb in a timely birth, far away at the centre of the earth, where the hoof of Pegasus kicked up the sacred waters, and Parnassus, uncovered from Deucalion's flood, pierces the heavens with its twin peaks, Clio, sadder than her sad sisters, thus began;

after "the battle fought between the rulers of Padua and Verona," which the Veronese lost "because of the ignorance and incompetence of a general who had never seen battles except the ones he had seen in pictures or read about in books" (probably referring to the Battle of Brentella, 1386, in which Francesco da Carrara of Padua defeated Antonio della Scala, whose field commander was Cortesia de Sarego). Libera, "a really excellent woman, reverent and god-fearing, and an example of chastity and decency first among married women and later among widows," brought Guarino up to respect his family name, and the virtues of the saint after whom he was given the name Guarino. Both Carbone and the Anonymous Veronese say that she made sure Guarino had the best possible schooling.

947-49: The *omphalos* or exact mid-point of the earth was commonly located by the Greeks at Delphi, site also of the Castalian spring sacred to Apollo, below two peaks called "The Shiners" on the southern side of Mt. Parnassus. In Ovid's account of the Flood (*Metamorphoses* 1. 211:421), Deucalion's ark ran aground on the twin peaks, which were the only parts of the earth clear of the waters. The fountain Hippocrene, sacred to the muses and said to have been started by a kick from the hoof of Pegasus (Ovid, *Fasti* 5. 7, etc.), is near Mt. Helicon in Boeotia, a condiderable distance from Delphi in Phocis. Ianus uses *medio orbe* loosely to include both locations.

"Cum bene, germanae, variantia supputo mecum
Tempora, vicinus cineri nimis esse supremo
Mundus et a ferro iam degenerare videtur.
Nam licet in chalybem defluxerit aurea quondam
Vita patrum, tamen egregios vel pace vel armis   955
Omnibus in terris late generabat alumnos,
Haudquaquam nunc vis eadem mortalibus aegris,
Improcera ferunt hebetes sed corpora sensus
Nec longum numeri fatalis vincula durant.
Interea pravi mores perversa voluntas   960
Segnibus ingeniis et in actus prona nefandos
Spernit turba deos ac vana tonitrua ridet
Nec putat ad Siculos sudare Pyracmona folles.

950. *Clio*: The muse of history, and therefore the appropriate choice to make the prognostication that follows. Ianus imagines all of this taking place just before Guarino's birth.

951-53. *Cum ...mundus*: Ianus is here drawing on the Stoic doctrine of the Great Year (Cicero, *De natura deorum* 2. 50–51; *De finibus* 2. 102, etc.), or period of 15,000 years (Macrobius, *In Somnium Scipionis*, 2. 11. 10-11), which is complete when all the stars and constellations have returned to the point they started from at the beginning of the cycle, at which point there is an *ekpyrosis* (Latin, *conflagratio*), or purgation by fire, the basic element to which the others (air, water, earth) must return. Seneca (*Quaestiones naturales* 3. 28. 7) says this happens when God decides to put an end to the old, and create a better order ("conflagratio fit, cum deo visum ordiri meliora, vetera finiri"): see also Cicero, *De natura deorum* 2. 20. 58. The universe is therefore permanent, but continually renewing itself in cycles. The souls of men perish in the *conflagratio*, to be remade, with everything else, by God, the *ignis artificiosus* (creating fire), in a similar but better way (Cicero, *De natura deorum* 2. 46. 118).

953. *ferro*: Hesiod, *Works and Days* 106-201, describes five ages through which man has come: the golden, silver, bronze, heroic, and

"Sisters, by careful calculation of the changing times, the world seems to me very near to its final ashes, and already degenerating from its iron age. Although our fathers' way of life, once golden, declined to one of iron, still it produced nurslings in every land, who were outstanding in war and peace. But now these sick mortals have nothing like the same energy; their stunted bodies have dull senses, and the links in the number decreed by fate do not last long. Meanwhile, their manners are depraved, and their lazy minds are possessed with perverse whims. The common crowd is inclined to sinful acts, it despises the gods and laughs at the thunder as meaningless, and it thinks there is no Pyracmon sweating at the Sicilian bellows.

iron, in the last of which he conceives himself to be living. Ovid, *Metamorphoses* 1. 88-210, omits the age of heroes. In general, the ancients took the view that mankind was gradually deteriorating.

957. *mortalibus aegris*: Adapted from Homer's *deiloisi brotoisi*, this phrase occurs in Lucretius, 6. 1, and Vergil, *Aen*. 2. 268 and *Geo*. 1. 237, with reference to the "weakness" of humans, compared to the gods. Ianus is using *aegris* in a double sense: as a goddess, Clio is disgusted by the physical degeneration of mankind; as a muse, she is disgusted by their ignorance. Cf. 941, where ignorance is said to bring disease, meaning an unsound intelligence, curable only by the light Guarino brings. Similarly, in the simile 339-50, in which students are compared to a flock of sheep, they are said to be sick (339, *aegrum*) and weak (340, *debile*) from starvation (lack of sound teaching) before Guarino's arrival. Throughout the poem, Ianus returns periodically to the theme of Apollo and Guarino as light-bearers and healers. Guarino had used similar imagery in his praises of Chrysoloras in, e.g., *Epistolario* 2. Ep. 862. 68-70: "And so Latin language and style, tarnished and blotched from long disuse, had to be purified by the simples of Chrysoloras, and brightened by the light he brought to it" ("Longa itaque desuetudine infuscatus

Sed non ulla magis quam nos despecta per orbem
Numina: multus adhuc Cererem veneratur arator, 965
Multus adhuc spoliis bellator Martia ditat
Templa nec artifici desunt sua dona Minervae,
Fulmineos dentes ramosave cornua cernas
Postibus In Triviae, Neptuno litore in omni
Votivae pendent tabulae, tibi, mater Amoris, 970
Centum vel sola fumant altaria Cypro,
At nobis iam nullus honos, communia nusquam

958 In procera *A*

---

ante latinus sermo et inquinata dictio Chrysolorinis fuerat pharmacis
expurganda et admoto lumine illustranda").
962. *Pyracmona*; The Cyclopes Brontes, Steropes, and Pyracmon
are named as Vulcan's three helpers in his forge under Mt. Etna by
Vergil, Aen. 8. 425. For Pyracmon, see also Claudian, *De raptu Pros-
erpinae* 1. 238.
969. *Triviae*: Artemis (identified by the Romans with their goddess
Diana) was goddess of wild creatures. Tusks and antlers were therefore
appropriate offerings to her. She is called goddess of Three Ways be-
cause she was sometimes identified with Hecate, a goddess of witchcraft,
whose symbol was the meeting point of three roads.
970. *votivae ... tabulae*: In classical times, sailors who had escaped
shipwreck would often hang up their garments as a thanks-offering in
a temple of Neptune. Accompanying them would be a tablet with an
inscription or perhaps a picture of the event (see Horace, *Odes* 1. 5. 13
and 3. 26, and the notes in the edition by T. E. Page [Macmillan: New
York and London, 1964] 148-49 and 378).
971. *Cypro*: Cyprus was a major centre of the worship of
Aphrodite.
977: The Turks captured Constantinople on May 29, 1453 but they
had made many incursions into Europe before that (see n. on 677).
978: Ianus loathed fratricidal war between Christian peoples, as is
evidenced by his early poem, *Pro pacanda Italia*, and his two poems
(Epigr. 1. 7 and 1. 2) to Mars (see Birnbaum, 148-49, and 154, n.
25 and 27). Guarino, too, had long seen that the real enemy were the
Turks. In 1416 he congratulated Venice for its victory over them at

But no deities are more looked down on in the world than we are: many a ploughman still respects Ceres, many a warrior still enriches the temples of Mars with spoils, and crafty Minerva is not short of her own gifts. You may see sparkling tusks and branching antlers at Trivia's doorposts, votive tablets to Neptune are hanging on every shore, and there are a hundred altars alone smoking on Cyprus for you, mother of Love. But for us there is no honor now. Nowhere do we share a shrine with

Gallipoli (*Epistolario* 1. Ep. 56), and in 1446 (*Epistolario* 2. Ep. 796. 7-11) he deplored the internecine wars in Italy that kept Christians from deploying their strength against foes abroad, meaning the Turks.

979: Cf. Vergil, *Aen.* 6. 879.

982. *viles ...lymphas*: Seaweed, not water, is the usual type of worthlessness in Latin: e.g. Vergil, *Ecl.* 7. 42 and Horace, *Sat.* 2. 5. 8. Pindar, in fact, had called water "best" (*Olympians* 1. 1). But the best of mortal drinks is not good enough for goddesses who want their due.

983. *Tempe*: A beautiful valley in Thessaly, between Mt. Olympus and Mt. Ossa. To a goddess denied the light of heaven, and harried from place to place on earth, even Tempe seems unattractive.

984. *Pyreneus*: A mythical king of Thrace, whose encounter with the muses is recounted by one of them in Ovid, *Metamorphoses* 5. 274–93. Meeting the muses on their way to Delphi, he invited them to shelter from the rain in his house. When they were inside, he attempted to rape them. They escaped by donning their wings. Pyreneus tried to follow them, jumping from a tower, but fell and was killed.

985. *picae*: Nine mortals, the daughters of Pieros of Pella and Euhippe of Paeonia, challenged the nine muses to a singing contest. A jury of nymphs voted for the muses, and the Pierides (daughters of Pieros) as a penalty for their presumption and their rudeness after the contest were turned into magpies (Ovid, *Metamorphoses* 5. 294–314 and 662–78). Ianus pictures them as still challenging the muses, who can find no better competition.

988. *Erigone*: identified with the constellation Virgo at Manilius, 5. 251 and Vergil, *Geo.* 1. 33. In myth, she was the daughter of Icarius, an Athenian who received the gift of wine from Dionysus, and gave it to

Herculeis delubra focis secretave saltem
Silvarum et rigui per amoena suburbia fontes.
Hos pridem in saltus toto velut orbe fugatae   975
Cessimus, hinc etiam pellit nos barbarus hostis,
Ignotos postquam Phrixea per aequora Turcos
Fraterna Eoi traxit discordia regni.
Heu, Pietas, heu, prisca Fides, nunquamne resurget
Clara sub obscuris facundia mersa tenebris,   980
Nunquamne ingenuae remeabunt amplius artes?
Quid viles nobis, genitor, pro nectare lymphas,
Quid caeli pro luce dabas horrentia Tempe?
Quas modo sacrilegus tentet violare Pyreneus,
Nunc inhonora vocent raucae in certamina picae.   985
Iam tandem emeritis requiem, iustissime divum,
Ac pacem largire poli. Quo dignior astris
Erigone et nitidi bis septem lumina tauri?
Sin minus, immitis patrui regna atra petemus,
Qua soror infernos servat Proserpina lucos,   990
Inter et Elysias veterum spatiabimur umbras
Cultorum exangues sine voce et corpore vultus,
Nulla adeo in vivis si iam solatia restant."

974 fontis *A*

his fellow citizens. Feeling its effects, they thought they were poisoned,
and killed Icarius. When Erigone found his body, she hanged herself
from grief. According to Hyginus (*Fabellae* 130 and *Astronomia* 2.4),
Icarius became a constellation (Bootes or Arcturus), Erigone the con-
stellation Virgo, and Erigone's dog, Maera, the Dogstar (for which last,
see Ovid, *Fasti* 5. 723).

     tauri: The cluster of fourteen stars that make up the constellation
Taurus (the Bull), said to have been the bull of the Europa–myth.

the altar fires of Hercules, or even have the secret places in the woods and the fountains that water charming suburbs. Long ago, when we were driven from the world at large, we withdrew to these glens, but a hostile barbarian is driving us even from here, now that quarreling among brothers in the eastern kingdoms has lured the strange Turks across the waters of Phrixus. Alas for Piety, alas for pristine Faith, will fair eloquence, sunk in murky darkness, never rise again? Will the liberal arts never again return? Why, father, did you give us cheap water instead of nectar? Why did you give us the rough spots instead of the vale of Tempe? Once impious Pyreneus would have been trying to rape us, but now the hoarse magpies challenge us to contests without honor. Most just of gods, grant us at last the rest we have earned, and the peace of heaven. In what way did Erigone and the fourteen lights of the shining bull deserve the stars more than we? Otherwise, we shall go to the dark realms of our ungentle uncle, where sister Proserpina keeps the infernal groves, and walk among the Elysian ghosts of our old worshipers as bloodless faces without voice and bodies, if there is no comfort left for us among the living."

989. *patrui*: The muses were daughters of Mnemosyne (Memory) and Zeus (Hesiod, *Theogony* 921 ff). Hades, as brother of Zeus, was therefore their paternal uncle.

990. *soror ... Proserpina*: Persephone (Latin, Proserpina) was the daughter of Demeter and Zeus (Hesiod, *Theogony* 912 ff), and therefore half-sister to the muses (see n. on 989).

992. *exangues ... vultus*: A phrase perhaps suggested by Ovid, *Metamorphoses* 5. 248-49, "oraque regis/ore Medusaeo silicem sine sanguine fecit." See n. on 994-1002. Cf. also Vergil, *Aen.* 6. 292, "tenues sine corpore vitae."

Talia dum queritur, procul aspicit Arcada fratrem
Caerula praepetibus scindentem nubila plantis.   995
Ille, ut Cirrhaeo paulisper colle resedit,
Castalios latices invisit et antra dearum:
Non illis citharae, non serta virentia cordi;
Plectra silent, disiecta solo crinalia marcent.
Ergo, ubi sive ultro (nam quid non sentiat Hermes?)   1000
Agnovit causas seu forte docentibus ipsis,
Cognatum tali solatur voce dolorem:

994-1002: Probably modeled on Ovid, *Metamorphoses* 5. 250-55,
with the difference that in Ovid it is Athena who travels through the
air, and she lights on Helicon to address the muses.

994. *Arcada fratrem*: Mercury was sometimes called Arcas by the
later poets, because he was born on Mt. Cyllene in Arcadia (Martial,
9. 35. 6; Lucan, 9. 661; Statius, *Silvae* 5. 1. 107). Since his father was
Zeus, he was half-brother to the muses (see n. on 989).

996. *Cirrhaeo ... colle*: i.e., Parnassus. Cirrha was a very ancient
town near Delphi. The adjective *Cirrhaeus* in later writers (e.g., Statius,
Thebais 3. 106) regularly means "sacred to Apollo."

1000. *Hermes*: Ianus cleverly chooses the figure of Hermes to ad-
dress the muses, because he is the devine messenger and as conductor of
souls he picks up much information about what is happening betweeen
the two worlds. Unlike Apollo, who knows everything (see 493-503),
Hermes must make shrewd guesses about the future. He is also a less
forbidding figure to address the slothful, apathetic muses than their au-
gust supervisor, Apollo, and his brisk banter is the perfect foil to Clio's
petulant complaints.

1003-04: *Solvite ...fero*: Hermes strikes an almost evangelical note,
evocative of Luke 2. 10, which is taken up again in 1025.

1006. *post lustra ducenta*: i.e., after 1000 years. Cf. Vergil, *Aen.*
6. 748 and Plato, *Republic* 10. 615A and *Phaedrus* 248C. Using *lus-
trum* here in its sense of a period of five years (cf. n. on 252), Ianus is
referring to the Platonic doctrine that contaminated souls must spend
1000 years in expiation of their sins before spending seven days on the
plain between earth and heaven, whence they procede after a journey of

While she was thus complaining, she saw her brother
Arcas far off splitting the clouds of heaven with his winged
feet. After a short rest on the Cirrhaean hill, he paid a
visit to the Castalian spring and the grottoes of the god-
desses: they had no interest in lyres or green garlands; their
quills were silent, their chaplets lying around wilting on the
ground. So whether he saw the reason for this for him-
self (for what would Hermes not sense?) or maybe because
they told him themselves, he consoled his relatives' grief as
follows.

four days to a place where a beam of light extends like a pillar through
all of heaven and earth. After another day's journey they can see that
this light is a kind of chain that holds the universe together (possibly
Homer's "golden chain," as interpreted by Guarino: see n. on 568).
From it extends the Spindle of Necessity, which turns all the revolving
spheres. The souls now choose their next life and a guardian spirit.
Lachesis gives each his or her lot, Clotho ratifies it, and Atropos makes
the events on the thread of destiny unalterable. The final step is to
drink from Lethe, the river of Forgetfulness, after which the souls go
to sleep, and are borne upwards like shooting stars to their new birth.
Plato puts this doctrine in the myth of Er, with which he concludes the
last book of his *Republic* (614B ff).
    1007. *bina ...limina*: See n. on 561.
    1008. *gemina de gente*: Probably Mercury means the Greeks and
the Latins. Alternatively, he is referring to the two classes of souls,
the just and the unjust, whom Er in Plato's *Republic* (614C-D) sees
ascending to the sky or descending into the earth, as judgement is passed
upon them.
    1011: Cf. Vergil, Aen. 6. 679.
    1012: This convocation of Life, Death, Genius, and the Fates seems
to be the product of Ianus' own fancy. Vergil, *Aen.* 6.277, locates
Death in the jaws of Orcus. Life does nor seem to be found as a per-
sonification in any classical writer; nor is Genius, although each indi-
vidual was thought to have his or her own *genius*, or tutular deity (Ho-
race, *Epistles* 1. 7.94; *Odes* 3.17.14, etc.), and *genius* is found, though

"Solvite tristitiam, luctus removete, sorores,
Gaudia certa fero. Nam cum modo forte recentes
A bustis animas pallentem duco sub Orcum,   1005
Ast alias iterum post lustra ducenta reduco
Ad superos et bina frequens per limina curro,
Vidi exultantes gemina de gente disertos
Tot veterum manes, quod iam meliora redirent
Tempora, dum studiis florerent omnia priscis;   1010
Vidi secreto vasta in convalle recessu
Cum Genio et Vita Parcas et Morte sedentes,
E quibus una retroflexa cervice silebat,
Altera perspicuum speculi intendebat in orbem,
Tertia prospectu lustrabat inane barathrum,   1015
Ducere cum subito varias coepere choreas:

1010 cum *A*

very rarely, in the sense of intellectual brilliance (Juvenal, 6. 562; Martial, 6. 60, 10 and 7. 78. 7). The concept of a transcendent Genius is barely discernible in Martianus Capella, *De nuptiis Philologiae et Mercurii* 2. 152–54, a passage Ianus might have seen, but is not fully realized before the twelfth century in Bernardus Silvestris, *Cosmographia: Microcosmos* 3. 11, a work which Ianus is unlikely to have known. As for the Fates, clearly Ianus had in mind Plato's discussion of them in the myth of Er (see n. on 1006). Plato places them on the Spindle of Necessity, the fly or whorl of which is hollow and contains eight concentric circles, fitting into each other like a series of bowls. A siren sits on each of the circles as it moves, sounding one note of the scale, all eight sirens thus producing a unified harmony. Round about at equal distances sit the three Fates on thrones, singing to the music of the sirens, Lachesis of the past, Clotho of the present, Atropos of the future. Clotho touches the outer circle with her right hand and helps to spin it; Atropos moves the seven inner circles with her left hand, spinning them in the direction opposite to that of the outer circle; and Lachesis touches and moves both the outer circle and

"Away with your grief, sisters, get rid of this gloom. I have happy and reliable news. From time to time I happen to lead the souls of the recently deceased from their funeral pyres to pale Orcus, and bring others back again to the upper world after two hundred lustra, and I often run through the twin thresholds. I have seen so many eloquent spirits from both of the ancient races rejoicing, because better times are now returning, until the moment comes when the whole world blossoms with ancient studies. I have seen the Fates sitting in secret seclusion in a vast valley with Life, Death, and the Guardian Spirit. One of the Fates was keeping quiet, with her head thrown back, another was staring into a clear round mirror, and the third surveyed the unfilled pit of the future, when suddenly they began to dance in different movements:

the seven inner ones alternating with each hand. Ianus draws on this complex imagery in 1013–1019.

1013. *una*: Lachesis, whose neck is turned backwards, because her thoughts are of the past. Plato, less effectively, makes her vocal (see n. on 1012).

1014. *altera*: Clotho, who is concerned with the present, the reflection of things as they are at any given time. The mirror motif probably derives from Martianus Capella, *De nuptiis Philologiae et Mercurii* 1. 7, where Sophia (Wisdom) gives Psyche (Soul) the mirror (*speculum*) of Urania, by means of which the soul can gain self-knowledge and the desire to recover its pristine condition.

1015. *tertia*: Atropos, who in Plato, *Republic* 10. 617 C sings of the future (see n. on 1012).

1016-20: This dance of Destiny, perhaps suggested by the dancing of the nymphs and the three Graces (e.g. in Horace, *Odes* 4. 5-6), seems to be Ianus' own invention. Atropos, foreseeing the imminent transfer of classical learning from Constantinople to Italy, signifies her vision by moving from East to West; her step is rather simple," because little else was needed for the transfer than the voyage of Guarino home. Clotho, whose seven-fold robe represents the Seven Liberal Arts, comes to meet her, signifying her eagerness for the

Atropos in Zephyrum vestigia movit ab Euro
Simpliciore gradu, cui protinus obvia Clotho
Multiplici torsit septena volumina gyro,
Ambabus similes Lachesis dedit ultima gestus.   1020
Tunc has divino sanxerunt carmine sortes
Candida inauratis volventes licia fusis:
'Quanta fuit, magnus Romam dum Augustus habebat,
Tanta per Europam doctorum turba redundet!
Tu vero, Oenotriis puer olim debite terris,   1025
Nascere tantorum princeps et causa bonorum.
Per te facundas iam dudum muta loquelas
Ora dabunt hominum, tu vitae mortua reddes
Nomina, tu nati revocabis ad oscula matrem.
Nascere, sic rerum leges, sic Iuppiter urget!'   1030
Haec cecinere deae; voces Natura dearum
Ferreis in tabulis adamante notavit acuto.

new learning; and finally Lachesis, who looks to the past, shows her ap-
proval by joining in the dance, her imitative gestures perhaps suggesting
imitatio veterum (imitation of the ancients).
    1021: Cf. Vergil, *Ecl.* 4. 46-47, where the Fates simply say "talia
saecla currite."
    1022: Ianus now presents the Fates in their more traditional role
as spinners.
    1025. *puer olim debite*: A clear reference to Vergil, *Ecl.* 4, in which
is prophesied the birth of a child who will restore the Golden Age. Even
in antiquity there was much speculation about his identity, and begin-
ning with Constantine of Nicea in 325 (Eusebius, *Oratio ad Sanctos*),
there were those who identified him with Christ. With startling audac-
ity, Ianus identifies him with the infant Guarino, soon to be born (*olim*
can refer to future time: see, e.g., Vergil, *Geo.* 2. 192).
    1029. *nati ...matrem*: Cf. Vergil, *Ecl.* 4. 60. The "mother" here
is classical antiquity, the "son" the humanist movement, or Latin letters
in general, which had gone astray (in the Middle Ages) and needed to
be restored.

Atropos progressed from East to West in a rather simple step; Clotho, meeting her right away, whirled her seven-fold robe in a complicated pirouette, and finally Lachesis made movements like both of them. Then as they turned the shining threads on their gold-inlaid spindles, they ratified these lots with divine song: 'May Europe abound with as many scholars as it did when great Augustus held Rome! O child long since promised to the lands of Oenotria, come to birth as the leader of such great men and the source of their blessings! Through you, the mouths of men long mute will speak with eloquence, you will restore their dead names to life, you will recall the mother to the kisses of her son. O come to birth! Such are laws of nature, such the will of Jove!' That was the song of the goddesses; and Nature marked their words on iron tablets with sharp steel.

1032. *adamante ...acuto*: Cf. Job, 19. 24.

1033: Cf. Vergil Ecl. 4. 52, "aspice, venturo laetentur ut omnia saeclo."

1034. *Uraniae*: As muse of astronomy, Urania would know the junctures of the heavenly bodies, just as Clio knows the patterns of history (951-53). Like their sisters, however, they have been depressed and distracted, and neither has grasped that a new Golden Age is about to dawn. Mercury, as god of intelligence, alerts them to the implications of their ciphering.

1035. *numeris*: This word means both "rhythms" and "numbers": Urania would naturally sing as she counted. Here Ianus is expressing poetically what Guarino himself states prosaically in *Epistolario* 2. Ep. 813. 65-105 and 2. Ep. 862. 13-70. In the first of these passages, drawing on Isidore, *Etymologiae* 9. 1. 6-7, he divides the history of the Latin language up to the time of his boyhood into four periods: the beginnings in the time of Saturn, Ianus, Picus, and Faunus; the period beginning with Latinus, the son of Faunus, when a still crude,

Nonne vides, eadem totus portendat ut aether
Uraniae numeris sibi respondentia faustis?
Quam bene fatorum concordant sidera pensis!   1035
Quare, age, deterso maeroris surgite laetos
Squalore ad thyasos! Iuvet in Paeana canorum
Contentas rupisse fides! Tibi tibia fletur,
Euterpe, et biforis Tritonia fistula buxi!
Argutos digitis, Erato, tu percute nervos!   1040
Tu grave, Melpomene, tu molle, Thalia, sonato!
Omnia Calliope concentu temperet uno!
Nunc et Pirene nunc et Libethrides undae
Ambrosia scateant, lactis Permessia rivos
Ripa det, Aoniae revirescant largius umbrae!   1045

1038 rapuisse *A*

but improved language was spoken by such early figures as Menenius
Agrippa (who led the secession of the plebeians to the Aventine) and the
compilers of the laws of the twelve tables; the third and most robust
period, when such writers as Plautus, Naevius, Ennius, Ovid, Vergil,
the Gracchi, Cato, and Cicero (whom he names as the best model)
flourished; and finally, the long period of decay and corruption started
by the barbarian invasions. In the second passage Guarino discusses
the revival that began in his own time (see n. on 899).
    1039. *Tritonia fistula*: Athena (Tritonia) is said to have invented
the flute, after hearing the high-pitched screams of the surviving gor-
gons, when their sister Medusa was killed (Pindar, *Pythians* 12. 6 ff).
    1040. *Erato:* The muse of lyric and amorous poetry (Ovid, *Fasti*
4. 195, etc.).
    1041. *Melpomene*: The muse of tragic (and sometimes also lyric)
poetry, whose instrument was the cithara (Horace, *Odes* 1. 24. 3, etc.)
    Thalia: The muse of comedy and pastoral poetry (Vergil *Ecl.* 6.
2, etc.).
    1042. *Calliope*: The muse of epic poetry, and generally regarded
as the chief of all the muses. The most famous poem to her is Horace,
Odes 3. 4. She stands for all the muses at Vergil, *Aen.* 9. 525.

Do you not see how the whole upper air is presaging the same events, and how consistent they are with the auspicious number of Urania? How well the stars agree with the threads of fate! So come, wipe away the ugly marks of grief and rise to join the glad congregation! Rejoice in breaking the tight strings to honor tuneful Paean! Our sympathy to your flute, Euterpe, and to the Tritonian pipe with the two holes in its boxwood! Strike the clear strings with your fingers, Erato! Strike a deep note, Melpomene, and you, Thalia, a soft one! Let Calliope mix everything in one harmony! Now let Pirene and the Libethridian waves gush with ambrosia, the banks of Permessus give rivers of milk, and the green shades of Aonia return in ever greater lushness!

1043. *Pirene*: A fountain in the citadel of Corinth, one of those said to have been started by a kick from the hoof of Pegasus (Pliny, *N.H.* 4. 4.5).

Libethrides undae: Libethra was a fountain near Magnesia in Macedonia, sacred to the muses (Servius on Vergil, *Ecl.* 7. 21, where the adjective *Libethrides* occurs).

1044-45. *Permessia..ripa*: The River Permessus, which rises in Mt. Helicon in Boeotia and flows into Lake Copais, was sacred to Apollo and the muses (Vergil, *Ecl.* 6. 64).

1048. *Vindelicas*: i.e. belonging to the Vindelici, a Germanic people whose chief settlement was Augusta Vindelicorum (Pliny, *N.H.* 3. 20. 24), the modern Augsburg.

1049. Athesis: The modern River Adige.

1050. *Brennum*: Brennus was a Gallic chieftain who defeated the Romans at the River Allia (Livy, 5.38.3), and is said to have captured and extracted a huge ransom from Rome in 390 B.C. The story that he founded Verona may be based on the false etymology *Vae Romae* (woe to Rome), modeled on his famous utterance *Vae victis* (woe to the conquered). Verona may have been founded by the Raeti, but it first appears in history as a town of the Cenomani (Livy, 5.35).

Quod si, quae tanto decoretur germine tellus,
Nosse ferunt animi, non longa ambage docebo:
Urbs est, Vindelicas qua plana assurgit in Alpes
Italia et patulos Athesis vagus exit in agros,
Verona auctorem referens cognomine Brennum.   1050
Dividit hanc fluvius, sed ruptum ponte quaterno
Continuatur iter; medio sublime theatrum
Eminet et longe templorum culmina vincit.
Inde olim vestrum scitis prodisse Catullum,
Plinius inde satus, sed nunc venit altior illi   1055
Gloria, Scaligeris nec se iactaverit aeque
Regibus et Magni Canis armipotentibus actis!
Illic iam toti reboant genialia montes
Carmina, iam glauca praevelat arundine crinem
Mincius et vitreo gestit Benacus in antro,   1060

1052. *theatrum*: The elliptical theatre at Verona dates from the first century. It has a brick foundation but otherwise is constructed of pure marble, and is still well enough preserved to be used today for operatic and other performances.

1054. Catullum: Gaius Valerius Catullus (?84-?54 B.C.), the famous writer of elegies and epigrams, was born in or near Verona.

1055. *Plinius*: This could refer to either Gaius Plinius Secundus (A,D. 23 or 24-79) or his nephew Gaius Plinius Caecilius Secundus (A.D. 61–c. 112), because Guarino held that both were born in Verona. The first, usually referred to as Pliny the Elder, was the author of at least seven large works, of which only the *Naturalis Historia* is extant. Pliny the Younger was the author of nine books of literary letters, and a tenth of correspondence with the Emperor Trajan on the administration of Bithynia; two volumes of verses in the manner of Martial; and a prose *Panegyricus*, in which he praised Trajan and denigrated his predecessor Domitian. In the Middle Ages no distinction was drawn between the two, until in the fourteenth century a Veronese priest named Giovanni wrote a *Brevis annotatio de duobus Pliniis* as the preface to an intended

But if your hearts long to know what land is graced with such fine seed, I shall tell you plainly and briefly: there is a city called Verona, also named the city of Brennus after its founder, where the plain of Italy rises up to meet the Austrian Alps, and the wandering Athesis goes off into open fields. The river divides this city in two, but continues its broken course under a succession of four bridges. A theatre rises high up from the centre and overtops the roofs of the temples by far. Your Catullus, you know, once came from this place, and Pliny was born here, but now there comes a glory greater than that, and it will not be mentioned in the same breath as the Scaliger princes and the warlike deeds of the Great Dog! Whole mountains there are echoing birthday songs, already Mincius is covering his head with greenish reeds and Benacus is in high spirits in his glassy cave,

edition of Pliny the Younger's letters. Giovanni saw that there had been two Plinies, but he mistakenly argued that both were from Verona, because in the *Naturalis Historia* Pliny the Elder had referred (*praefatio* 1) to Catullus as his *conterraneus* (fellow countryman), and the phrase *Veronensibus nostris* (our Veronese) occurs in Pliny the Younger, *Epistulae* 6. 34. 1. Giovanni argued away the notice of Suetonius in the codices of the *Naturalis Historia*, in which the author is called *Plinius Novocomensis*, by taking it to mean "Pliny, a new inhabitant of Como." In 1424 Sicco Polentone, working on the lives of the two Plinies for his *Descriptoribus linguae latinae*, referred to Guarino (*Epistolario* 1. Ep. 265) the question of their place of origin. We do not have Guarino's reply, but evidently he convinced Polentone that they were both from Verona, not Como, because this is what he finally printed. The case for Como was settled, at great length but definitively, by Antonio Giuseppe della Torre Rezzonico in his *Disquisitiones plinianae* (2 vols., Parma, 1763). For Guarino's part in the matter, see Sabbadini, *La scuola e gli studi di Guarino* 146-47 and G., *Epistolario* 3. 164-65.

1056. Sc*aligeris*: The della Scala family, whose coat of arms included a ladder (Italian, *scala*), were lords of Verona from 1277 to 1387.

Dummodo laxatae fusum de ventre parentis
Ipsa liquore sacro fovet Ilithyia Guarinum,
Fasciola ligat ipsa manus et crura nitenti.
Audio Maenalia salientes Pana cicuta
Hortantem Satyros plenis et flore canistris   1065
Ludentes video circum cunabula Nymphas.
Vos mora lenta tenet? Nunc, o, nunc ite citatis
Gressibus et cupidis ereptum auferte Napaeis!
Velate aerio nimbi rutilamtis amictu!
Quis Charitum gremiis, vestro quis dignior infans   1070
Ubere? Hyanteos iam nunc, sine, reptet ad amnes
Parvulus et Phoebo velit advagire canenti!"
Sic ait et dictis parent Heliconides ultro.

1057. *Magni Canis*: Can Grande della Scala (1291-1329), Lord of Verona from 1311 until his death in 1329, was the most distinguished of his family. His reign was filled with warfare, most of it with Padua, from which he had wrested Vicenza. In the end, he won ascendancy over Padua, and with his additional acquisitions of Feltre, Belluno, and Treviso, ruled one of the most powerful states in northern Italy. He was a patron of artists and writers, among them Dante, who fled to his court at Verona after his exile from Florence. Dante dedicated his *Paradiso* to Can Grande (whose name means "Big Dog" in Italian), and immortalized him in Canto 27 of that part of his *Commedia*.

1060. *Mincius*: The River Mincio issues from Lake Garda at Peschiera and flows in a slow, wide, and deep current about 40 miles before emptying into the Po. The greenish reeds that line its banks are mentioned in Vergil, *Aen.* 10. 205; cf. also *Ecl.* 7. 13 and *Geo.* 3. 15. At Mantua it breaks up into a series of large, shallow pools that surround the city on three sides.

Benacus: i.e. "Father Benacus" (Vergil, *Aen.* 10. 205, *patre Benaco*), the tutelary spirit of Lake Benacus (Garda), the largest in Italy.

1062. *Ilithyia*;: A Greek goddess of childbirth.

1064. *Maenalia*: Cf. Vergil, *Ecl.* 8. 21. Maenalus, a mountain range in Arcadia extending from Megalopolis to Tegea (see n. on 930), was sacred to Goat-Pan.

while Ilithyia herself is nursing Guarino, just emerged from his unburdened mother's womb, with her own sacred milk, and is personally binding his hands and legs with clean swaddling clothes. I hear Pan encouraging the dancing Satyrs on his Maenalian pipe, and I see the Nymphs, with baskets full of flowers, playing around the cradle. Why the slow delay? Now, oh go now, with speedy steps, and get him quickly out of reach of the greedy Napaeae! Coddle him in the airy blanket of a pink cloud! What infant deserves the laps of the Graces and your breasts more? Even now the little lad is crawling—let him alone—to the Hyantean streams, and trying to cry in tune to Phoebus' song!"

So he spoke, and the daughters of Helicon obeyed his commands forthwith.

1065. *Satyros*: Wood-spirits, regularly attendant on Pan, with ape-like torsoes and goat-like legs, and frequently depicted in art as sexually aroused.

1066. *Nymphas*: Female spirits of the woods and dells mostly, they were regarded as well-disposed to mortals, and in some authors (e.g. Ovid, *Metamorphoses* 8, 771; Servius on Vergil, *Ecl.* 10. 62) they are said to be themselves mortal, though extremely long-lived. They also represent, however, the wilder and more mysterious forms of nature.

1068. *Napaeis*: The Napaeae, or nymphs of the dell, are called *faciles* (easily appeased) by Vergil, *Geo.* 4. 535, precisely because they were thought not to be, on the same apotropaic principle by which the conciliatory term *Eumenides* (The Well-Disposed Ones) was sometimes used to avert the Furies. Theocritus, 13. 44, refers to the abduction of Hylas and bormus by nymphs who loved them.

1069: Cf. Homer, *Odyssey* 7. 14 and 13. 189, and *Iliad* 3. 380; Vergil, *Aen.* 1. 411-12. In these passages mortals are wrapped by a deity in a protective cloud.

1071. *Hyanteos*: i.e., Boeotian, and thus belonging to the muses: cf. Martial, 12. 3. 12.

Completed camera–ready pages were generated with TeX. The typefaces selected are Old Times Roman and Dunhill, both converted by Donald Knuth to the Computer Modern family for use with TeX. Although Dunhill is an experimental typeface, its spiky, ragged quality echoes the tall, narrow Gothic letters used in the fifteenth century. The decorative initials are French–area designs from the same period, courtesy of the Dover Pictorial Archives. This book was designed and typeset by Elena Fraboschi.